ENCYCLOPAEDIA OF INDIAN GOVERNMENT: PROGRAMMES AND POLICIES

ENCYCLOPAEDIA
OF
INDIAN GOVERNMENT:
PROGRAMMES AND POLICIES

Vol. 10

Environment and Forests

Edited by

Satish Tiwari

ANMOL PUBLICATIONS PVT. LTD.

NEW DELHI - 110 002 (INDIA)

ANMOL PUBLICATIONS PVT. LTD.
4374/4B, Ansari Road, Daryaganj
New Delhi - 110 002

Encyclopaedia of Indian Government: Programmes and Policies

First Edition, 2000
ISBN 81-261-0515-1 (Set)

PRINTED IN INDIA

Published by J.L. Kumar for Anmol Publications Pvt. Ltd., New Delhi - 110 002 and Printed at Mehra Offset Press, Delhi.

Contents

Preface

Encyclopaedia of Indian Government: Programmes and Policies contains authoritative information on about fifty departmental policies and their future developmental programmes.

Organised to be completed in 40 volumes, this gigantic work covers Agriculture; Atomic Energy; Chemicals and Fertilizers; Coal; Commerce; Communication; Culture; Defence; Education; Environment and Forests; External Affairs; Finance; Food & Consumer Affairs; Food Processing Industries; Health and Family Welfare; Home Affairs and Internal Security; Human Resources; Industry; Information and Broadcasting; Labour; Law, Justice and Company Affairs; Non-conventional Energy Sources; Ocean Development; Parliamentary Affairs; Personnel, Public Grievances and Pensions; Petroleum and Natural Gas; Planning and Programme Implementation; Planning and Statistics; Posts and Telegraphs; Power; Rural Development; Science and Technology; Social Justice and Empowerment; Space; States Affairs; Steel; Steel and Mines; Sugar and Edible Oils; Surface Transport; Textiles; Tourism; Urban Development; Water Resources; Women and Child development etc.

Based on the information derived from authoritative sources, this work contains authentic facts and figures. I am deeply beholden to all the scholars whose writings are cited or substantially made use of in the present work. I am also thankful to Anmol Publications Pvt. Ltd. for undertaking publication of this encyclopaedia. I am solely responsible for shortcomings in presentation of matter.

Encyclopaedic in nature, this will prove a dependable reference work for scholars and academics besides those appearing for different competitive examinations.

—Satish Tiwari

1

Introduction

Role and organisation

In the administrative structure of Central Government for the planning, promotion, coordination and overseeing the implementation of the environmental and forestry programmes, the Ministry of Environment and Forests is the nodal agency in the Govt. The Ministry is also the nodal agency within the country for the United Nations Environment Programme (UNEP) International Centre for Integrated Mountain Development and looks after the follow-up of the United Nations Conference on Environment and Development (UNCED)including Agend 21.

The mandates of the Ministry are conservation and survey of flora, fauna, forests and wildlife, prevention and control of pollution, afforestation and regeneration of degraded areas and protection of environment. These tasks are being fulfilled through environmental impact assessment, eco-regeneration, assistance to organisations implementing environmental and forestry programmes; promotion of environmental and forestry programmes; promotion of environmental and forestry research, extension, education and training to augment the requisite manpower, dissemination of environmental information, international cooperation and creation of environmental awareness among all sectors of the country's population.

The aforesaid objectives are well supported by legislative and regulatory measures which are aimed at the preservation and protection of environment. Some of them are the Air (Prevention and Control of Pollution) Act, 198 1, the Water (Prevention and Control of Pollution) Act, 1974, the Environment (Protection) Act, 1986 the Public Liability Insurance Act, 1991, the National Environment Tribunal Act, 1995 the National Environment Appellate Authority Act, 1997, Wildlife Protection Act, 1972 and Forest (Conservation) Act 1980. Besides the legislative measures, a National Conservation Strategy and Policy Statement on Environment and Development, 1992, National Forest Policy, 1988 and a Policy statement on Abatement of Pollution, 1992 have been evolved.

The Ministry is in the process of formulation of a National Action Plan on Conservation of Biodiversity and National Environment Policy. The Organisational structure of the Ministry indicating various divisions, associated and autonomous offices/ agencies is given in Annexure-1.

Allocation of Business

— Environment and Ecology, including environment in coastal waters, in mangroves and coral reefs but excluding marine environment on the high seas.

— Botanical Survey of India and Botanical Gardens.

— Zoological Survey of India.

— National Museum of Natural History (NMNH).

— The Water (Prevention and Control of Pollution) Cess Act, 1977.

— The Air (Prevention and Control of Pollution) Act, 1981.

— The Indian Forest Act, 1927.

— The National Environment Tribunal Act, 1995

— The Wildlife (Protection) Act, 11972.

— The Forest (Conservation) Act, 1980.

— The Environment (Protection) Act, 1986

— The Public Liability Insurance Act, 1991

— Biosphere Reserve Programme

— National Forest Policy and Forestry Development in the country, including Social Forestry.

— Forest Policy and all matters relating to forests and forest administration in so far as the Andaman and Nicobar Islands are concerned.

— Indian Forest Services

— Wildlife preservation and protection of wild birds and animals.

— Central Zoo Authority

— Fundamental research, including coordination thereof and higher education in forestry.

— Padmaja Naidu Himalayan Zoological Park.

— National Assistance to Forestry Development Schemes.

— Central Ganga Authority

— The National Environment Appellate Authority Act, 1997

— Indian Plywood Industries Research and Training Institute, Bangalore

— Forest Survey of India, Dehradun

— National Afforestation and Eco-Development Board.

" Desert and Desertification.

An overview of the activities of the Ministry and its associated offices/organisations during the year:

Survey of Natural Resources

Flora

— Seventy-nine exploration tours were undertaken by various circles and units of the Botanical Survey of India (BSI) in different priority areas of the country during which about 25,000 specimens have been collected and about 11,791 of them were identified.

— 1075 plants belonging to 230 species from wild were introduced to preserve the germplasm.

— 24 species of threatened and endangered plants were conserved and multiplied.

— Seeds of 56 species of economic and medicinal importance were preserved in the seed bank.

— An All India Coordinated Project on Taxonomy has been initiated.

Fauna

— A total of 68 surveys covering different ecosystems in various states of the country were conducted by the Zoological Survey of India (ZSI).

— The National Zoological Collections were further enriched by the addition of 10,595 identified examples belonging to 834 species.

— During the year detailed taxanomic studies resulted in the discovery of two genera and 26 species new to science.

— A total of 3,409 examples (10 species) of Chaetogantha were identified out of the material obtained during the cruises of Sagar Sampada

— Three volumes under the Fauna of India series and one volume each of Records of ZSI and Fauna of Mahanadi were published.

— Undertaken a pilot project of Global Environment Facility on the biodiversity of coral reef associated fauna in Andaman and Nicobar Islands.

Forests

Action are being initiated for publication of the State of Forest Report, 1999 the seventh in the series of biennial reports by the Forest Survey of India.

Conservation of Natural Resources including Forestry and Wildlife

Biosphere Reserves

During the year the 10th Biosphere Reserve has been set up at Dehang-Debang area of Arunachal Pradesh.

Wetlands, Mangroves and Coral Reefs

— During the year an amount of Rs. 140 lakhs has been released to the State Governments for the management action plans of Pongdam in Himachal Pradesh, Wullar in Kashmir, Loktak in Manipur, Rudrasagar in Tripura and Kolleru in Andhra Pradesh.

— One more wetland has been identified for conservation viz Rudrasagar from Tripura increasing the list to twenty wetlands for intensive conservation and management in the country.

— Wetland Strategy has been drafted.

— A review workshop and a meeting of the reconstituted National Committee on Conservation and

Management of Mangroves and Coral Reef were held during September 1998. The Committee has recommended the establishment of a Network of Mangrove Information and data base centres along the East and West Coasts of India and Indian Coral Reef Monitoring Network (ICRMN). A PDF-B Project on strengthening of Gulf of Mannar Biosphere Reserve with financial assistance from UNDP/GEF is being implemented.

Bio-diversity Conservation

— The National Policy and Action Strategy for Biodiversity has been finalised.

— The legislation on bio-diversity is under finalisation.

— The report to the Secretariat of the' Convention on Biological Diversity highlighting the measures undertaken for conservation and sustainable use of biodiversity was released on 2911 December 1998 on the occasion of International Day for Biodiversity.

Combating desertification

— The Ministry participated in two international meetings, held to discuss the Thematic Programme Networking on the six areas identified for regional cooperation amongst Asian countries.

— India has been identified as the focal point for Thematic Programme Area-2 on agroforestry and soil conservation in arid, semi-arid and dry subhumid areas.

Forest conservation

— During 1998, 854 proposals from various States and UT Governments were processed under the Forest (Conservation) Act 1980, out of which 365 were given stage II approval and 346 were given stage I approval and 143 were rejected on merit.

— All other schemes aimed at the conservation and management of the forests of the country were continued.

— Revised guidelines have been used under Forest (Conservation) Act for proposals for development projects.

— An expert committee for development of a long term strategy on forest conservation vis-a-vis mining activities was constituted.

— A high level committee has been constituted on 'Jhudpi Jungle'.

— A Joint Forest Management monitoring cell has been created to assess the impact of JFM Programme in the Ministry on the protection and development of forests.

Wildlife conservation

— The network of protected areas now comprises 84 National Parks and 447 Wildlife -Sanctuaries covering about 1.50 lakh sq. km. Area of the country

— One meeting of the Indian Board for Wildlife was held during the year.

— Financial assistance was provided to 28 National Parks and 107 Sanctuaries in 23 states for development of National Parks and Sanctuaries.

— Award in the name of Amrita Devi Vishnoi has been instituted for showing valour and courage in protection of wildlife

— During the year two new tiger reserves were created in Karnataka and Mahrashtra respectively.

— An amount of Rs. 893.13 lakhs was provided upto Dec, 1998 as Central assistance for development and maintenance of the Project Tiger areas.

— An amount of Rs. 4.50 crores was allocated to the elephant range states to provide for habitat management, management of man-elephant conflicts etc.

— A technical workshop to formulate collection plan of endangered species in Southern Indian Zoos was organised in Chennai.

Environmental impact assessment

— A total of 250 projects were appraised for environmental and site clearance during the year, out of which, 80 were cleared 88 were either rejected or exempted and the rest are pending.

— Coastal Zone Authorities have been set up both at National and State/Union Territory levels to take measures for protecting and improving the quality of coastal environment and preventing, abating and controlling environmental pollution in coastal areas.

— The Ministry has constituted a committee to identify areas adversely affected due to mining and to commission specific studies for the development of action plans for environmental protection vis-a-vis mining activities.

— A committee has been constituted under the chairmanship of Director General of Hydrocarbons, Ministry of Petroleum and Natural Gas to formulate guidelines for management of wastes emanating during offshore drilling.

— A draft Notification was issued in September 1998, notifying Pachmarhi region in Madhya Pradesh as an eco-sensitive zone with the intention of regulating industrial mining and tourism activities in the area and to conserve the natural and man-made heritage.

Prevention and control of pollution

— Steps were taken to control pollution from 17 categories of highly polluting industries. Out of a total of 1151 industries identified in 1991, now only 155 units are not having adequate facilities to comply with the standards.

— 24 critically polluted areas have been identified and Action Plans have been prepared for 22 areas and are being implemented by CPCB/SPCBs,

— River basin-wise surveys conducted to identify the polluted streteches and their sources. 14 major rivers are included under the River Action Programme.

— Environmental guidelines for siting and operation of industries were brought out.

— Public hearing has been made mandatory for all projects requiring environmental clearance.

— Environmental audit in the form of environmental statement has been made mandatory for all the polluting industries.

— To promote pollution prevention in small scale industries, 15 waste minimisation circles have been set up in various parts of the country and about 100 such more circles are being established for adoption of clean technology, better work practice and energy conservation techniques.

— Environmental Epidemiological Studies have been initiated in different parts of the country to find out impact of pollution on human health and suggest mitigative measures.

— For control of pollution from automobiles, stricter emission standards, introduction of unleaded petrol in major cities, installation of catalytic converters, introduction of low sulfur fuels and improvement in the fuel quality have been undertaken;

— Preparation of zoning atlas for siting of industries based on environmental considerations in various districts of the country has been taken up. So far 19 such districts have been covered.

— A scheme for setting up of Common Effluent Treatment Plants (CETP) in cluster of small industrial units has been taken up. About 7 CETP projects have been approved which are at various stages of implementation.

— A Network of Ambient Air (290) and Water (480) Quality Monitoring Stations has been set up throughout the country.

— Effluent and Emission Standards have been notified under the Environment (Protection) Act, 1986 for 'about 40 categories of industries. Besides, standards 'for ambient air and water quality have also been notified.

— Fiscal incentives are provided for installation of pollution control equipment and also for shifting of industries from congested areas. These include depreciation allowance at 100%, investment allowance, custom and excise duty exemptions for pollution control/monitoring equipments. Excise duty exemptions on utilisation of fly ash, phosphogypsum etc. are also provided.

— The White Paper on status of pollution in Delhi with a Action Plan for its control prepared earlier for Delhi is being implemented. The respective state governments of Maharashtra, Tamil Nadu and West Bengal had been advised to prepare similar Action Plans for Mumbai, Chennai and Calcutta respectively. Out of these, Mumbai Action Plan has been prepared and the authority to implement the Action Plan is being constituted. The Action Plan for Chennai is awaited.

— Six Environment Authorities have been constituted under the EPA, including the National Environment Appellate Authority.

— Emphasis is being laid on the collection and treatment of waste water before its disposal on land or on surface waters. For this purpose, a sewage tre- nent plant with proper collection and con nce system is being promoted.

— Prom n of waste minimisation techniques to conser aw material by recovering solvents is encouraged which also leads to reduction of pollution at source.

— Vehicular pollution being the main reason for air pollution in the major cities, stricter emission standards for automobiles fuel quality standards etc. have been notified. Use of clean fuel such as CNG and Propane is being promoted specially for plying of commercial vehicles in the major cities.

— Noise pollution control is being is given due importance specially in metropolitan cities to deal with the problem of traffic noise, industrial noise, noise generated through loudspeakers, bursting of crackers, DG sets etc.

— Inventorisation (quality and characteristics) of hazardous wastes is being taken up to develop a common facility for disposal of hazardous wastes and chemicals at pre-determined sites.

— Implementation of monitoring of Bio-medical Wastes (Handling & Management) Rules, 1998 for providing necessary facilities for safe disposal of bio-medical wastes generated by hospitals, nursing homes and clinics.

Hazardous Substances Management

— Draft ammendments to the Chemical Accident (emergency, planing, preparedness and response) Rules, 1996 have been notified.

— Final notification banning import of Waste Asbestos has been gazetted.

— The draft for the revision of Rules for manufactures, import, export and storage of Hazardous Micro organisms/ Genetically Engineered Organisms or Cells, 1989 has been vetted by the Law Ministry and is in the process of being notified.

— The Bio-medical Waste (Management and Handling) Rules, 1998 have been notified.

— The Ministry has issued draft Recycled Plastics Usage Rules, 1998 inviting suggestions and objections.

— Fourth edition of the Red Data book containing details to be performed during emergency, names, addresses etc. of the experts has been published and circulated.

— A National Poison Information Centre has been set up by the Ministry in the Department of Phamacology, All India Institute of Medical Sciences, New Delhi for dissemination information in the treatment and management of poisoning due to chemicals and other products.

— Three institutions viz. FICCI, HRD Foundation, New Delhi and Disaster Management Institute, Bhopal have been financially assisted for conducting training programmes on emergency preparedness and accident prevention.

— Final Act of the UN-Sponsored Convention on the Prior-Informed Conscent Procedure for certain hazardous chemicals and pesticides on international trade has been adopted at the conference of Planipotentiaries at Rottardam, Netherlands during 10- 11, Sept, 1998.

Regeneration and development

National river conservation directorate

— Out of the 261 schemes of pollution abatement sanctioned under Ganga Action Plan (GAP) Phase-I, 254 schemes have been completed upto 30.9.1998.

— A capacity to treat 728 mid of sewage has been commissioned as against the target of 873 mid.

— The National River Conservation Plan (NRCP) covers 141 towns located along 22 inter-state rivers in 14 States. The total cost of the schemes is Rs. 2014.39 crores.

— To improve implementation of GAP in Bihar, directions were issued on June 11, 1998 through the Centre Pollution Control Board (CPCB) to the State Pollution Control Board, Bihar to initiate action against the dafaulting Government Departments/ Local Bodies under the Water Act, 1974.

— A Standing Committee of the National River Conservation Authority (NRCA) has been constituted under the Chairmanship of Minister (E&F) to enable more frequent review of the progress of river cleaning programme.

— A Project Advisory Committee under, the Chairmanship of Shir K.C. Sivaramakrishnan, Member NRCA has been constituted to advise on issues such as speedy implementation of the programme, proper operation and maintenance of assets improving resource recovery from sewage treatment and enhancing public participation in the programme.

— Chief Minister of the three GAP State have been requested to constitute review committees under them with Members of Parliament, MLAs of the concerned towns along with Chairmen/Mayors of local bodies to review the progress of the Action Plan on regular basis.

— The Standing Committee of NRCA has decided that assets being created under the River Action

— Plans would be handed over to the local bodies after completion and that the construction agency may continue to maintain the assets on contract basis till such time as the local body acquires the necessary technical expertise for this purpose. The construction agency may maintain the assets under the supervision of the local body who may be financially assisted by the State Government.

— A committee of NGOs is being constituted for suggesting improvement in the programme.

— Guidelines for better public participation in River Action Plans were issued to concerned state governments.

National afforestation and Eco-development Board

— Seed Development Scheme was revised to add Pasture seeds of grasser and legumes in addition to tree species.

— Financial assistance of Rs. 5.87 crores has been provided to State Forest Departments for purpose of raising 50 trees in every village under the Swam Jayanti Kunj Scheme.

— The four Eco-Task Forces of ex-servicemen funded by NAEB continued to work on afforestation, pasture development, soil and water conservation and other restorative works in their areas of deployment.

— The seven Regional Centres of the NAEB located in Universities and other national level Institutions continued to assist the Board in implementing the various schemes throughout the country. These Centres also carried out problem-specific studies, evaluated the programmes and workshops.

— The Guidelines of the scheme for financial assistance to Non Governmental Organisations (NGO's) and Voluntary Agencies (VAs) for afforestation and tree planting activities have been revised to provide for improved cost-norms and simplified procedures.

Research

Environmental Research

— Under the three major research schemes viz., Man and Biosphere Programme, Environment Research Programme and the Action-oriented Research, Demonstration and Extension Programmes on Eastern and Western Ghats, a total no.of 45 new projects were sanctioned, 45 projects were completed and 112 projects were serviced and monitored for their progress during the year.

— Under the Environment Management Capacity Building Technical Assistance Project funded by the World Bank on Advisory Committee has been constituted to guide and monitor the 'activities of a sub component on Environment Research.

— Ethnobotanical investigations in tribal areas under All India Coordinated Research Project on Ethnobiology (AICRPE) revealed that the tribals have specific knowledge about use of over 10,000 wild plant species which includes 8000 medicinal plant, 4000 ediblle species etc.

— A delegation leld by the Minister (E&F) participated in the 4th, Conference of Parties (COP) to the

Framework Convention on climate change (FCCC), held during November, 1998 at Buenos. Aires, Argentina.

— India participated in the fourteenth session of the Inter Governmental Panel on the Climate Change (IPCC) held during October 1998 at Vienna.

— The G.B. Pant Institute of Himalayan Environment and Development (GBPIHED) continued with its various projects and activities aimed at sustainable development of the Himalayan region.

— The GBPIHED has utilized the strengths of Geographical Information System (GIS) and Remote Sensing Technology for the assessment of biodiversity, analysis and land use, land cover changes and resources management.

— An inventory of Indian Himalayan medicinal plants prepared by GBPIHED has resulted in identification of 1748 species belonging to angiosperms (1685 opp), gymnosperm (12 spp) and pteridophytes (51 spp).

— Large scale propagation or selected plant using conventional and biotehnological techniques continued in GBPIHED and *in vitro* protocols have been established for tea, malu, maggar, ringal, butter tree and some medicinal plants.

Research under the national River Conservation Plan (NRCP)

— The stretch-wise research projects undertaken for bio-conservation and bio-monitoring the river Ganga using indicator species approach were completed during the year.

— The Central Pollution Control Board in collaboration with the State Pollution Control. Boards of the coastal States has initiated surveys and studies to assess the actual pollution load in the 26 medium and minor rivers in the States of Goa, Tamil Nadu, Gujarat, Kerala, Orissa and Karnataka, Similar proposals from Andhra Pradesh and Maharashtra are likely to be taken up shortly.

Forestry research

— The Indian Council of Forestry Research and Education (ICFRE), Dehradun continued to coordinate, direct and oversee the research activities of the 11 research institutes/centres under its administrative control.

— The thrust area of forestry research is on increasing productivity through genetic and silvicultural improvement, treatment of waste land, conservation of forest ecosystems, wood substitutes, tribal development and social forestry.

— A modified ACA technology for preservative treatment of Eucalyptus hybrid was developed through treatment at elevated temperature. This resulted into reduction of treatment time from 7 days to just 4 hours.

— A protocol for mass clonal multiplication of superior phenotypes of *Eucalyptus fereticomis via* Micropropagation was developed.

— About 1200 wood samples were examined and identified received from various Govt. departments, Public undertakings, Central Bureau of Investigation (CBI)/Police Deptts.

— Seed collection, extraction and germination procedure were standardized for commercially important forestry medicinal plants namely, *Feronia elephantum, Ternlinalia spp. and Syzygium cumini.*

— 4000 rhizomes of bamboo (Dendrocalamus stictus) and 2000 plants of neem, babool, shisham and mulberry along with 300 fruit yielding tree species were distributed amongst farmers.

— Parthenium weeds were successfully controlled in experiments using extracts of Eucalyptus bark and leaves. Spraying of the extracts 'resulted in immediate wilting and blackening of the weeds.

— Protocols have been developed for 3 species viz., Acacia nilotica, Prosopis cineraria and Dalbergia sissoo for seed viability by TTC method.

— Collection and *ex-situ* conservation of 35 ethnomedicinal plants has been made and demonstrated to the people.

— Clonal propagation of neem through tissue culture has been successfully achieved and the plants so raised have already been planted out in the field.

Wildlife research

— The Wildlife Institute of India (WII), Dehradun continued to conduct research on the ecological, biological, socio-economic and managerial aspects of wildlife conservation in various parts of country.

— Initiated collaborative project with US Forest Service on Management of Forests in India for biological diversity and forest productivity a new perspective.

— Initiated a project on Ecology of the Asiatic Wild dog (Cuon alpinus) in Central India in collaboration with Institute of Terrestrial Ecology.

— The Salim Ali Centre for Ornithology and Natural History (SACON) continued with its research and extension activities relating to different aspects of ornithology and natural history during the year.

National Natural Resources Management System (NNRMS)

— A Standing Committee on Bioresources and Environment (SC-B) constituted by the Planning Commission advises the Ministry on the methods of using remote sensing technology for optimal use and management of natural resources of the country.

— During the year 6 projects have been sanctioned and the progress of 23 ongoing projects have been monitored.

Education, training and information forestry education, training and extension

— The Indian Council of Forestry Research and Education (ICFRE), Dehradun continued to organise, direct and manage the activities related to forestry education, extension and training.

— During the year, 28 candidates were awarded doctorate degree.

— Seventeen tested technologies developed by ICFRE have been prioritised on the basis of clients demand for extension.

— Financial assistance of Rs. 10 lakhs has been extended to various universities to strengthen education in forestry discipline.

— The Indira Gandhi National Forest Academy (IGNFA) continued to impart in-service professional training to IFS probationers. The Academy has so far trained 1793 IFS probationers and 231 foreign trainees.

— The IGNFA commemorated India's 50 year of Independence by organising two-day workshop on 25' and 26' May 1998 in which senior forest officer upto the 1970 batch participated.

— The diploma of Associate of IGNFA (AIGNFA) have been revived.

— The convocation of IGNFA was held on 30. 5.1998, after a lapse of 11 years.

— The Directorate of Forest Education, Dehradun continued to control, co-ordinate and manage all the regular training courses of the State Forest Service and the Forest Range Officers of the Country.

— The India Plywood Industries Research and Training Institute (IPIRTI), Bangalore continued with its training in saw milling and plywood.

— The Indian Institute of Forest Management (IIFM), Bhopal continued with its activities in education, training, research and consultancy related to forest management.

— The Management Development Programme (MDP) of IIFM continued to impart training to serving forestry personnel from various State Forest Department (SFDs) as well as officials from NGOs and other departments.

— During the year four new consultancy assignments were undertaken by IIFM.

Wildlife education and training

— The Wildlife Institute of India (WII), Dehradun continued to conduct the regular degree and diploma courses, long and short term training courses, workshops, seminars etc., on various' aspect of wildlife conservation and management.

— The WII organized one week capsule course in Wildlife Management during September 21-25, 1998.

— The WII conducted two short orientation courses (two weeks each) in Wildlife Tourism and Conservation during October-November, 1998.

— A training workshop on the Application of Geographic Information System (GIS) and Remote Sensing in Wildlife Conservation was organized by WII during I ' - 101 May, 1998.

Non-formal environment education, awareness and training

— A major initiative has been taken by the Ministry to review ad expand the existing components of environment education at all levels of formal education i.e. secondary, senior secondary and tertiry levels.

— The Minister (E&F) has written to all the Chief Ministers urging them to introduce environment education as a compulsory subject in the school curriculum from the next academic session. Copies of this Paper have also been forwarded to all the vice-chancellors, proponent NGOs working in the field of environment and eminent educationists of the country.

— The National Environment Awareness Campaign 1998 focussed on the theme, "keep our water resources clean". Twenty seven Regional Resources Agencies (RRAs) assisted the Ministry in conducting this campaign.

— During the year 1998-99, 1600 Eco-clubs have been set up in different parts of the country.

— White paper on National Environment Education Policy is being prepared by the Ministry.

Centres of excellence

— The Centre for Environment Education (CEE), Ahmedabad and the CPR Environment Education Centre (CPREEC) Chennai continued to organise activities aimed at creating environmental awareness among all sections of the society, especially students and teachers.

— The CEE and CPREEC brought out a number of environmental educational resource materials for different target groups during the year.

— The Centre for Ecological Sciences (CES), Bangalore continued to conduct research in front line areas of basic and applied ecology with special reference to the Western Ghats.

— During the year CES has carried out 21 projects in the broad areas of Biodiversity of India, Ecology and Conservation Biology, Animal Behaviour, Mathematical Ecology and Conservation, etc.

— The Centre for Environmental Management of Degraded Ecosystems (CEMDE) Delhi pursued research on the ecological rehabilitation of degraded ecosystems.

— The CEMDE has developed a bio-pesticide of microbial origin in controlling termites infestation to combat major biotic stress for forest tress and crops particularly in semi-arid regions.

— The CEMDE is in the process of patenting bio-molecule (chemical) isolated from leguminous plant.

— The CEMDE has also developed a simple, cost effective, low-input technology for the prevention of dust blow as well as for the mobilisation of toxic elements.

— During the year the Salim Ali Centre for Ornithology and Natural History, Coimbatore completed various ongoing -research projects and initiated several new ones.

— The Tropical Botanic Garden and Research Institute (TBGRI), Thiruvananthapuram has been designated as a Centre of Excellence for conservation and sustainable utilisation of tropical plant diversity.

— TBGRI has initiated work on economic evaluation of biodiversity, conservation and re-introduction of certain rare and endangered species.

— The Centre of Mining Environment (CME), Dhanbad carried out extensive investigations on the environmental engineering characterisation of fly ash.

— The CME has developed an EIA methodology for open cast mining projects.

National Museum of Natural History (NMNH)

— The NMNH continued to promote non-formal environmental education and create conservation awareness among the people through various in-house and out-reach activities.

— A Tableau on the theme of 'Save the Environment' was prepared by NMNH for participation in the Republic Day celebration, 1999 on behalf of the Ministry.

— The NMNH and its Regional Museum of Natural History (RMNH), Mysore participated in the 6' World Wilderness Congress from 24' to 29' October, 1998, at Bangalore.

— Director, NMNH participated in the Triennial of the International Council of Museum at Melboune, Australia from 10- 16 October, 1998 and was also elected as the Vice President of the International Committee of Natural History Museums (COM-NatHist) for the next three year term.

— The NMNH and its RMNH, Bhopal participated in the 2nd World Science Centre Congress at the Science City, Calcutta from 11-16 January, 1999

Fellowship and awards

— The Pitamber Pant National Environmental Fellowship Award 1998 has been given to Dr. U.C. Mishra, Director, Health, Safety and Environment Group-Bhaba Atomic Research Centre, (BARC) Mumbai.

— The B.P. Pal National Environment Fellowship Award, for Biodiversity for the year 19.98 has been awarded to Dr. Shashi Kant, Department of Bio-Sciences, University of Jammu, Jammu.

Environmental information

— One new Environmental Information System (ENVIS) centre in the field of 'electronic media and communication' has been set up at the Centre for Media Studies (CMS), New Delhi. The ENVIS network thus consists of 25 network partners now.

— The ENVIS network responded to a total number of 12,756 queries during the year, of which 11,660 were national and 1096 were international.

— Home page developed by ENVIS could be browsed through Internet at URL : http// www.nic.in/ envfor/envis.

— ENVIS, since October' 98 has started publishing the ENVIRO NEWS newsletter of the Ministry on monthly basis, with the main objective of disseminating information to all concerned on various important policies, new rules/legislations, important notifications and other important decisions taken by the Ministry from time to time.

— The Sustainable Development Networking Program (SDNP) Secretariat has started functioning in the Ministry during the year and the personnel required to man the secretariat for performing the activities of SDNP has been recruited.

—qA website for SDNP is being developed for accessing information by a wide cross section of users.

—qENVIS associated itself in publishing various publications of the Ministry.

— All the ENVIS Centres continued their activities related to collection, collation, storage, retrieval and dissemination of information in their respective subject areas.

Legislation and institutional support

— The Ministry is currently preparing a comprehensive National Policy on Environment. A White Paper will be published first to be followed by the National Environment Policy.

— The Water (Prevention and Control of Pollution) Cess Act, 1977 is being amended again so as to enhance the water cess rates thereby augmenting the resources of Pollution Control Boards.

International co-operation

— A National Steering Committee under the Chairmanship of Secretary (E&F) has been set up to review the progress of India : Environment Management Capacity Building Technical Assistance Project.

— A Programme Management Board PMB) has been constituted to recommend, implement and manage Programme Support Document under UNDP Country cooperative Framework-I. So far, 15 projects have been approved out of which 5 have reached implementation stage.

— The first ever Global Environment Facility (GEF) Assembly meet, hosted by India was held at the Vigyan Bhawan, New Delhi 1 -3 April 1998.

— On September 8, 1998, an MOU with Federal Republic of Germany was signed during the visit of President of India to Germany for the field of Environment Protection.

— Bilateral cooperation programmes and follow up of MOUs/Joint Statement of Intent have been signed with Brazil, China, Iran, Russia, Tajikistan, Turkmenistan, USA and Vietnam.

— Minister (E&F) participated in the 'Athens Summit'98 held in Greece from 11 - 13) September, 98 and delivered a speech on "Environment and Development : The Indian Perspective."

— Minister (E&F) also had bilateral discussion with the Kenyan Minister for Environmental Conservation in May 1998 who envinced interest in sharing of expertise through the wealth of the existing institutions.

— A meeting with North-Eastern (NE) States and External Funding Agencies was held on 30.11.98 to disseminate information regarding procedure for funding from external Agencies. Representatives of NE States, World Bank, UNDP, JICA, WHO, FAO, ICEF, DFID, UK and officers of this Ministry attended this meeting.

— Minister (E&F) led Indian delegation in the several international meet/conventions viz, the sixth session of Commission on Sustainable Development, (CSD), in New York, the special session of the Governing Council of UNEP, in Nairobi, the 7" Governing Council meeting of South Asian Environment Cooperation Programme (SACEP), etc.

— A delegation led by the Minister (E&F) participated in the Tenth Meeting of Parties to the Montreal Protocol, held during November, 1998 at Cairo, Egypt.

— A bi-monthly newsletter on ozone issues is being published by the Ozone Cell of the Ministry to disseminate information on ODS phase out to industry and others.

— An international children's painting competition was organized and the best entries were awarded by the Minister of State (E&F) on the occasion of International Ozone Day celebration on 16.9.98. Three best paintings were sent to UNEP-IE Ozone Action Programme for participation in the international competition in Paris. Mr. Maharshi Bhupender Jesalpur of Ahmedabad bagged the special merit award on the International competition for his planning.

— UNEP-IE Ozone Action Programme, Paris held its first South-Asia ODS officers Network Meeting in Delhi.

— Custom/excise duty exemption continued to be provided for ODS phase out projects.

— Detailed guidelines and procedure were finalized to implement Government notifications to grant benefit of duty exemption for new investments with non-ODS technologies.

— Draft Rules on ODS phase out under the Environment (Protection) Act, 1986 have been notified for public suggestions/comments.

Administration, plan co-ordination and budget

Administration

— Under IFS cadre management, cadre review revising the strength and composition of the Sikkim cadre was carried out during the year and the necessary notification has been issued by the Department of Personnel and Training on 29th January and 141 October respectively.

— Six offices under the Ministry were inspected during the year to ensure effective implementation of the Official Language Policy.

— Seventeen employees were nominated for Hindi typing stenography, Probodh, Praveen and Pragya courses under the Hindi teaching schemes.

— The Minister (E&F) convened a series of meeting with Hon'ble Member of Parliament belonging to different segments of society which is unprecedented in nature.

Civil Construction Unit (CCU)

The CCU of the Ministry has taken up 96 major works so far with a total estimated cost of Rs. 152.12 crores.

Plan Co-ordination and Budget

— The budget allocation of the Ministry for 98-99 was Rs. 704.09 crores against Rs. 543.7 crores for 97-98.

— The total outlay for the Ministry for 1999-2000 is Rs. 700.00 crores.

2

India's Environment

At the time of India's Independence, our priority was the provision of the basic human needs of food, fuel, shelter, health, employment, etc., to our vast population. As such the focus of our Five Year Plans was on agriculture, health, family welfare etc. In the Fourth Five Year Plan, problems related to environment received direct attention and a Committee was set up in 1972 to look into these problems and suggest a solution in consulation with experts and concerned minstries/departments of the government. Another Committee was set up in January 1980, for reviewing the existing legislative measures and administrative machinery for ensuring environmental protection and for recommending ways to strengthen them. On the recommendation of this high-powered Committee, the Department of Environment was set up in 1980. Consequently in 1985, it was upgraded to a full-fledged Ministry of Environment and Forests to serve as the focal point in the administrative structure for the planning, promotion and coordination of environmental and forestry programmes.

Environmental problem in India can be classified into two broad categories: (a) those arising as negative effects of the very process of development and (b) those arising from conditions of poverty and under-development. The first category has to do with the impact of efforts to achieve rapid economic growth and development. Poorly planned developmental projects are usually environmentally destructive. The second category has to do with the impact on the health and integrity of our natural resources such as land, soil, water, forests, wildlife, space, etc., as a result of proverty.

There are about 30 major enactments related to protection of environment now being administered by the Central and state governments. Prominent among these are: Wildlife (Protection) Act, 1972; The Forest (Conservation) Act, 1980; The Water (Prevention and Control of Pollution) Act, 1974; The Air (Prevention and Control of Pollution) Act, 1981; The Water (Prevention and Control of Pollution) Cess Act, 1977; The Environment (Protection) Act, 1986; The Public Liability Insurance Act; 1991; The Motor Vehicle Act, 1938 as amended in 1988; The Factories Act and the Insecticides Act. These are implemented through several organisations like Central and state pollution control boards, chief inspectors of factories and insecticides inspectors of agriculture departments, etc.

The Environment (Protection) Act, 1986, brought into force from 19 November 1986 is a landmark legislation as it is an umbrella Act for the protection of environment and aims at plugging the loopholes in the other related Acts. The salient features of this Act are as follows: (a) conferring powers on the Central Government to; (i) take all necessary measures for protecting quality of environment; (ii) coordinate activities of states, officers and other authorities under the Act or under any other law related to the objects of this Act; (iii) Plan and execute a nationwide programme for prevention, control and abatement of environmental pollution; (iv) lay down standards for discharge of environmental pollutant; (v) empower any person to enter, inspect, take samples and test; (vi) establish or recognise environmental laboratories; (vii) appoint or recognise analysts; (viii) lay down standards for quality of environment; (ix) restrict areas in which industries, operations or process may not be carried out or shall be carried out subject to certain safeguards; (x) lay down safeguards for prevention of accidents and take remedial measures in case of such accidents; (xi) lay down procedures and safeguards for handling hazardous substances; (xii) constitute an authority or authorities for exercising powers; (xiii) issue directions to any person, officer or authority including the power direct closure, prohibition or regulation of any industry, operation or process or stoppage or regulations of supply of electricity, water or any other services; (xiv) require any person, officer, state government or authority to furnish any prescribed information; and (xv) delegate powers to any of a state or authority; (b) it confers powers on persons to complain to courts regarding any violation of the provisions of the Act, after a notice of 60 days to prescribed authorities; (c) the Act makes it obligatory for the person incharge of a place to inform the prescribed authorities regarding any accidental discharge or apprehended discharge of any pollutant in excess of prescribed standards. Authorities on receipt of such information or otherwise shall take remedial measures are recoverable with inerest from the pollute; (d) it prescribes penalties for violation of the provisions of the Act. No distinction is shown between government department and other companies; and (e) jurisdiction of civil courts is barred under the Act.

Government has taken several steps to provide adequate legal and institutional basis for implementation of the Act. These include issue of rules, notification of standards, action regarding environmental laboratories, strengthening of state departments of environment and pollution control boards, delegation of powers, identification of agencies for carrying out various activities for hazardous chemical management and setting up of environemtn protection councils in the states. The Water (Prevention and Control of Pollution) Act, 1974 and the Air (Prevention and Control of

Pollution) Act, 1981, have been made more stringent. Steps have been taken to: (i) prevent pollution at source; (ii) encourage, develop and apply the best available practicable and technical solutions; (iii) ensure that the polluter pays for the pollution and control arrangements; (iv) focus protection on heavily polluted areas and river stretches; and (v) involve the public in decision-making.

One in every seven persons on this planet lives in India. With 16 per cent of the world's population and only 2.4 per cent of its land area, there is obviously a great demand on the natural resources including land. This is so in spite of the fact that an average Indian consumes a much lower quantum of resources than a person in the developed world. If an average person in the South were to consume as much as an average person in a developed country, the environmental crisis would be unimaginable. While, to a large extent, the lower per capita consumption is due to poverty, an important reason is also that a majority of the population in India follows a sustainable lifestyle which is based on environmentally sound practices evolved over thousands of years.

The environmental problem today is being precipitated partly because practices which were appropriate earlier, like shifting cultivation and unrestricted cattle grazing, are not so anymore. For instance, as a result of increasing population and decreasing availability of land, crop-fallow cycles in shifting cultivation have been reduced to a mere five years from a more sustainable 20-40 years in the past.

But just as there were learnings and difficulties with regard to traditional practices, so was the case with newly introduced technologies. Many measures, at one time seen as solutions, are today extracting an unanticipated price. The Green Revolution of the 1960s met India's growing demand for food. While it helped India to dramatically increase foodgrain production, what was not fully appreciated then was that the Green Revolution would on the one hand affect the country's natural resource capital, and on the other, create dependencies on inputs such as chemical fertilizers and pesticides. There are indications of soil health problems such as deficiency of micronutrients and organic matter, incidence of soil salinity and damage to the physical structure of the soil, apart from increasing dependence on chemical inputs, many of which are imported.

Today there is widespread realization that there can be no readymade solutions, that technology alone cannot solve problems, that we have to use all our ingenuity to find solutions which combine the best of the old practices with the benefits that modern science and technology can offer.

The challenges are staggering in number, scale and complexity. We need to develop and to modernize in less wasteful ways than is the current paradigm, but not lose our sound traditional values and practices. India will have to leap-frog over wasteful and polluting technologies and go for technologies which are the most environmentally sound, and are based on maximizing recycling and efficient use of resources practices which are inherent in India's traditions. It is when such development comes about that the population pressures will ease, as development brings down demographic growth rates.

The task is stupendous. For while the challenge of development might seem to be 'how to get there' the real challenges is 'how not to get there'. Urbanization, industrial growth, transportation systems, agriculture, housing... all have to stop imitating practices that are already being phased out in the developed world. With the North becoming more conscious about the condition of their own environment, 'dirty' factories are moving South. To cite only one example, the production of harmful and toxic dyestuff intermediates such as H-acid, K-acid, gamma acid and metanilic acid taken up in the 60s stands at over 41,000 tonnes in the country today, with an estimated Rs. 6 billion worth for export to the developed countries.

The forces which are taking India, and much of the developing world, on the conventional and largely imitative and unimaginative development path are many. But this path is not sustainable—for India or for the world. As Mahatma Gandhi remarked over 60 years ago. "God forbid that India should ever take to industrialism after the manner of the West. The economic imperialism of a single, tiny... kingdom is today keeping the world in chains. If an entire nation of 300 million took to similar economic exploitation, it would strip the world bare like locusts.

When the West developed, it did so perhaps in ignorance of the environmental impact of its activities. Today we know that such a path is neither practicable nor desirable for countries which are raising their standards of living. We, along with other developing countries, have to find alternative paths to an alternative goal. A goal which ultimately is the true goal of development—an environmentaly sound and sustainable quality of life, which is socially just and equitable. A goal that must be common to all citizens of the planet. A goal that is perhaps as distant from the developing world as it is from the over-consuming, wasteful societies of what is currently referred to as the 'developed' world.

It is this goal of development that we seek together as people, as organizations and as governments at the United Nations Conference on Environment and

Development. It is this intermeshing of environmental and developmental concerns that must form the goal of humankind.

The world is rapidly realizing that environmental issues such as global warming and ozone depletion, acid rain, marine pollution and the threat to biodiversity are global and not merely national issues. But in a world where per capita GNP varies from US $ 80 in Mozambique to US $ 29,880 in Switzerland; where life expectancy at birth varies from 42 years in Sierra Leone to 79 years in Japan; and where literacy rates vary from about 12 per cent in Somalia to over 95 per cent in the United States, what is not as explicitly understood is that development too is a global issue. And perhaps even less understood is the fact that a sustainable and viable planet requires that development be global. As Mrs. Indira Gandhi, then Prime Minister of India and the only visiting head of government to attend the UN Conference on the Human Environment in Stockholm in 1972, said, the removal of poverty is an integral part of the goal of an environmental strategy for the world.

It is towards this goal that several efforts are under way in India. These are environmental initiatives—not merely of government at various levels, but of people and organizations outside the government. They are efforts which may not all succeed, but they represent initiatives that are continuously under review and change. They represent the broad base of concern and the vibrancy of environmental efforts in India. These initiatives need to be shared in an effort to find the alternative paths that will lead all nations towards the true goal of development without environmental and social damage.

According to Planning Commission estimates, population figures are expected to go up from 856 million in 1991-92 to 938 million in 1996-97, showing an annual average growth rate of 18 per cent . If the growth rate remains around two per cent, this figure will go up to 955 million, According to current indications, the actual figure will be in between these two figures since the death rate has fallen below even the 2000-2001 and in any case will be below the rate of around two per cent as estimated by the current UN projections, of around 1,042 million in that year. If India is able to achieve a population growth rate of around 1.6 percent in the decade 2000-2001 to2010-2011, its population will reach 1,171 million, if the Planning Commission projections are used as a base. Even if this target is exceeded, the figure will be less than 1,224 million as estimated by the UN. These projections have not incorporated the detail of the 1991 census. The Registrar—General's Working Group on Population Projections set up conventionally by the Planning Commission, will have to firm up these alternative conjectural projections, in terms of underlying fertility, mortality and expected life span-behaviour, by age—group and rural-urban categories.

The other major category needing examination on this kind of perspective is the land or resource base of the economy. The Planning Commission has correctly projected that the net area sown or arable land of the country will remain constant at 141 million hectares. Growth in net area sown at around one per cent annually in the early period of planing fell to around 0.6 per cent and then to 0.3 per cent in subsequent decades and is now not growing at all. It is reasonable to assume that the exploitation of the geographical area of the country or the extensive land frontier has reached its limits. This is an important issue, the implications of which are not being realized with the urgency they deserve, since at a basic level resource constraints of a more severe kind faced by certain East Asian economies are now being approached in India. Organizations, communities, households and individuals will have to grasp this fact and live with it.

The intensive frontier for land use, however remains. It has been known for example that cropping intensity depends on irrigatin. Thus gross cropped area or harvested area has been shown in the past to be strongly determined statistically, in an econometric sense, by net irrigated area and irrigation intensity. This fundamental relationship can be used to project the intensive resource base of the economy.

Water management: Recognizing these problems the Finance Minister has been persuaded to introduce an Accelerated Irrigation Benefit Programme in the Annual Plan for this year. An outlay of Rs. 800 crore has ben provided for large irrigation project where substantial achievement can be expected—say in completing a section of the canal systems in the next two or three years and Rs. 100 crore for delivering water to the field in the next two agricultural years. These programmes will be strictly monitored. More important, a blue ribbon commission has been set up with the following terms of reference:

- To prepare an Integrated Water Plan for development of water resources for drinking, irrigation, industrial, flood control and other uses;
- To suggest modalities for transfer of surplus water to water-deficit basins by interlinking of rivers for achieving the above objectives;
- To identify important ongoing projects as well as new projects which should be completed on a priority basis together with phasing;
- Identify a technological and interdisciplinary research plan for the water sector with a view to maximizing the benefits;

- To suggest physical and financial resource generation strategies for the water sector; and
- Any other related issue.

The projections assume a vastly improved performance on the land and water management frontiers. It needs to be remembered that the balance ground water reserves towards the later half of the nineties will be nore and more limited. A very dramatic effort will be needed to harvest and carefully use the available water. Otherwise, the projected increase in cropping intensity will simply not take place. Cropping intensity increased from around 1.3 in the early nineties. In the nixt two decades, this effort needs to be considerably strengthened, so that cropping intensity can increase from 1.3 to 1.5. Harvesting of rainwater, recycling water from agricultural drainage systems, more judicious use of water for cropping, will all be required, Non-agricultural use of water will have to be far more econmical.

Another way of looking at the severe land constraint is to see that a net area sown per person will go down from around 0.17 ha to around 0.10 ha. The gross area sown per person currently around 0.2 ha will, even if cropping intensity increases very rapidly, go down to around 0.15-0.18 ha.

It has been shown elsewhere that limited co-operation in waer use has been successful in many watershed projects in resolving the land constraint. The same is true of lower level surface irrigation systems. Community involvement is also important for judicous management of aquifer systems and ground water use. In many cases, land management questions are equally important and are inextricably linked with water management, eg land shaping in hill slopes and on farm investment in irrigation commands.

The technology interface is important, both for land and water management and for cropping and non-crop farm systems that are optimal, in this class of issues. While a lot of research has been done and is available, the real issues are policy rules for fast replicability of existing knowledge and success stories. Community institutions have to be at the heart of this process. ICAR, its centres and sponsored institutions, have not easily participated in this process.

This kind of development is simply not possible if the functional literacy skills of the farm population arenot improved and if the peasant who works on the land, does not have rights to make improvements on it. There are a number of significant examples where based on local initiative, educational and training institutions led to knowledge-based growth in rural areas. These include the Charotar Vidya Mandal at Vallabh Vidyanagar (later Sardar Patel University), Dharamasthala Educational Trust (efforts of Veerendra Heggade) and many co-operative sponsored institutions in Maharashtra (for example the Pravara Ecucational Trust at Loni). Recognizing the importance of such efforts, the government of India has set up a National Council for Rural Institutes. The ICAR and its affiliates must be one of the major thrust institutions in this effort and its educational and extension wings must sponsor, acredit and support the effort.

The government's Basic Minimum Services (BMSDs) Programme also has the same objective. It consists of the following programmes which need integration with our agricultural strategy:

- 100 per cent coverage of provision of safe drinking water in rural and urban areas.
- 100 per cent coverage of primary health service facilities in rural and urban areas.

- Universalization of primary education.
- Provision of public housing assistance to all shelterless poor families.
- Extension of mid day meal programme in primary school to all rural blocks and urban slums and desadvantaged sections.
- Provision of connectivity to all unconnected villages and habitations.
- Streamlining the public distribution system with the focus on the poor.

The challenges

India is a land of physical, ecological, social, cultural and linguistic diversity. Bounded by the Himalayan mountain ranges in the north and the Indian Ocean in the south, it has a multitude of climates, soil types and geographical areas—and consequently of habitats and wildlife. But it is not only the physical and biological diversity that is enormous. The census reports 1,652 languages as mother tongues. Of these, 33 are spoken by over a 100,000 people each. India is also home to many religious communities and its ancient tradition of secularism is manifested in its Constitution.

Each of these languages and religions contributes to the vibrancy and variety of Indian life, and to the mosaic of India's social, cultural and economic life. 'Unity in Diversity' has been the maxim of cultural pluralism in India. But at times of resource shortages and allocation, it is not always easy to keep regional or sectorial aspirations subservient to national ones. To maintain the unity of India with all its diversity remains a challenge—but the binding forces evolved over centuries help meet this challenge.

India's population of 844 million is today growing at 2.11 per cent every year. This is expected to stabilize only in the second half of the next century, when India will be the most populous country in the world. Adding over 17 million people each year puts considerable pressure on the country's natural resources and reduces the gains of development.

The challenge underlying limiting population growth was brought out by Prime Minister P.V. Narasimha Rao who stressed recently the need for the country to "take upon itself the challenge to deal with population-related issues whish are inextricably linked to the total development of our nation." The `link' is usually misunderstood. It is not that population control will lead to development, but that development leads to a decrease in population growth rates.

High population growth rate is usually an indicator of poverty, and not the cause of it. This is perhaps best seen in the case of women's development. Taking just one indicator—female literacy—some trends become clear. States such as Kerala and Tamil Nadu which have among the highest female literacy rates in India (86.93 per cent and 52.29 per cent, respectively) are also among the states with the lowest decennial population growth rates (13.98 per cent and 14.94 per cent). This is just one development factor out of the many which act together to affect population.

Based on ideals long cherished by its people, the Constitution of India defines India as a 'Sovereign, Socialist, Secular, Democratic Republic'. the system of government is parliamentary with a federal structure, power and responsibility being shared between the Central and State Governments, and in turn with many local and district level authorities. The cooperation between various levels of government is crucial to development.

A challenge before a large country like India is to find the right blend between centralized and decentralized decision-making and between micro-level planning and macro-level planning. Decision-making that involves people at various levels brings in different perceptions and enriches the process. The importance of involving local people in decision-making, to bring in a better perspective of their requirements and in finding implementable solutions, is also being recognized. Starting from colonial times, several policies, laws and procedures have tended to alienate people from their natural resources. Evolving methods for the participation of local people in the management of common property resources is a major challenge for natural resource management.

The floodplains of the great rivers are India's food bowls. So far, food production has kept abreast of population increase. But the Green Revolution, which was largely responsible for this, has raised some questions of environmental costs. High-yielding varieties, making crops more vulnerable to disease. Soil health problems such as deficiency of micro-nutrients and organic matter, incidence of soil salinity, and damage to the physical structure of soil have arisen in the intensively cultivated areas. The need for higher inputs has resulted in chemical inputs going up from about 1.9 kg per ha of gross cropped area in 1960 to over 72 kg per ha by 1990-91. The challenge is not only to sustain and increase agricultural growth, but to do so without damaging the environment.

Of the total 329 million hectares (mha) of land, it is estimated that only 266 mha possess any potential for production. Of this, 143 mha is agricultural land and it is estimated that 85 mha suffers from varying degrees of soil degradation. Of the remaining 123 mha, 40 are completely unproductive. The balance 83 mha are classified as forest lands, of which over half are denuded to various degrees.

India has the world's largest cattle population. The 406 million head of livestock have to be supported on 13 mha, or less than 4 per cent of the land which is classified as pasture lands, most of which is overgrazed. Thus, out of 266 mha, about 175 mha or 66 per cent is degraded to varying degrees. Water and wind erosion account for the degradation of almost 150 mha of this. The challenge of prevention of erosion, and indeed of restoration of India's land resources, is intricately related to strategies for the management of land, water and vegetative cover.

Forests in India have been shrinking for several centuries owing to pressures of agriculture, commercial and industrial use, urbanization and other uses. The process continued after Independence. Vast areas that were once green are today wastelands. Bringing these back under vegetative cover is a major challenge.

Like indigenous people all over the world, the tribal communities that live in forests respect the trees, and the birds and animals that give them sustenance. Strategies are being developed for a greater degree of people's participation in forest management. The role of forest-dwelling communities in restoring and conserving forests is now being increasingly recognized. The challenge is to attempt to integrate the modern knowledge and skills of the Forest Department with the traditional knowledge and experience of the local communities, and to evolve strategies for the joint management of forests.

As in most places in the world, the forests and the agricultural plains have an intimate relationship. Forests usually act as catchments for rivers. With the increasing demand for water, plans were made to harness the mighty rivers through large irrigation projects. Typically, these would submerge forests, displace local communities and benefit agriculture in the plains. Today some of these, like the dam on the river Narmada and the Tehri dam, have become areas of debate. This is an issue which poses very difficult questions regarding the relationship between environment and development, and resolving these is a challenge the country faces.

If the world's rainfall were averaged over its landmass, it is seen that India receives more than one-and-a-half times the rain that other parts of the world get. But this rainfall has a large spatial and temporal variation and is highly seasonal. Eighty per cent of the country gets 80 per cent or more of the annual rainfall during the four months of the monsoon.

Managing water so that it is available when and where it is required is a major issue. Of the total 400 million hectare metres (mham) annual precipitation that India receives, approximately 150 mham percolates into the soil, 180 mham joins the surface flow and 70 mham evaporates. Of the 150 mham which enters the soil, about 110 mham constitutes soil moisture while 40 mham percolates into groundwater aquifers. Of the 180 mham run-off, major and minor irrigation projects have so far succeeded in trapping 17 mham in their reservoirs. Another 4 or 5 mham are stored in tanks and small reservoirs. Thus only about 16 per cent of the annual rainfall is available for irrigation.

Large dams which replaced traditional water-harvesting techniques in modern India were initially seen as the solution. But today the problems of displacement, submergence and drainage are subjects of serious debate. Increasing demands and new technologies are leading to the over-exploitation of groundwater, leading to an alarming drop in water tables in certain areas. This has even led to the problem of extreme salinity in some parts of the country. Rationalizing the use of groundwater is another important issue.

Community wastes, industrial effluents and excessive use of chemical fertilizers and pesticides are polluting surface water and affecting the quality of groundwater. The implications of this on human health and aquatic life are obvious. Finding optimal strategies for the conservation of water, provision of safe drinking water and keeping warer bodies clean are difficult challenges.

India is very rich in biodiversity. Preserving this heritage is a major challenge, as also utilizing this for development. With the considerably large financial resources and research capabilities available with the North, the benefits emanating from this biodiversity are being exploited more rapidly by the North than by the countries of its origin.

Although India is largely rural and agricultural, the 27 per cent Indians who live in urban areas constitute a large number in absolute terms. A very large number of these are the urban poor who live in highly degraded slums. Urbanization and industrialization pose a host of environmental problems that need urgent attention. Over 30 per cent of urban Indians live in slums. Out of India's 3,245 towns and cities, only 21 have partial or full sewerage and sewage treatment facilities. Coping with rapid urbanization is a major challenge facing the country today.

Several of India's cities started out as trading towns centred in agricultural area. As these grew, urban land requirements ate into some of the best agricultural lands. Location policies for urban and industrial growth from this point of view are other challenges to planning in India.

While on the one hand India has some of the most sophisticated industrial plants, there are many more using outdated, polluting technologies and makeshift facilities, with negligible provision for treating their wastes. As a result, there are many cities and industrial ares that would perhaps be classified among the worst in terms of their air and water pollution. Major initiatives are however being taken. The Environment Protection Act (1986), the Water (Prevention and Control of Pollution) Act, 1974, and the Air (Prevention and Control of Pollution) Act, 1981, have set standards that certain industries must fulfill. Much pollution control equipment is now available in the country. The Central Pollution Control Board and State Pollution Control Boards have their own machinery to monitor emission and pollution levels.

The choices, however, are difficult. Substantial resources, technical expertise, political and social will, awareness among the people and their support are required to implement these rules. Industries may need to be relocated, and new equipment added to treat the wastes. New, clean technologies need to replace older ones. In some cases plants may even need to be scrapped. These measures may involve loss of jobs in the short run and have an immediate consequence on the cost of products. These are difficult choices, especially in a developing country.

The Challenges of meeting India's growing energy requirements are many. presently, commercial and non-commercial sources contribute almost equally to fulfilling these needs. The current use of bio-resources for meeting energy requirements is far in excess of their regenerative capacities. Each source of commercial energy-hydel, thermal or nuclear—has major environmental consequences and the challenge is to utilize these resources with the least environmental damage. This involves determining the optimal technology, scale and location of such projects.

There is considerable scope for energy saving. For instance, the inefficiencies of the system can be seen from the fact that 100 tonnes of coal mined for the purpose of power generation provide only the energy equivalent of 5 tonnes of coal in the form of actual irrigation when we use electric pumping in the agricultural sector. A full 95 tonnes of coal is lost in energy euqivalent terms in the process of power generation, transmission and distribution, inefficiencies in the pump set itself and the irrigation system which finally reaches water to the farmer's field. Major investment would be required in the area of technology upgradation for increasing efficiency of generation, transmission and utilization of commercial energy. There are also technology constraints in using existing sources. Huge quantities of natural gas estimated to be worth about Rs. 50 million a day are today flared, rather than utilized for power generation, domestic fuel or feedstock for the production of fertilizer.

Another challenge is that of reorienting to today's conditions and needs, institutions, attitudes and infrastructures essentially built up during the colonial times. This change must take into account India's traditions of resource use, management, education etc. The change needs to come about in education, in attitudes, in administrative procedures and in institutions, for it affects the way people view technology, resources, and indeed development itself.

Poverty, however, remains the central issue and the biggest challenge. While the annual per capita income has been slowly rising over time, about 40 per cent of the people are below what is considered the poverty line. The challenge is therefore not only to find development paths and models which are environmentally sustainable but that are also socially just and culturally acceptable. For a very large number of the poor who depend on the resources of their immediate environment, poverty has been compounded by environmental degradation. Not only does the natural resource base of the immediate environment provide their basic requirements, it is also the basis of their livelihood and security. The challenge of poverty and the challenge of environment are therefore not two different challenges but two facets of the same challenge.

The problems are complex and the choices difficult. Each issue needs its own resolution, not a borrowed solution. A large number of areas need research and constant monitoring. Citizens and decision-makers need to become more aware of their environment and the intricate relationship it bears to development. Today in India we see the seeds of this effort. A national Ministry of Environment and Forest was set up in 1985. Most states have set up Departments of Environment and associated agencies. Several hundred institutions and several thousand NGOs are today, in one way or another, working towards coping with the challenges of environment and development. But the most hopeful sing perhaps is an increasing number of people who, individually and through their communities, are taking action—action that leads to a better environment and a better life. It is these efforts that need to be shared widely. The efforts of the people, NGOs and the Government.

The rapid increase in industrialisation and urbanisation has exerted extra pressure on the infrastructural facilities of human settlements manifesting in environment problems like increased incidence of air, water and noise pollution.

The ambient aire quality major towns and cities in the country is being monitored under the National

Ambient Air Quality Monitoring (NAAQM) programme. The monitoring results indicate that Sulphur Dioxide and Nitrogen dioxide levels are mostly within the permissible limits whereas Suspended Particulate Matter (SPM) values are higher than the prescribed limits at some places due to vehicular and air pollution, burning of fossil fuel and natural dusty conditions. The pollution caused by vehicles contributes significantly towards air pollution. The problem of suspended particulate matter is more acute during the summer due to local dusty conditions. During the winter months, lower ambient temperatures, lower mixing depth temperature inversion, higher traffic density, higher consumption of domestic fuels, aggravate the pollution problems.

The data on ambient water quality of rivers indicates that levels of coliform count and Biological Oxygen Demand (BOD) are generally high resulting in deterioration of water quality. This is primarily due to inadequate sanitation facilities and discharge of waste water into the surface water bodies without proper treatment.

Urban noise levels in major cities also indicate and incresing trend due to rise in human population, automobiles and industrial activities. Specific studies reveal that noise levels in industrial areas are generally within the prescribed limits but exceed the standards in respect of commercial, residential and silence zones during certain hours. The problem is more conspicuous near the traffic intersections and commercial centres.

The on-going initiatives of Government to improve environment include preventive as well as promotive measures. Fiscal incentives are provided by the Government to encourage the installation of appropriate pollution abatement equipment in the form of custom waive off and soft loans. While the industries are encouraged and the fiscal incentives are provided for installing equipment for control of pollution, punitive measures including legal action is taken against the defaulting units.

To achieve the goal pollution abatement, emission and effluent standards for air, water and noise have been notified. Regular monitoring is carried out and the enforcement efforts have been intensified. At present, a majority of identified units have already installed the requisite pollution control equipment. According to the data collected by the Central Pollution Control Board (CPCB) on September 30, 1996, out of 1,551 units belonging to 17 categories of highly polluting industries, 1,259 units had facilities to comply with the environmental standards, 112 were closed and 180 were not having adequate facilities. Show cause notices under Section 5 of the Environment (Protection) Act 1986 have been issued to all the defaulting units.

Apart from notifications of effluent and emission standards for the major categories of polluting industries, national ambient air quality standards including ambient noise standards have been notified. Industries have been directed to instal necessary pollution control equipment within a stipulated time frame. More stringent norms for vehicular emissions have been notified under the Central Motor Vehicles Rules which have come into effect from April, 1996. Supply of unleaded petrol in four metropolitan cities of Mumbai, Calcutta, Delhi and Chennal has been introduced with effect from April 1, 1995 for use in four wheel vehicles fitted with catalytic converters. The use of unleaded petrol will be gradually expanded to other cities in the country.

Twenty-four critically polluted areas in the country have been identified and action plans have been drawn up to improve the quality of environment in these areas.

Adoption of clean technologies of production and formation of Waste Minimisation Circles is being encouraged to minimise environmental pollution. Under the World Bank aided Industrial Pollution Control Project, technical and financial assistance is provided for setting up Common Effluent Treatment Plants (CETPs) in clusters of small scale industrial units. An "Eco-Mark" scheme has been launched to certify various products of the industries which fulfil the prescribed pollution control standards to achieve the objective of environment-friendly production, packaging and waste disposal. To increase public awareness and participation, several public awareness campaigns on effects of pollution and measures to control it have been launched.

The Polity Statement for Abatement of Pollution indicates adoption of best available clean and practicable technologies, rather than end-of-the-pipe treatment, as the key elements for pollution prevention. As a part of this thrust, the Ministry of Environment & Forests has set up a Clean Technologies Division for identifying cleaner technologies that can be introduced in different development sectors. Techniques like coal beneficiation are being promoted. The programme envisages setting up a National Clearing House for cleaner technologies as the overall co-ordinating agency and sectoral centres in different areas of development to focus on their activities. Another initiative taken to motivate environmentally oriented technologies and practices is mandatory submission of Annual Environmental Statements which would be subsequently evolved into environmental audit.

Prior environmental clearance of development projects based on impact assessment is being increasingly emphasised. Such clearance has been made mandatory for 29 specified categories of development projects through a statutory notification issued in January, 1994.

This has been done with a view to mitigating the adverse environmental effects of these projects and in integrating the environmental concerns into development. This mechanism is also of help in catalysing the process of inducing cleaner environment-friendly technologies into the developmental process.

The success of the Ganga Action Plan has encouraged its replication for water pollution abatement in tributaries of the Ganga (Yamuna, Gomati and Damodar) under Ganga Action Plan Phase-II. A wider scheme called the National River conservation Plan covering pollution abatement works for grossly polluted stretches in 18 major rivers in 10 States of the country has also been initiated. Further, a programme for conservation of selected lakes has also been formulated by the Ministry.

The National Environmental Tribunal Act, providing relief, compensation and restitution to victims of accidents while handling hazardous substances, and for environmental damages, came into force from 17 June, 1995. The Act provides (i) strict liabilitiy for damages arising out of any accident occurring while handling any hazardous substances and (ii) Establishment of National Environmental Tribunal for effective and expenditious disposals of cases arising from such accidents with a view to give relief and compensation for damage to persons, property and the environment and (iii) matters connected therewith or incidental thereto.

The National Environment Appellate Authority (NEAA) has been set up by the Government in January 1997. Public hearings have now been built into the environment impact assessment. The machinary for hearing appeals against environment pollution impact assessment is also being set up. The measures are to ensure greater transparency and faster decision-making in matters concerning the environmental impact of industrial projects.

With loss of forest cover and natural lands, the socio-economic and ecological impacts on local indigenous communities are sizeable, some of which are listed below.

Loss of habitat due to drastic reduction in forest areas the has led to increased socio-economic problems of local communities; diverse functions of forest ecosystems such as watershed properties and micro-climatic regulations have been affected, thereby affecting lives and livelihood of local communities. Accelerated deforestation has affected livelihoods of local people. The local women are also required to walk longer distances for collection of fuel, fodder, food, etc.

Exploitation, expropriation and threats from outside agencies have increased where some local communities have been forced to forfeit their lands and join the ranks of the landless. In the case of constitutional rights of local people, they get violated most often and, in practice, they stand to lose in the existing socio-economic and political set-ups, which tend to be repressive, and most often, work to their disadvantage.

Large areas of forests have been formally kept virtually out of reach of forest people who have managed forests sustainably for subsistence and income. Such actions or policies have led to tensions in social control of forests and have become acute. Increased pressure on forests in making for low resilience of forest systems leading to firewood and fodder problems for local communities. Social and economic problems of local people have increased and so also are the areas of conflict. As an illustration, let us consider the case of India. The colonial laws have led of State ownership o nearly 97 per cent of India's forest land which limit people's accessibility to forests. Local communities having limited access to forests without ownership rights face increased pressure of livelihood. This leads to tension and conflict between foresters and local communities where the latter's need for forest resources is overlooked and not acknowledged in practice.

Meeting the challenge

Such destruction of environment has resulted in disturbance or breakdown of their support-base and has led to immense hardship especially because of limited substitution possibilities available for alternative sources of livelihoods. There are also those local communities, whose traditional access and rights have been denied to such local resources thus paving the way for their increased impoverishment.

However, on the brighter side, there are many cases where local communities have accepted the challenge of natural resource depletion and are participating at local levels, either by themselves, or in collaboration with developmental agencies, to organize themselves for regenerating trees, forests and water bodies while conserving and preserving the existing ones.

Such a state of affair in the lives of local indigenous communities calls for better management of natural resources by redefining their access to forest resources and clarifying roles and responsibilities of local communities. With drastic fall in forest cover, local communities/groups, in many areas, are also associated with tree/grass plantation for restoration of degraded forests. A new concept of social forestry (also known as community forestry/agro-forestry) has been introduced to influence people's behaviour towards trees. Defining a need for trees, communities are directly involved in tree planting and management. The concept of social forestry is a broad term covering roadside strip planting, community woodlots, farm forestry, and tree planting on marginal lands by the landless. The concept of social forestry recognizes that if such programmes are designed appropriately to motivate people to plant trees, they promote such trees which provide essentials like firewood, small timber and income to the small producers and lead to increased benefit to poorer sections of the society. A variant of social forestry is Joint Forest Management in which local forests are protected by local communities in collaboration with the Forest Department.

Although such small beginnings have been made, a lot remains to be done in the rebuilding of safety net which forests provided to local indigenous communities. Their loss of habitat cannot really be compensated for in full but their deprived status can be improved upon by giving them a chance to be involved in decision-making regarding regeneration of forest wealth. Not only their accessibility to forests but also their rights to forest produce have to increase substantially and their roles need to be redefined in control and use of such resources. Otherwise, any collaboration of the State with indigenous communities on natural resource management cannot create appropriate stakes and involvement. In can at best create temporary interest which does not augur well for sustaining community efforts in preserving and conserving natural resources.

With approximately 27 per cent of its population living in urban areas, India is one of the least urban countries, but with an urban population of 217 million (1991) it is also a country with one of the largest urban populations. India's towns and cities could, by themselves, make up the third largest nation of the world.

Urban India consists of close to 3500 towns varying in size from the smallest district towns with a population of 5,000 to the large urban agglomerations exceeding 10 million people. Nearly two-thirds of the urban population is concentrated in 317 'Class I' towns, or cities with a population of over 100,000 of which half lives in 23 metropolitan areas with populations exceeding 1 million. The four largest cities—Bombay, Calcutta, Delhi and Madras—between them account for one sixth of the urban total. the Class I towns are the fastest growing urban areas in India. Greater Bombay, with apopulation of 12.57 million, and Calcutta with 10.86 million, are among the largest metropolitan areas in the world.

While over the past four decades the popultion of India has more than doubled, during the same period the urban population has more than quadrupled. The growth has come as much from net migration as from natural increase (about 40 per cent each), with the balance due to reclassification and inclusion of new towns.

The National Commission on Urbanization (1988) states that "these urban centres have also generated tha most brutal and inhuman living conditions, with large sections of the citizens living in squatter settlements. The overcrowding in the slums and the desperate lack of water and sanitation leads not only to severe health problems but to abject degradation of human life." It further remarks that "in the decades to come, who knows how much political tension and physical viloence will be triggered off by the flrgrant display of wealth which coexists with the rising expectations of the poor and with the appalling conditions of congestion and pollution which form their environment?"

The estimate of proportion of urban people living in slums varies from about 20 per cent to 30 per cent. Looked at by class of town, the highest percentage of people living in slum areas is in the cities with a million plus population and the least in towns with less than

100,000 population. The growth rate of the slum population, largely through continuing in migration, is significantly faster than that of other segments of the urban population. While this phenomenon is in no way unique to India, it is the sheer size of the problem in India that is staggering.

About 27 per cent of the urban population lives below the poverty line, 30-40 per cent of the population of the larger metropolitan areas live in slums, 27 per cent does not have access to water-borne sanitation. Indian cities also have very high levels of air and water pollution. As a result, the environment that the rural migrant has to live in, is as harsh a choice between environment and development as one can pose.

And yet the choice is made. It is made by over 13,500 people each day who move from rural to urban environments and the several million who continue to live in the highly degraded areas of urban India. The urban slum is their 'gateway'. It is the 'solution' rather than the 'problem' of urban living. It is both a low cost housing solution and a low cost transportation solution, as the slum is usually close to the place of work. But it makes nevertheless for squalid surroundings. It is a price that is paid, and paid consciously—because the option, where it even exists, is worse. Urban poverty is preferred to rural poverty.

Air pollution is a problem in some urban areas. Heavy vehicles cause 47 per cent of the pollution while accounting for 8 per cent of the total number of vehicles on Indian roads. The production of automobiles in India has increase from 1,891 in 1955 to 116,564 in 1988. Two and three wheelers constituting 63 per cent of the number of vehicles cause 13 per cent of the total pollution. While this pollution does cause localized problems, the number of vehicles is so small that it has negligible impact at the global level. Efficient public transport options, which will cut down on both fossil fuel consumption and pollution need to be explored.

The noise levels in many of the Indian cities is much above the safe limit. This is due to diverse factors which include industrial manufacturing activities, excessive use of vehicle horns, and unregulated use of loudspeakers at social, political and religious events. Awareness must be created in this regard.

The question that is difficult to understand is not so much why the poor decide to stay in slums, but rather how much remains to be done about improving conditions in these areas. The Report of the National Commission on Urbanization feels that "For whatever reason, resource allocation in the urban field seems to follow a problem rather than anticipate it." Furthermore, "the inefficiency of our cities and towns is being perpetuated by obsolete, rigid and irrational laws, regulatory provisions and norms. The urban centres, with their concentration of diverse activities, should be generators of wealth; instead, they have degenerated into parasites looking elsewhere for support."

There are a host of human interventions including development activities which have resulted in considerable environmental degration. Major human interventions in forests are deforestation, commercial logging, setting up protected area, partial closure of forests, etc which are described below:

* There is increasing deforestation due to commercial exploitation, building of dams, mining and construction activities. Of the world's estimated 8.4 billion hectares of forests in 1990, tropical forests covered 1.76 billion ha. During 1981-90, tropical forests were lost at the rate of 0.8 per cent (15.4 million ha) a year, as per estimates of the World

Resources Institute. The net annual deforestation during 1981-90 exceeded two per cent in 10 tropical countries of Asia and Africa.

* Commercial logging for industrial activities is increasing rapidly. Eighty-four per cent of such logging took place in closed tropical broadleaf forests in primary (undisturbed forests) during the 1980s. Logging activity is a causal factor for forest degradation and is reflected in rough wood production which increased by 19 per cent between 1979-81 to 1989-91. Globally, almost 50 per cent of such rough wood is used for industrial purposes, the rest for heating and cooking.

* Setting up of protected areas for conservation purposes has led to complications and conflict-situation with indigenous communities and also denial of many of their rights and privileges.

* Closure of parts of forests for setting up of industries or agro-based activities for private, semi-private lands, construction of railways, roads and new settlements has led to shrinkage of forest cover and increased hardship for local communities in their day-to-day existence.

* Interventions for adhering to international agreements have also alienated many local communities and some of their practices, eg, tribal hunting of wild animals which goes against biodiversity agreements.

* Policies of economic liberalization, privatization and globalization have both, directly and indirectly, led to reduction of forest cover and cuts in subsidies and grants affecting food subsidies and other welfare schemes involving poor and marginalized communities.

Prevention and control of environmental pollution

As per the Policy Statement of Abatement of Pollution announced in February 1992, the key elements for pollution prevention are adoption of the best available clean and praticable technologies rather than end of the pipe treatment. The focus is on source reduction and substitution of chemicals, with safe alternatives. The thrust has, therefore, been made for considering process changes which involve significant improvements in energy and water conservation. To follow up on the various issues covered in the Policy Statement for Abatement of Pollution, the National Conservation Strategy and the Forest Policy Statement, several new programmes and studies have been initiated and commissioned. An Environment Action Programme has been formulated covering a wide ambit of subjects such as clean and low-waste technologies, improvement of water quality, institutional and human resources development, forestry and natural resources accouning.

To integrate natural resource accounting into the national accounting process, collection and analysis of environmental data has been initiated. It is proposed to produce a computerised map of the critically polluted areas through digitisation, on a format based on Geographic Information System. Base thematic maps on 1.6 M scale have been prepared for the country on the following themes: (i) major river basins and drainage network; (ii) administrative divisions; (iii) designated best use classification of streams; (iv) location of water and air pollution monitoring stations; (v) location of critically polluted areas; and (vi) major cities of India (above one lakh population).

The gazette notification on environmental audit issued in 1992 has been amended and now applies to all units seeking environmental clearance, and such units are required to submit environmental statements for the period ending 31 March on or before 30 September every year beginning from 1993 To facilitate industries in preparing environmental statements, model environmental statement reports for six categories of industries have been prepared. A booklet titled "Environmental Statement as part of environmental audit" has also been prepared by the Ministry. A software package 'Paryavaran' along with a user manual, has been prepared for analysis of information submitted in these environmental statements and is being distributed to all the SPCBs.

An 'Eco-Mark' label has been introduced to label consumer products that are environment friendly. Sixteen products have been identified for labelling and standards for toilet soaps and detergents, paper, paints, architectural paints and laundry soaps have been notified for awarding this label. The procedure for granting consent to small scale industries has been simplified. A new format for the consent application and for authorisation required under the Environment (Protection) Act, 1986 has been developed and notified. Under the scheme "Adoption of clean technology in the small scale industries and to extend necessary technical support", training and awareness programmes for personnel in small Industry Development Organisation and entrepreneurs are being organised. A manual "From Waste to Profits" giving guidelines for waste minimisation has been prepared.

The Central Pollution Control Board (CPCB) is the national apex body for assessment, monitoring and control of water and air pollution. The executive responsibilities for enforcement of the Acts for Prevention and Control of Pollution of Water (1974) and Air (1981) and also of the Water (Cess) Act, 1977 are carried out through are Board. Twenty three states and union territories have already adopted the Act and respective state pollution control boards have been constituted. These states are Andhra Pradesh, Assam, Bihar, Goa, Gujarat, Haryana, Himachal Pradesh, Jammu and Kashmir, Karnataka, Kerala, Madhya Pradesh, Maharashtra, Meghalaya, Mizoram, Orissa, Punjab, Rajasthan, Sikkim, Tamil Nadu, Tripura, Uttar Pradesh, West Bengal, Delhi and Pondicherry. Arunachal Pradesh has adopted the Act, but is yet to constitute the board. Enactment of the Enviornment (Protection) Act, 1986 has further extended the scope of the activities of the Board. Under the Environment (Protection) Act, 1986, effluent and emission standards in respect of 61 categories of industries have been notified. So far, 84 laboratories have been recognised as environmental laboratories. Minimum National Standards (MINAS) for effluents and emissions from specific industries have been formulated and control measures are being implemented in a phased manner. A notification consolidating all the environmental standards including general effluent, emission and noise standards has been issued. It also includes standards for waste water generation in respect of 11 categories of industries. Further mass emission norms which would come into effect from 1 April 1996 have also been issued for petrol and diesel driven vehicles under the Central Motor Vehicles Rules of the Ministry of Surface Transport. Unleaded petrol of Delhi, Bombay, Madras and Calcutta from 1 April 1995. Petrol with a maximum lead content of 0.15 g/l has been introduced at all the retail outlets of these four metro cities since June 1994.

Seventeen categories of heavily polluting industries have been identified namely, cement, thermal powre plants, distilleries, sugar, fertilizer, integrated iron and steel, oil refineries, pulp and paper, petrochemicals, pesticides, tanneries, basic drugs and pharmaceuticals, dye and dye intermediates, caustic soda, zinc smelter, copper smelter and aluminium smelter. Action is taken against the defaulting units in these categories on priority. On the basis of the designated best use of criteria CPCB has identified 13 grossly polluted stretches of Sabarmati, Subernarekha, Godavari, Krishna, Indus (tributaries), Sutlej, Ganga (tributaries), Yamuna, Hindon, Chambal, Damodar, Gomati, and Kali rivers to formulate short-term result oriented programmes. The CPCB, in consultation with SPCBs has identified 22 critically polluted areas in the country which need special attention for control of pollution. These are Vapi (Gujarat), Singrauli (U.P.), Korba, Ratlam, Nagoda (Madhya Pradesh), Digboi (Assam), Talcher (Orissa), Bhadravati (Karnataka), Howrah (West Bengal), Dhanbad (Bihar), Pali and * Pataucheru (Andhra Pradesh), Chembur (Maharashtra), Najafgarh (Delhi), Govindhgarh (Punjab), Udyog Mandal (Kerala) and Parwanoo and Kala Amb (HP). The progress in abatement of pollution in these areas is being reviewed. A Bill has been introduced in the Parliament for establishing a National Environment Tribunal.

In India, as in most traditional societies, people lived a life that rarely, if ever, threatened their environment. For centuries populations were more or less steady and local resources were sufficient to meet the demands of food, fuel, shelter and other basic requirements of life. Practices specifically suited to each area evolved over hundreds of years. Practices that ensured utilization of natural resources without degrading them.

While these systems were environmentally sound, life was vulnerable to many externaly factors. This was reflected in the low life-expectancy at birth, which was about 30 years at best. Communities were highly vulnerable to disease, epidemics and calamities like floods and drought. It is estimated that about 2.5 million people died during the Bengal famine of 1943. During the decade 1911-1921, the great influenze epidemic took a toll of 12 million lives. In fact, during this period the number of deaths exceeded the number of births, resulting in a population decline.

At the time of independence in 1947, the challenges before the new nation were many. Prime in importance was the task of decreasing human vulnerability to natural calamities. India needed not only to become self-sufficient in food production, but also to build enough reserves to tide over a drought year. Changes were also required in policies laid down during colonial times which dealt with the use and distribution of basic requirements.

With better health services and sanitation, increased food production and better nutrition, life expectancy at birth went up from 32 years at Independence to 64 years in 1991. Death rate decreased rapidly from 22.8 per thousand in 1951 to 10.9 in 1988. Birth rates have also decreased with overall development, but these have been slower in coming down. The net effect was a rapid increase in population from 361 million in 1951 to 844 million in 1991, a 134 per cent increase.

To meet the challenge of sustaining this increased population, nes land was brought under the plough. The total cultivated area went up from 118.75 mha in 195-51 to 140.90 mha in 1984-85, levelling off thereafter. Irrigation potential went up from 22.6 mha in the '50s to 74.3 mha by 1989-90. New seeds and higher inputs brought about the Green Revolution, and India's agricultural growth rate went up from a mere 0.3 per cent in pre-Independence years to 3.5 per cent after 1977. Between 1950-51 and 1988-89, the country's foodgrain production rose from 50.8 million tonnes per annum to 170.2 million tonnes per annum, an increase of 235 per cent.

Milk production has gone up from 17,406 thousand tonnes in 1950 to 44,300 thousand tonnes in 1986—an increase of 180 per cent. Largely operating through producers cooperatives, India has a sophisticated dairy industry. However, despite a livestock population of over 400 million—the world's largest—India milk yield per animal is still very low. Bullocks are used for traction in fields and for rural transport, making for a close relationship between cattle and agriculture. Animal dung acts as a source of fertilizer as well as fuel.

India is no longer dependent on import of foodgrains. While gains in food production have taken India towards self-sufficiency, the country still depends on imports of certain agricultural inputs. While floods and drought are a recurrent reality, no longer do they lead to mass starvation deaths. A buffer stock of foodgrains, with rice and wheat amounting to about 15 million tonnes, has been built up.

While achievements have been considerable, the gains in the quality of life have been slow. The increasing population continues to erode the net benefits. Although they spend 85 per cent of their income on food, the poorest 20 per cent of the population are still unable to consume more than 1,500 calories a day, as against the 2,300 considered a necessary minimum by the Planning commission.

Efforts are on to ensure that all 600,000 villages in India, have a safe and protected source of drinking water. The implications of this on health and sanitation, and on the amount of time and energy spent by women on fetching water are enormous. While the challenge of vulnerability has been met, poverty remains an issue central to India's development.

But while the effect of population increase in decreasing the net benefits of development was understood, there was something else, less noticed, which was threatening the gains of development. This was the erosion of the biological and environmental base of the country. Many of the gains of the first few decades had come at the cost of India's biological and environmental 'capital'. Intensive agriculture led to problems like land deterioration, water depletion, pest infestations and loss of genetic diversity of crops. Excessive use of chemical fertilizers and pesticided, and poor drainage have led to pollution in several rural areas.

Land, water and the biological resources which support agriculture and animal husbandry and provide the essential requirements of food, drinking water and fuel are all under severe pressure. Protecting and reclaiming these and managing them more carefully is essential to sustaining India's life-support systems.

Removing obstacles

These wastelands and degraded lands are not sufficiently utilized under agricultrual land use, because of several reasons. Fortunately, most of the wastelands are fit for growing trees which are renewable resources. Experience of the past confirms that trees have been successfully used to reclaim and improve various kinds of wastelands and degraded lands (Gupta and Deepinder, 1982). Afforestation of such lands through proper financial assistance by various agencies in India can provide substantial income and employment opportunities to villagers especially the rural poor and improve the quality of environment. The Central and State governments in India have recognized the need for afforestation of such lands and have launched various projects for the purpose. Besides governmental organizations, numerous non-govermental organizations (NGOs) including Tree Growers' Co-operative Societies (TGCS) are also now engaged in the task of afforestation problem of non-availability of wastelands for afforestation programmes due to a variety of procedural and legal complications. The government can play a facilitating role by removing obstacles in the way of NGOs acquiring degraded revenue and forests lands on lease for afforestation. Faced with the gigantic task of developing over 100 m ha of wastelands in the country, the Ministry of Rural Development has written to the States to set up their own wastelands development board which would identify wastelands, chalk out projects and render assistance to the NGOs (Anonymous, 1994).

Ambitious Targets no Solution: To develop the 175 m ha of degraded and wastelands in the country, a high-level committee on wastelands development has recommended framing of a perspective master plan for the next 10 to 15 years. According to the recommendations made by this committee, in the next 15 years about 12 million hectares would need to be ameliorated every year (Dharia, 1995). This master plan has to be the part of the Ninth Five Year Plan. An afforestation plan was laid out in the year 1985 by NWDB to rehabilitate 5 m ha of wastelands every year. However, the targets were never achieved. During the VII Five Year Plan (1985-90), only 8.466 m ha of wastelands were afforested (Kapoor, 1992). Merely by setting big targets of afforestation, it is not possible to achieve the aim of bringing 33 per cent of the total geographical area of the country under tree cover as laid down in the national Forest Policy of 1988.

In the absence of reliable data base any conclusion on the availability of wastelands for bringing under vegetative cover would not be more than crude guess. This lack of ground level data/information has dampened the progress of formation, implementation and financing of afforestation programmes. Along with availability of wastelands for afforestation programmes in

India, there are many other technical, financial and institutional constraints which have to be overcome in the coming years to give an impetus to afforestation in the country.

It is estimated that 175 mha of India's land is degraded. This includes 85 mha under agriculture and 35 mha of forest land. Among the various reasons for the land losing its productivity are the over-application of chemical fertilizers in agriculture, waterlogging as a result of over-irrigaiton, canal seepage, poor drainage, overgrazing of common grazing lands and deforestation. The seriousness of deforestation has been dramatically brought out through the use of modern monitoring and mapping thechnologies.

Land, water and biological resources are intricately linked to one another. With excessive pressure on the biomass, the vegetative cover starts to disappear. As a consequence, the runoff of water during the rains increases and groundwater recharge is diminished. Without vegetation, the topsoil that has taken centuries to form is washed away and the land gets eroded. In hilly areas, the process starts an almost irreversible cycle of degradation.

Two of the main pressures on the vegetative cover are the need for fuelwood and fodder. In India almost 87 per cent of energy for cooking is obtained from firewood, agricultural wastes and cow-dung, and only 13 per cent cooking energy is from commercial sources. Firewood alone provides 50 per cent of the cooking energy in cities and 70 per cent in villages. This dependence on firewood has put a great pressure on forest, and in fact on all vegetative matter. The demand, estimated at 157 million tonnes in 1986-87, is far in excess of the supply. With the consequent disappearance of trees and other vegetation, women, who are the principal collectors of fuelwood, have to spend a much greater amount of time on collection thereby putting up the 'cost' of fuelwood.

The other pressure is the need for fodder. With the world's largest cattle popultion of over 400 million animals, fodder availability in India is grossly inadequate. Pasture land only constitutes 3.9 per cent of the land and as a result is degraded. The pressure on forests is once again heavy. The cattle which are undernourished produce low quantities of milk. In degraded environments people find it easier to keep goats, and the increase in te goat population has been much more rapid than that of cattle, buffaloes and sheep. But goats in fragile ecosystems are as much a problem as a solution and, unless properly managed, can further degrade the environment.

Realizing the urgent need to increase biomass production, social foresty programmes were started in the late 1970s. These included raising rural fuelwood plantations and village wood lots, starting tree nurseries, distribution of tree spalings, encouragement to plantations around agricultural fields, as well as promotion of farm forestry and strip plantation on roadsides and canel banks. But while there were many successes, this programme was not able to arrest the increasing degradation of land caused by over-exploitation.

By 1985 about half of India's land was estimated to be wasteland—land which had hardly any vegetation left on it. Rajiv Gandhi, who was then Prime Minister, announced the development of wastelands as a major thrust area. The social forestry experience had shown that such programmes were more effective if carried out with the participation of the local communities at every stage. Without this it would not be possible to protect the plantations. The National Wastelands Development

Board was set up to encourage wastelands development and, working with a number of voluntary agencies, to involve people in this process.

While these programmes were being initiated several experiments were underway, including the one at Arabari in West Bengal, in which people were being involved in managing forest areas along with the Forest Department. The cumulative experience of such efforts led to a Government circular in 1990, asking all state forest departments to try the Joint Forest Management model. It will be some time before such a concept can be fully implemented, but the circular itself represents a significant recognition regarding the management of forests.

When the forest regulations, and indeed the Forest Department, were established during the colonial period, they were seen as agencies for the controlled exploitation of forests for wood and revenue. The growing pressure on forests has seen the gradual transformation of the Department into a conservation agency. The recent circular speaks not of protecting forests from the people, but rather of conserving forests for the people, with the help of the people. While there is a long way to go in strengthening this partnership, the new initiative marks the beginning of a new era in the management of forests India's largest publicly held biological resource.

The initiatives for conserving biological resources have not come from Government alone. The Bishnoi example and movements like Chipko have been based on local communities protecting these resources and taking up afforestation programmes. people are involved in selecting the species most relevant to them, and take the responsibility for their protection which leads to high survival rates of the saplings.

While greater generation of biomass is one way of dealing with the pressure on this resource, its more efficient use is another. Several initiatives have been taken in this direction by both NGOs and the Government. But changing practices is a slow process. New technologies need to be explored while certain old practices need to be reaffirmed. There are practices that were once beneficial but are no longer sustainable. An example is that of shifting cultivation, practised in north-east India, parts of Andhra Pradesh etc. This used to operate under cycles of 20-30 years or more, but with increased population and reduced availability of land the cycle has been shortened, making the practice unviable today.

New improved chulhas (wood-fuelled stoves) can, if used properly, reduce the requirement of firewood by as much as 40 per cent. New experiments such as those under the Programme of Integrated Energy Systems for Villages of the Department of Non-Conventional Energy Sources go even beyond this. their aim is not only to make the village self-sufficient in cooking energy but also to fulfil its energy requirements for agriculture, pumping, lighting and heating. Experiments such as those by the Gujarat Energy Development Agency (GEDA) have made villages like Methan and Kalyanpura self sufficient in energy. The strategy is based on growing biomass on village fallow land and using a wood gasifier to generate motive power. This is combined with direct solar-thermal power for heating water. The gasifier uses the biomass five times as efficiently as conventional methods. The key to this success story, as in the case of forest management, is a self-managed system controlled by the local community.

Biogas is a low-cost appropriate energy technology with major potential in rural areas. The National Biogas Development Programme has, as its main objectives, the maximisation of recycling of organic wastes in order to provide gas for cooking, and small decentralized power generation systems for operating water pumps, flour mills and other rural industries. At present 1.4 million family-size biogas plants generate energy for cooking in village households across the country. The progress with community biogas plants has been less encouraging, with only around 300 such plants operating in the country today.

The shortage of fodder would similarly have to be dealt with through a combination of more production and better utilization. The current estimate of availability of green and dry fodder in the country is 250 million tonnes and 440 million tonnes respectively, while the requirement is about 932 million tonnes and 780 million tonnes respectively. About 100 million head or 25 per cent of the cattle population is estimated to be grazing on forest land. To close the gap between demand and supply and to reduce pressure on grazing land, practices like stall feeding of cattle need to be promoted.

The problem is, however, that with a large number of unproductive cattle, stall feeding is not always viable. The livestock issue is complex because of the very intricate relationship cattle have with life in rural India. The cow-dung is used for manure or as fuel. Bullocks are used as drought animals. The social status of a family is often linked to the number of animals owned by it. Cows are not slaughtered for meat. The unproductive animals graze on public lands, and are maintained at virtually no cost to the owner. But the price is paid in terms of the pressures on the local environment. Excessive grazing leads to land deterioration, soil erosion and the suppression of the regeneration of useful species.

Just as excessive pressure on bio-resources leads to land denudation and decline in groundwater recharge, the excessive demand for water leads to a decrease in land and agricultural productivity due to waterlogging and salinity. In addition, the large projects to supply such quantities of water can lead to several environmental problems.

Harnessing the water resources of India was identified as a major task at the time of Independence. Large dams were seen as a solution. But India's first Prime Minister Jawaharlal Nehru in 1957 cautioned. "We have many large scale river valley projects which are carefully worked out by engineers. I wonder, however, how much thought is given before the project is launched to having an ecological survey of the area and to find out what the effect would be to the drainage system or to the flora and fauna of the area. It would be desirable to have such an ecological survey of these areas before the project is launched and thus avoid an imbalance of nature.

Nehru's apprehensions have today become major environmental issues. They are central to the debate over large dams. Issues of resettlement of affected persons and rights of tribal communities, the impact on biodiversity and fragile ecological systems, the correctness of assessment of parameters like siltation rates, drainage and waterlogging are at the centre of the debate. The imbalance perceived as to who pays the cost and who benefits has led to arguments on equity. The whole issue of scale, of small irrigation projects compared to large projects, is a major environmental debate in India.

Sustainable utilization of groundwater resources necessitates a shift from extraction-focused development to conservation and creation of management systems. To date, most development efforts have concentrated on ways to increase groundwater extraction. Nationwide the number of diesel and electric pump sets have grown from 87,000 in 1950 to 12,581 million in 1990. Over 20 per cent of the electricity generated in India is currently used for pumping. Groundwater accounts for 42 per cent of India's irrigation potential and for nearly 48 per cent of the net area actually irrigated. Over exploitation of groundwater is causing the water table to drop in most hard-rock and aridzones, and saline intrusion is occurring in extensive areas along the coasts.

3

Natural Resources

Survey of Flora

Botanical survey of India (BSI)

In order to explore the plant wealth of the country and identifying the species having economic potentiality for the welfare of mankind the Botanical Survey of India. (BSI) was established in 1890. Its mandate has been modified recently to meet the commitments of the Convention on Biological Diversity (CBD) which are based on three primary principles viz.,

— the exploration, inventorisation, monitoring and conservation of plant species, populations and ecosystems,

— the sustainable utilization of plant resources, and

— the fair and equitable sharing of benefits arising from utilisation of plant resources.

BSI, with its Headquarter at Calcutta, has several well equipped Laboratories viz., Indian Botanic Garden (IBG), Central National Herbarium, Industrial Section at Indian Museum at Calcutta and nine regional stations located in different phytogeographical regions viz., Jodhpur, Allahabad, Dehra Dun, Pune, Coimbatore, Gangtok, Itanagar, Shillong and, Portblair which are self reliant to meet the challenges of CBD & Patenting.

Objectives of BSI

Primary Objectives

— To explore plant resources of the country.

— To inventorise and monitor phytodiversity.

— To document phytodiversity in the form of Flora of India, State Floras, District Floras and Floras of Fragile ecosystems, protected areas, hot spot areas and in the form of technical research papers.

— To identify species, populations and ecosystems which are under threat and need conservation including endemics.

— To undertake *Ex-situ* conservation of critically threatened taxa in the Botanical gardens through conventional and biotechnological methods.

— To explore the bioperspectives of the plant wealth of the country for sustainable utilisation through ethonobotanical studies.

— To identify economically important species which are under threat due to over exploitation, for trade etc. and to conserve them.

— To identify wild relatives of crop plants and preserve the germplasm in the form of seed banks.

— To prepare National Data Base of all the above mentioned information including herbarium collections, types, live collections, plant distribution etc.

Secondary objectives

— To undertake Environmental Impact Studies (EIS) as may be specifically called for.

— To carry out pharmacological studies of medicinal plants used by tribals.

— To carry out phytochemical, palynological and cytogenetical studies-to provide additional information to determine systematic position and taxonomic status of certain confusing taxa.

— To collect and preserve the plants ad products used for various purposes in the country in the form of Museum exhibits to create awareness among the people.

— To impart training and education to the people in the methodology for phytodiversity studies.

— To provide public service and create awareness among the people regarding role of plants in the updegradation of polluted environment.

The activities of the BSI during the year are summarized below :-

Botanical exploration, Inventorisation, monitoring and documentation of phytodiversity : Seventy-nine exploration tours to inventorise and monitor the phytodiversity and bioresources of forest ecosystems, fragile ecosystems, protected areas etc. including lower group of plants were undertaken. As such, about 25,000 plant specimens were collected and about 11,791 of them were identified. The identification of rest is under progress. After identification the plant species are inventorised and documented in the form of Floras.

National Flora/Flora of India

To provide detailed information regarding the phytodiversity of nation as a whole, the organisation is engaged in the revision of Flora of India which will be completed in 35 volumes. During the year under report about 350 species belonging to fifteen families were documented.

State Flora : Die manuscripts of 8 State Floras viz.,

Andaman and Nicobar Islands (Vol. 1), Arunachal Pradesh (Vol. 3), Cold Desert (Vol. 1), Nagaland (Vol. 3 & 4), Madhya Pradesh (Vol. 3), Jammu & Kashmir (Vol.1), Maharashtra (Vol 1 & 2), Kerala (Vol. 1), were completed and edited. The Mosses of Central India and Pteridophytic Flora of North East India were also completed and edited among the lower group of plants. Further, the work on 9 volumes of State Floras viz. Andaman & Nicobar Vol. II, Haryana Vol. 1, Sikkim Vol. 1, Mizoram Vol. I, Assam Vol. II, Bihar Vol. 1, West Bengal Vol. III, Karnataka Vol. I, Kerala Vol. II is under various stages of progress and about 730 species were studied during the year. Work on the Flora of Govind Pashu Vihar, Mumbai City and Pench National Park are also under progress.

About 180 species belonging to Lichens, Fungi, Algae, Mosses and Liverworts were collected, identified, inventorised and documented.

Palynological/Cytological/Photochemical studies: Pollen morphology of about 54 Indian species of Capparaceae, Rhamnaceae, Asclepiadaceae, Gentianaceae and Thalictaridaceae have been worked out. Further, phytochemical screening of 3 species of family Tiliaceae (seeds) was done.

Threatened taxa documentation : BSI has published so far three volumes of "Red Data Book" and two volumes (Vol. 4 & 5) are under preparation during the year under report. Further, data sheets for 50 species were prepared under negative list of export in reference to Convention on International Trade in Endangered Species of Wild Fauna and Flora (CITES).

Ex-situ Conservation : The conservation activities during the year include :

— 1075 plants belonging to 230 species from wild were introduced to preserve the germplasm.

— 24 species of threatened and endangered plants were conserved and multiplied.

— Seeds of 56 species of economic and medicinal importance were preserved in the seed bank.

— Live germplasm from wild of 39 species of high medicinal value were preserved in the "Charak Udyan" in Indian Botanic Garden (IBG), Howrah.

Bioperspectives/Ethonobotanical Studies: To provide more information about the economic potentiality of phytodiversity of different phytogeographical regions, studies were conducted in four States viz., Tripura, Assam, Orissa and West Bengal. Six tours were undertaken an about 500 species have been identified which have potential for utilisation for various purposes, especially for medicinal purposes. A book "Ethnobotany of Rajasthan" has been published which deals with about 610 species. An "All India Co-ordinated project on Ethnobotany" has been initiated to provide information regarding bioperspectives of megadiversity areas of the country viz., Western Ghats, N.E. India, Eastern Himalaya etc. The work is in progress.

Environmental Impact Assessment: Environmental Impact studies in Pandiyar-Purinapuzha Hydro Electric Project (HEP) of Tamil Nadu Electricity Board (TNEB), Motia Copper open cast Project, Purulia Pumped Storage project, Bansagar Canal project and Chota Nagpur Coal field project were conducted and reports prepared. Besides these, a report on 20 projects throughout India was monitored.

National Data Base: Data from Indian flora, herbarium holdings, type specimens, Taxonomic bibliography, rare and threatened plants of Indian flora, medicinal plants, live plants of botanical gardens of India was computerised at Coimbatore, Dehra Dun and Pune.

An Environmental Information System (ENVIS) Centre has also been engaged in the above work at Calcutta.

Public Services and Environmental Awareness: BS provides services not only to various scientific and academic institutions but also to individuals.

— About 1000 species were identified.

— Information on distribution, flowering and fruiting period of about 100 species were provided.

— About 25 0 students and teachers were provided training on phytodiversity methodology at various centres of the BSI.

— On the occasion of 50th Anniversary of India's Independence an exhibition was organized at New Delhi on collaboration with other institutions of the Ministry which was awarded a Shield.

— About 5 exhibitions to promote scientific consciousness and reflecting role of plants in the control of pollution and the products provided for food, clothing, shelter and health were organized to educate the people.

— A symposium on "Role of Gardens in the life of Man" was organized at IBG Howrah, for school going children and parents.

— A seminar on "Development, Reforms of Indian Botanic Garden and its Hindrance" was organized for sharing ideas and creating awareness among the beneficiaries of this historic garden.

— Sit and draw, painting and quiz competitions were organized at IBG, Howrah for students of various age groups and winners were awarded prizes.

— On the occasion of World Environment Day plantation of about 500 plants was done in different botanical gardens of the BSI.

— An exhibition reflecting "aims, objectives and achievements of BSI was also organised in the Botanical Gallery.

— Plant material, literature and other information was provided to various institutions and individuals.

— A Parliamentary Standing Sub-Committee of 7 MPs led by Hon'ble Member of Parliament Shri R.R. Pramanikji visited IBG and Central National Herbarium.

Publications of the BSI brought out during the year :

— Flora of India, Vol. 4.

— Flora of West Champaran District, Bihar.

— Jaiba Baichitra Convention - O - Bharater Jaiba

— Baichitra (Bengali).

— Plant Diversity in the Tiger Reserves of India.

— Plants for human consumption in India.

— Paschim Banglur Udvid, Vol. 2 (Bengali).

— Flora of Bilaspur Dist., Vol. II

— Flora of Buldhana District, Maharashtra.

— ENVIS Newsletter, Vol 4.

— Vanaspati Vani, Vol. 8 (Hindi).

— Parijat (Hindi).

— Brochure of Sikkim Himalayan Circle.

— About 25 research papers were published in different national and international journals.

Survey of fauna

Zoological Survey of India (ZSI)

With a view to carry out exploration, survey and

inventorisation of faunal resources of the country the Zoological Survey of India (ZSI) was established in 1916. While the headquarters of ZSI is in Calcutta, it has 16 regional stations located in different parts of the country.

Highlights of various activities of ZSI during the year.

Exploration and Survey of Faunal Resources

A total of 68 surveys covering different ecosystems in various States were conducted, during which collection of voucher specimens of almost all groups of non-scheduled animals as well as detailed field observations on scheduled animals were undertaken. Several periodical trips to selected areas were also undertaken for ecological studies.

Ecosystem survey

Tropical Rainforest Ecosystem: Surveys were conducted in Quilon District of Kerala.

Cold Desert Ecosystem: Several areas of cold desert of Ladakh were surveyed.

Wetland Ecosystem: Some important wetlands of the country were surveyed for their faunal composition which included Pong Wetland in Himachal Pradesh, Kondakarla Lake in Andhra Pradesh and Nath Sagar Wetland in Maharashtra.

Estaurine Ecosystem: Krishna estuary in Andhra Pradesh was further surveyed for the collection of benthic fauna and fishes.

Marine Ecosystem: Faunal explorations in the marine and coastal waters of Tamil Nadu, Andhra Pradesh and West Bengal were undertaken.

Conservation areas survey

National Parks: Faunal explorations were carried out in Pench National Park and Tadoba National Park, both in Maharashtra.

Biosphere Reserves: Gulf of Mannar Biosphere Reserve was surveyed for faunal component.

Wildlife Sanctuaries: Bhim Bandh (Bihar), Kaimur (Bihar) and Asola Bhatti (Delhi) Wildlife Sanctuaries were explored for their faunal component and general ecological studies.

Reserve Forests: Anaimalai Reserve Forest (Tamil Nadu) was surveyed for faunal occurrances.

State Fauna Survey: Under this programme surveys were conducted in several districts of Andhra Pradesh (Srikakulam, Vijayanagaram and Vishakhapatnam), Andaman Islands, Gujarat (Kheda, Pench Mahal and Vadodara), Maharashtra (Kolhapur), Manipur, Mizoram, Nagaland (Kohima, Wokna and Mokokchung), Rajasthan, Sikkim, Tamil Nadu, Kerala (Thriuvananthapuram), and Uttar Pradesh (Bundelkhand and Terrai Region).

Ecological Surveys: Chandrika Wildlife Sanctuary (Orissa), Hugly Matla estaurine system in Sunderban delta, coastal waters of Bay of Bengal near Digha, several areas of North Bengal forests, (West Bengal), Forest of Gujarat and several man-made lakes and ponds of Andhra Pradesh and West Bengal surveyed in connection with ecological studies and status survey of some important species/groups.

Other Surveys: Kopili River in North Cachar Hills (Assam), was surveyed for its faunal composition to formulate a suitable strategy for environmental safeguards.

Scientists participated in Panchchuli Multidimensional Expedition (Uttar Pradesh) and Jarwa Contact Programme (Middle Andaman).

Identification of New Taxa : During the year detailed taxonomic studies resulted in the discovery of a total of'; two genera and 26 species new to science. These include three species of Amphibia, one species of fish, three species of Diptera (Insecta), two genera and 17 species of Hymenoptera (Insecta), one species of Thysanura (Insectal and one species of Scolopendromorpha, (Diplopoda).

Taxonomic Studies : The research work carried out on fauna collected from different states, conservation areas and other ecosystem is as follows :

State Fauna : Details of the number of species identified (under major groups) based on the collections made from different state surveys, are given in Table - 1.

Fauna of Conservation Area

National Parks

Tadoba National Park : 6 examples, 4 species of Crustacea ; 9 examples, 3 species of Thysanoptera (Insecta) and 3 examples, 3 species of Reptilia were identified.

Pench National Park, Maharashtra: 10 examples under 2 species of Thysanoptera (Insecta) were studied.

Eraviculam National Park, Kerala : 13 examples species) of Arachinida, 33 examples (7 species) of Odonata, and 49 examples (4 species) of Hemiptera were studied and recognised. This includes 3 new species of Hymenoptera.

Govind Pashu Vihar, U.P. : 21 examples (5 species) of Chilopoda were studied.

Melghat Tiger Reserve, Maharashtra : 4 examples (I species) of Arachinida, 8 examples (4 species) of Mollusca, 3 examples (2 species) of Amphibia and 8 examples (3 species) of Reptilia were identified.

Asola Bhatti Wildlife Sanctuary, Delhi : 85 examples (2 species) of Amphibia were studied

Indira Gandhi Wildlife Sanctuary, Tamil Nadu : 11 examples (9 species) of Diptera, 75 examples (8 species) of Scorpionida, 290 examples (5 species) of Millipedes, 137 examples (2 species) of Mollusca, 673 examples (18 species) of Pisces, and 35 examples (5 species) of Amphibia were identified.

Parambikulam Wildlife Sanctuary, Kerala: 2 examples (1 species) of Hymeniptera were determined.

Anaimalai Reserve Forest, Tamil Nadu : 4 examples (4 species) of Rotifera, 16 examples, (4 species) -of Diptera, 4 examples (4 species) of Crustacea, 29 examples (18 species) of Pisces and 2 examples (2 species) of Reptilia were identified.

Fauna of Ecosystems

Wetland Ecosystem

Harike Wetland, Punjab : 34 examples (4 species) of Pisces and 12 examples (2 species) of Amphibia were identified.

Pong Wetland, Punjab : 25 examples (4 species) of Oligochaeta (Annelida) and 50 examples (14 species) of Lepidoptera (Insecta) were identified.

Asan Reservoir, Dehra Dun : 18 species of migratory Aves were observed and recorded.

Doon Valley Wetland, Dehra Dun : 167 examples (17 species) of Pisces, 7 examples (1 species) of Amphibia, 3 examples (3 species) of Reptilia were identified.

Ladakh Cold Desert Ecosystem, Jammu & Kashmir: 23 examples (3 species) of Annelida (Oligochaeta) and 40 examples (7 species) of Pisces were determined.

Himalayan Ecosystem: From Western Himalayan Region of Himachal Pradesh 32 examples (6 species) of Annelida (Oligochaeta) and 10 examples (2 species) of Pisces were identified.

Tropical Rainforest/Western Ghat Ecosystem, Kerala : 390 examples (41 species) of Hymenoptera, 86 examples (35 species) of Lepidoptera, 24 examples (7 species) of Odonata, 97 examples (26 species) of Pisces, 68 examples (9 species) of Amphibia, 4 examples Q species) of Reptilia and 2 examples (2 species) of Mammalia were identified These include 14 species new to science.

Krishna Estuary, Andhra Pradesh : 16 examples (2 species) of Crustacea were determined.

Andhra Pradesh Coast : 11 examples (6 species) of Polychaeta and 19 examples (3 species) of Sipunculata were identified.

Tamil Nadu Coast : 91 examples (20 species) of Crustacea and 25 examples (75 species) of Pisces were studied.

Deep Sea : A, total of 3,409 examples (10 species) of Chaetognatha were identified out of the material obtained during the cruises of Sagar Sampada.

Ecological Studies

The following research studies/projects pertaining various ecosystems were continued during the year.

Study of Limnology, biological productivity and ecology of plankton, benthos and necton of two man made lakes and a few ponds of Calcutta.

Studies on the fauna associated with the coral reefs of Andaman and Nicobar Islands.

Studies on Intertidal fauna of Hugli River.

Faunal succession in a newly emerged Island at Sunderban delta.

Biomonitoring in the Coastal areas of West Bengal.

Studies on the ecology and behaviour of the Asian elephant, Elephas maximus indicus (Linnaeus) at Chandrika Wildlife Sanctuary, Orissa.

Studies on the ecology and behaviour of Macaca assamensis (Mc Lelland) at Jalpaiguri and Coochbehar, West Bengal.

Studies on the ecology and behaviour of giant squirel *Ratufa* bicolor gigantea (Mc Lelland) in the forest of North Bengal.

Status survey of Chinkara and Desert cat in Gujarat.

Environment Impact Assessment (EIA) Studies

During the year detailed faunal studies, including site surveys, were made in respect of the following EIA projects referred to the ZSI by various Agencies for expert opinion.

Kalpong Hydro Electric Project.

Tehri Dam Project.

Kudali Irrigation Project.

Pipalpanka Dam Project.

I.B. Valley Coalfield Project.

Kolhapur Indian Aluminium Co. Ltd. Bauxite Project.

Development of National Zoological Collections

The ZSI, which is the National repository of Zoological specimens, maintains a collection of large number of identified species belonging to almost all groups of animals occurring in the country. The National Zoological collections were further enriched by 10,595 identified examples belonging to 834 species, including 26 species new to science.

Publications : During the year, three volumes under the Fauna of India series and one volume each of Records of Zoological Survey of India and the Fauna of Mahanadi were published.

Other activities

World Environment Day and Wildlife Week were celebrated at ZSI, Calcutta.

Sixth Training Course in Field Ornithology and Thrid Refresher Course on collection and Preservation Techniques were conducted at ZSI, Calcutta.

An Advanced Training Course in Nematode Taxonomy was conducted at Jodhpur by the Desert Regional Station.

Scientists participated in two joint expeditions viz., Panchchuli Multidimensional Expedition and Jarwa Contact Programme. At present one scientist is participating in 18' Antarctica Expedition.

Four scientists attended Plan Training Programme on Management of Natural Resources and Environment (9th and 10th series) organized by the Indian Institute of Public Administration (IIPA), New Delhi.

One Scientist participated in Geographical Information System (GIS) Training at Dehra Dun

One scientist participated in Training on GCRMN, South Asia Biophysical Methods in Maldives and another participated in a Symposium on Antarctic Fauna at Christchurch, New Zealand.

The Department has undertaken a pilot project of GEF on the biodiversity of Coral Reef associated Fauna in Andaman & Nicobar Islands.

Northern Regional Station, ZSI, participated in an exhibition AGRASAR organized by Department of Science and Technology (DST) in Delhi.

The Director, ZSI, participated in an International Workshop on Global Taxonomic Initiative in Darwin, Australia.

Scientists of ZSI attended a number of seminar/ symposia/workshops in different parts of the country and presented papers.

The holdings of the library of ZSI at the Headquarters has been enriched by the addition of 694 books/ periodicals during the year. A total of 7500 copies of periodicals/books have been exchanged with partner institutes of the country and abroad. Journals/books of ZSI worth about Rs. 2.0 lakhs were sold during the year to both book sellers and individuals.

Forest Survey of India (FSI)

Established in June, 198 1, the Forest Survey of India (FSI) is entrusted with the responsibility of survey of forest resources in the country. The FSI has four zonal offices located at Bangalore, Calcutta, Nagpur and Shimla with headquarters in Dehra Dun.

The objectives of FSI are as follows :

To prepare a comprehensive State of Forest Report (SFR) inciuding National Forest Vegetation Map (NFVM) once iii every two years; also prepare thematic map through use of remote sensing data with minimum essential ground truth verification in 10 years cycle.

To collect, store and retrieve necessary forestry and forestry related data for national and state level planning and to create a computer based National Basic Forest Inventory System (NBFIS).

To design methodologies relating to forest surveys and subsequent updating. This would include methodology for

Vegetation mapping including thematic maps through use of satellite imagery/aerial photographs.

Ground truth verification

Growing stock and volume assessment.

To undertake work in regard to preparation of forest inventory in selected States/UTs on agency basis until establishment of their own resources survey units.

To impart training in modem forest survey techniques to foresters at various levels of responsibility in States/ Uts/GOI.

To support and oversee technique/inventory work undertaken by State/UT forest departments.

The activities of FSI during the year were as follows :

Vegetation mapping

One of the main objectives of FSI is to assess the extent of forest cover the monitor on A two years cycle, the broad changes in forest vegetation cover of the country by using multi-satellite data on 1:2,50,000 scale. The first attempt to assess the forest cover of the country by visual interpretation of satellite imageries was made in 1984-85 and the first NFVM was prepared in 19 8 7 on 1: 1 million scale. FSI which used Landsat satellite data earlier, has now completely switched over to the Indian Remote Sensing Satellite (IRSS) for the assessment of the forest cover. Besides visual interpretation of the satellite data, the FSI is gradually switching over to digital image analysis. SFR 1997 is the sixth report in the series of biennial reports, published by the FSI since 1987 and presents a comprehensive account of forest cover of the country and its dynamics over the previous assessment (SFR 1995).

The total forest cover of the country has been estimated to be 63.34 million ha. i.e. 19.27% of the geographic area of the country. While the dense forest (crown density more than 40%) and open forest (10%-40%) occupy about 11 % and 8% of the geographic area respectively, mangroves occupy 0. 15% of the total geographic area.

The country has lost about 5,482 sq.km. of forest cover since the 1995 assessment. Major losses have been recorded in the states of Andhra Pradesh (3,822 sq. km.) and Madhya Pradesh (3,969 sq. km.) while Maharashtra has shown a significant increase of 2,300 sq. km. The North Eastern states, which have rich forest cover (67%), have lost 316 sq.km. forest cover compared to the loss of 783 sq.km. recorded during the 1995 assessment.

Survey of Non-forest Area

Keeping in view the important role played by forestry plantations and to assess the impact of social forestry and other forestry extension programmes in meeting fuelwood, timber and raw material requirement of the wood based industries, survey of plantation outside conventional forest has also been initiated by the FSI. The survey completed in Harayana reveals that the total growing stock of wood in the state is 10.3 million cu.m. as compared to 1.4 million cu.m. in the natural forest areas. Though the two situations are outside the forest areas reflects the great potential that the plantations programmes have in wood production.

Field inventory

Since its inception as Preinvestment Survey of Forest Resources (PISFR) in 1965, field inventory has been one of the most important activities of Forest Survey of India. During the sixteen years of existence, PISFR has carried out ground inventory over a forest area of 2.28 lakhs sq.km. in India and 0.38 lakhs sq.km. in Nepal and Bhutan. After creation of the Forest Survey of India (FSI) in 1981, it has carried out field inventories in an additional area of 4.01 lakhs sq.km. till 1995. Methodology adopted by the FSI for carrying out field inventories is based on the two stage stratified random sampling with standard error ± 10%.

An inventory report prepared by the FSI gives details of area estimates, topographic description, classification, rate of forest (healthy or degraded), ownership , pattern, estimation of volume and other growth parameters such as height and diameter in different types of forest, estimation of growth, regeneration and modality of important species, volume equation and wood consumption of the area studied.

The annual target of field inventory is about 25,000 sq.km. and data pertaining to 25,000 sq.km. is processed every year. The reports of inventory are being brought out every year.

Thematic Mapping

FSI is engaged in preparing thematic maps on a scale of 1: 50,000 by interpretation of aerial photographs. These maps depict the forest types, species composition, ground density of forest cover and other land use classes. These maps are prepared for the entire country on a ten year cycle. Every year about 5,000 aerial photographs corresponding to 260 topographical sheets (1:50,000) of Survey of India are interpreted.

Electronic Data Processing

The objective of the Electronic Data Processing unit is to provide qualitative and quantitative information about the forest resources of the country. This unit functions as the national forest data bank by storing relevant data on forest inventory.

Training

FSI organises a number of training programmes for

forestry personnel on various aspects such as application of remote sensing techniques in forestry including GIS, forest inventory and electronic data processing. The duration of training varies from one week to four weeks depending on the level of personnel and the objective of the training. One week training is imparted to officers of the Indian Forest Service (IFS) and 2 weeks training to State Forest Service (SFS) Officers for exposing them to remote sensing techniques and its application in forestry. Two weeks training is imparted to Working Plan Officers to train them on the use of remote sensing techniques in preparation of working plans, updating stock maps, ground inventory and data processing. Four weeks training is imparted to Forest Range Officers to train them in interpretation of aerial photographs and satellite data, forest inventory and electronic data processing, The skills of the technical staff of FSI are also updated through suitably designed trainings courses.

The Andaman & Nicobar Islands Forest and Plantation Development Corporation Ltd., a Government of India Undertaking has a authorised capital of Rs. 600 Lakhs out of which Rs. 35 Lakhs is subscribed and paid up. During the year the Corporation have declared a dividend of Rs. 14.37 Lakhs. During the year the Corporation has also contributed a total sum of Rs. 390 Lakhs to the national exchequer by way of income tax and royalty. The Corporation has created assests worth Rs. 19.0 crores. The Department of public Enterprises has also conferred the status of mini Ratna to the Corporation.

4

National Natural Resource Development

India has a total geographical area of 3287263 sq. km. The officially recorded forest area is 765210 sq. km., which constitutes 23.8% of the total geographical area. Over 45000 species of plants occur in the country and several thousand species of them are endemic to India. Their range of distribution is confined only to this country and not reported from any other part of the world. India is equally rich in fauna. The country has about 350 species of birds and qmqore than 20,000 species of insects.

Various sources give different figures of the land use pattern in the country. However, the task of reconciliation of these figures has been assigned to National Remote Sensing Agency (NRSA) and in all probability it would be completely reconciled in the beginning of Ninth Plan, which is to begin from April 1997. Presently, the land use pattern have been quoted from the report published by Directorate of Economics and Statistics (1996), a nodal agency in the country to compile the data related to various departments in the country.

The total area recorded as forest in 1950-51 was 404800 sq. km. Over the years recorded forest area continuously rose and touched the figures of 765210 sq. km. This was on account of unoccupied government lands being declared as the Forest area by state/UT governments. Most of these lands were non-productive and came under the category of wastelands. A unique situation exists in the North-Eastern states of the country. These forest lands are unclassed i.e. without any legal status. In India the total unclassed forest is 125385 sq. km. which constitutes 3.8% and 16.38% of the geoographical area and recorded forest area of the country respectively.

The transfer of forest land to non-forest uses is also one of the important factors which has depleted India's natural forest ecosystem. In between 1951 to 1980, 4.328 million ha. of forest land were officially diverted for non-forestry uses. It would be proper to mention here that the transferred forest lands were highly productive lands and would have contributed much towards enrichment of forest ecosystem, if retained.

While analysing the state-wise forest cover of India it is revealed that owing to specific problems the country may be broadly divided into two regions namely, North Eastern region and rest of the country.

North Eastern region consists of seven states. There has been a decrease in the dense forest and open forest cover in almost every state and there is an alarming proportion of forest degradation in this region.

The loss of forest cover in N-E region because of the practice of shifting cultivation accounts for 1526 sq. km. and for other reasons the loss is 377 sq. km.

In most of the states as mentioned in preceding para, the dense forest cover has shown a deslining trend thereby setting in a chain reaction in the degradation of ecosystem.

In 1995 assessment (fifth cycle) the State wise and above forest category wise detail are not given but it has shown that in totality there has been an increase in the dense forest and Mangrove but open forest has shown a declining trend. Presently, the Forest ecosystem is under tremendous pressure on account of excessive removal of biomass in all forms including diversion of forest lands to non forest uses.

Our forest cover has dwindled notwithstanding three successive National Forest Policies. A scientific land use policy alone can ensure sustained production, ecological balance and environmental benefits. It is time that the Forest Policy is reviewed and a new strategy adopted keeping in view that conservation includes preservation, maintenance, sustainable utilization, restoration and enrichment of the environment. Man depends on natural resources from his forest environment for all his basic needs. No doubt, the majority in the industrialized countries is no longer dependent on the natural living resources but the bulk of the rural and a section of the urban population in India and the rest of the developing world continue this dependence, especially for their fuel, fodder and timber needs. The forest serves many valuable functions as has been reflected in the national forest policies. Moreover, forest plays an active role as a storehouse of living organisms of potential use and as a regulator of rainfall, soil and water regime, source of many basic needs of the weaker sections of the rural population. The relationship between land, climate and forest is such that if the soil is allowed to deteriorate or lost, degradation of both land and vegetation becomes inevitable. Unfortunately, in the developing countries like India, biotic pressures are intense.

Problems with India's forests:

The situation is worsening in spite of the lofty aims propagated by the three successive national forest policies. In India, although the first policy is nearly a century old, the present forest cover is worse than when it was originally proposed. The failure of the national forest policies is perhaps due to their focus on government forests rather than to the land and soil in general. There has been a lack, of scientific land use policy having legal backing and public support. For these reasons, the definition of 'forest' has come to imply land area constituted as reserve forests and not general tree cover.

Biotic Pressure: The tremendous increase in human population, the resultant poverty nd the heavy dependence on agriculture have resulted in the use of wood as the main fuel. India's ecology is today no better with the deficit of firewood at 145 million m^3 and 43 million ha of land brought under the plough between 1951 and 1976 for the extension of agriculture. The loss of forest area for various purposes during 1951-76 was substantial. The situation has still remained the same and the condition has not changed as is evident from the cases of some of the States. The problem has worsened due to excessive grazing coupled with forest fire. About 52 per cent of India's forests are incapable of regenration largely due to the combined effects of biotic pressures. In a developing country like India, forests have suffered badly because of the failure in land management practices. To what extent can we put the blame on forest policies? Are the policies wrong or inconsistent or is it that the policies have remained merely ceremonial documents devoid of the will to implement or people's support? An analysis of the forest policies of India would reveal that the main cause of failure has been, perhaps, viewing forests in isolation rather than taking into consideration the country's soil as a whole. It is after all the soil which supports all kinds of plant life in the biosphere.

Forests are a renewable source and contribute substantially to economic development. They play major role in enhancing the quality of environment. The country has an area of 752.3 lakh hectare notified as forests, of which 406.1 lakh hectare is classified as reserved and 215.1 lakh hectare as protected. Unclassified forest area is spread over 131.1 lakh hectare. About 19.47 per cent of the total geographical area of the country is under actual forest cover.

India is one of the few countries which ahs a forest policy since 1894. It was revised in 1952 and again in 1988. Main plank of the revised forest policy of 1988 is protection, conservation and development of forests. Its aims are: (i) maintenance of environmental stability through preservation and restoration of ecological balance; (ii) conservation of natural heritage; (iii) check on soil erosion and denudation in catchment area of rivers, lakes and reservoirs; (iv) check on extension of sand dunes in desert areas of Rajasthan and along coastal tracts; (v) substantial increase in forest/tree cover through massive afforestation and social forestry programmes; (vi) steps to meet requirements of fuel wood, fodder, minor forest produce and soil timber of rural and tribal populations; (vii) increase in productivity of forest to meet the national needs; (viii) encouragement of efficient utilisation of forest produce and optimum substitution of wood, and (ix) steps to create massive people's movement with involvement of women to achieve the objectives and minimise pressure on existing forests.

The entire gamut of forest activities are being given a new orientation in the light of the National Forest Policy of 1988. Some of the important areas for immediate and effective protection of forests include afforestation and development of wastelands, reforestation and replantation in existing forests, settlement, restriction on grazing, encouragement for wood substitutes and supply of other kinds of fuel, elimation of forest contractors, discouragement of monoculture practice etc.

Increasing destruction and degradation of forests and treelands especially in the Himalayas and other hilly areas, is contributing to heavy erosion of top soil, erratic rainfall and recurring floods. It is also causing acute shortage of firewood and loos of productivity due to eroded and degraded lands. The Forest (Conservation) Act, 1980 enacted to check indiscriminate deforestation/ diversion of forest lands for non-forestry purpose was amended in 1988 to make it more stringent by prescribing punishment for violations.

Another area of concern has been degradation of forests due to biotic pressure. Guidelines have been framed for preparation of working plans and felling in forests. Some of the salient features are: (i) working plans shoudl be up-to-date and stress conservation; (ii) preliminary working plan should have multi-disciplinary approach; (iii) tribal rights and concessions should be highlighted and with control mechanisms; (iv) grazing should be studied in detail and specific prescriptions should cover fodder propagation; (v) shifting cultivation and encroachments need to be controlled; (vi) clear-felling with artificial regeneration should be avoided as far as possible and clear felling blocks should not exceed 10 hectare in hills and 25 hectare area in plains, and (vii) banning all felling above 1,000 metre altitude for a few years should be considered to allow these areas to recover. Critical areas in hills and catchment areas prone to landslides, erosion etc., should be totally protected and quickly afforested.

Guidelines have been issued in June 1990 to state governments for involving village communities and voluntary agencies for regeneration of degraded forest lands on usufruct shraing basis. As a follow up of these guidelines, 14 states have issued appropriate orders. These states are: West Bengal, Orissa, Bihar, Madhya Pradesh, Rajasthan, Gujarat, Maharashtra, Tripura, Himachal Pradesh, Haryana, Jammu and Kashmir, Andhra Pradesh, Karnataka and Tamil Nadu. Other states are being persuaded to issued such orders.

Firewood occupies a predominant place as an energy source in rural areas. As against the estimated requirement of about 15.7 crore tonnes of fuelwood per annum, recorded production is only 5.8 crore tonnes. Due to scarcity of firewood, considerable quantities of cowdung and agricultural residues are burnt as fuel leading to air pollution. It is expected that programmes of renewable energy sources and augmenting fuel growth in wastelands will help in closing the gap.

Fire is one of the major factors responsible for destruction of forests in the country. In India, most of the fires are man-made and are generally deliberate and on rare occasions accidental. The causes of deliberate fire incidences are grazing, mahua seed and flower collections, tendu leaf collection, poaching and shifting cultivation, etc. In order to reduce the incidents of fire in India, the following steps have been undertaken by the forest department: (i) development of firelines and (ii) establishment of watch towers besides employing fire watchers during fire seasons. In order to develop the techniques for detection, prevention and suppression of fire in the country, a UNDP assisted Modern Forests Fire Control Project was initiated in 1984 in Chandrapur, Maharashtra and Haldwani/Nainital, U.P. Techniques like development of better communication network and effective use of hand tools and other equipments developed under the projects have proved successful in reducing the fire damage. In addition, fire danger rating system, wireless network, fire reporting system and hand tools etc., were designed. This scheme is being continued in 11 states of the country.

The National Wildlife Action Plan adopted in 1983 provides the framework of strategy as well as programme for conservation of wildlife. At present the protected area network comprises 80 national parks and 441 sanctuaries covering 4.5 per cent of the total geographical area of the country. The Wildlife (Protection) Act, 1972 adopted by all states except Jammu and Kashmir (which has its own Act), governs wildlife conservation and protection of endangered species. The Act prohibits trade in rare and endangered species. India is also a signatory to the Convention on International Trade in Endangered Species of Wild Flora and Fauna. Under this, export or import of endangered species and their products is subject to strict control. Commercial exploitation of such species is prohibited. The Centre provides finanacial and technical assistance to states for: (i) development and improved management of national parks (ii) protection of wildlife and control of poaching and illegal trade in wildlife products; (iii) eco-development in areas around national parks and sanctuaries; (iv) conservation of elephant and its habitat; and (v) conservation of rhinos in Assam. The Wildlife (Protection) Act, 1972 has been amended to make the provisions more effective. Endangered species of plants and animals have been brought under the purview of the Act. A Central Zoo Authority has been set up to look after the management of zoological parks in the country. The Authority has since notified rules for recognition of zoos which stipulates the standards for upkeep, maintenance and veterinary care of animals. It coordinates the activities of over 200 existing zoos and also supervises the exchange of animals on a scientific basis. Project Tiger, one of the premeir conservation efforts of the country has completed 20 years in April 1993. Under this scheme 21 Tiger Reserves have been set up all over the country. A Global Tiger Forum has been set up for Tiger Range countries and an interim secretariat has been set up at New Delhi. A Tiger Crisis Cell has been set up to obtain all the information essential for conservation of the tiger.

The Animal Welfare Board of India, established in 1962 under the provisions of the Prevention of Cruelty to Animals Act, 1960 is an autonomous organisation of the Ministry of Environment and Forests working for the cause of animal welfare in the country. A series of camps for training the members of SPCAs and Animal Welfare Organisations are being held all over the country, in collaboration with the Royal Society for Prevention of Cruelty to Animals, London. The Board also celebrates Animal Welfare Fortnight from 14 January every year.

Forest policy—precedence of agriculture: The first National Forest Policy initiated nearly a century ago, while stressing the important role played by forests in conserving the ecology of the country, had expressed in no uncertain terms that the role of forests was secondary to that of agriculture. However, it suggested that, except for the reserved forests (the preservation of which was essential on climatic and physical grounds), if the demand for permanent agriculture arose, forests should give place to it and even in the case of economically rich forests, the considerations of forests income were to be subordinate to that of satisfying the needs of the local population for forest produce. Further, the areas excluded from reserved forests should be managed in the interests of the local population for forest produce as distinct from the general public.

The National Forest Policy of 1952 was framed at a time when pressure on land had begun to be exerted and the slogan 'grow more food' was at the cost of forest covered areas. It stressed that a system of balanced and complementary land use was of permanent importance,and contradicted the considerations that neighbouring areas and agricultural requirements should be entitledto a prior and preferential claim over forests. It supported the necessity of forest not only on the slopes but also in flat areas with dry conditions.It countered demands for the clearance of forests for extension of agriculture, saying that the solution to the food problemof an increasing population lay in intensive cultivation. It suggested that India should aim at maintaing one-third of its land area under forests.

The current National Forest Policy (1988) recommneds increased afforestation in view of the wide gap between demand and supply and the evident allround degradation of the land, and the desire that the mountainous region should have forests over 66 per cent of the land area. The policy also stresses that the poorer people should be encouraged in the afforestation programmes, and that land grant rules and land ceiling laws should not be subverted. Giving first priority to the local needs, the policy recommends sharing of forest revenues with local communities from social forestry plantations. It is also against the supply of forest raw materials from natural forests to industry, implying mismanagement in the forestry sector, and holding forest-based industries and contractors partly responsible for the deterioration of forests.

The only aspects of land use touched upon are the afforestation of denuded wastelands nd the ban on diversion of good agricultural land to forestry plantations. The policy generally refers to blocks legally constituted as reserve forests with no recommendations or restraints on the use of the remaining 77 per cent of the land area outside the reserve forests. There is no suggestion on prohibition of cultivation on steep slopes in the Himalayas on the Western Ghats, or in the semi-arid and arid regions. Tree-covered government land not classified as reserve forest continues to be released for cultivation. This includes government land in the mountain belt also.

Regularisation of encroachment on government land is a priority issue with the Centre and many State governments. It recommends that revenue from forestry plantations should be shared with the local people. While acknowledging that 29 per cent of all energy consumed in the country is from firewood, compared with 55 per cent from commercial energy, the document has pointed out that the share of the forestry sector in the VII plan was around three per cent of the commercial energy sector. The afforestation contemplated in the 1988 policy is more in the nature of poverty alleviation schemes rather than through development of forests. While the policy advocated strict grazing practices, entry of cattle into reserve forests continues to be free and unregulated.

In the developing countries like India, classification of land use is adopted with the focus on conservation and prevention of forest sites being used for agriculture rather than for promoting afforestation in sites unsuited for agriculture. Hence the extent under forests invariably refers to the area of the government forest, the minor distinction being reserved forest and unclassified forests. It does not necessarily imply are under tree cover. The position is different in the developed countries where the areas designated as forest are fully clad with tree growth and can belong to government, companies, co-operatives or private individuals. The imperative of wage structure as in Canada; tax incentives and agricultural pricing policies as in the UK; strong tax support as in Brazil, legal requirements with tax incentives as in Sweden, or simply the requirement by law as in Switzerland has promoted private forests mainly in land unsuited for agriculture in these countries. Presently, Japan is promoting increased use of wood for house construction. Such wood, mainly produced through private enterprises, will far exceed its consumption and Japan does not wish the afforestation programme to suffer a set-back for economic reasons. Development has unfortunately implied increased agricultural production, mainly through the expansion of the area under agricultural crops. In many regions and terrains, soil and climate may not be suited for sustainable agriculture. Therefore, proper scientific land classification alone can provide for sustained production, ecological balance and environmental benefits.

Our economic and ecological sustenance can be ensured only through the care of the soil involving several factors including population growth and poverty. Redemption from poverty cannot be through indiscriminate extension of agriculture in unsuitable areas but through intensification of production. This could be through industry, handicrafts or production of the best suited crop for the site. A forest policy has more meaning if it prescribes specific scales for the use of land based on site factors, rather than deliberating on the advantages of ecological equilibrium. The government must devise measures and means to implement the land use policy with as much concern as it devotes to the protection of the country's frontiers. Wherever a tree crop is the best alternative, it should be grown.

It is time to assess the results of the 1988 policy, because of the steady decline in both the extent and quality of forests, occurrence of floods and droughts, which result in the national loss of 600 million tonnes of soil annually and the widening gap between demand

and supply for firewood which will increase from 144 million m^3 to 300 million m^3 in the next evolve a new strategy of forest conservation keeping in mind that conservation includes preservation, maintenance, sustainable utilization, restoration and enhancement of the natural environment.

Forestry is one of the cheapest option to bring about a change in rural economy of the country. Forests not only give fuelwood, small timber, timber, and fooder to the people but it also conserves water and soil moisture for the agro-eco system. Development and conservation of forest area will help rural people to improve their level of loving. The forest wasteland has immense potential in this respect. Degradation of forest has been going on because of various pressure groups on the forest eco-system. Today, various agencies give different figures for the extent of waste land avaliable in the country. Forest Survey of India has given 31 million hectares of degraded forest in the country, though the actual figure may be higher. The Ministry of Environment and Forest considers and extent of forest wasteland around 35 million hectares. The problem of increasing wasteland becomes more complex if the non-forest wasteland is also taken into consideration. The National Commission on Agriculture (1976) has given a figure of 176 million hectares of wasteland available in the country while Society for Promotion for Wasteland Development has given 129 million hectares as wasteland in the country. To arrive at the actual figure the job for assessing wasteland in the country has been assigned to National Remote Sensing Agency (NRSA) and it is believed that a conclusive figure would be provided in the beginning of Ninth Five Year Plan (1997-98).

Regardless of the extent of wasteland available in the country, it becomes all the more important to develop them on priority basis so that the basis requirement of the local populaltion is fully met. The total annual availability of fuelwood and small timber from the forest is 26290 thousand cum. and 8 million cum. respectively whereas the total requirement of fuelwood, fooder and small timber of the country has been estimated and found to be much higher than their annual availability.

All eco-systems develop a set of specialised and integrated structural and functional properties which are in delicate balance. In a stable ecosystem, all the system variables may return to the initial equilibrium, if the disturbance is moinor. The stability of a system, however, may be exclusively or collectively determined by the extent of its resistance and/or resilience. Exploitation of natural resources beyond the threshold limits imposed by the resistance and resilience of the ecosystem warrants immediate attention. Any further mismanagement can lead to damages beyond repair. For example, tropical moist forests, rich in genetic resources, are continuously under biotic pressure resulting in soil erosion, floods,l loss of species, loss of biomass and many others. Therefore, the management of each ecosystem should be site and problem specific if the forests have to be conserved an developed on the principle of sustainability. This has also been seen after a very careful review of the various schemes in the Forestry sector that this sector has not been dealt with adequate attention from planning point of view. For example, the scheme titled "control of forest fire" covers only five states in the country though it is a menace which not only disturbs the existing ecosystem but also leads to extinction of many flora and fauna. Likewise, control of poaching, rhino conservation, forest protection, natural regeneration are many areas where regular efforts or schemes are needed to strengtrhen the infrastructure in general and capacity building in particular.

Non-timber forest products (NTFP) and non–wood forest production (NWFP) are terms that are being widely used currently to denote what was termed minor forest produce earlier. The term NTFP as is used now broadly includes fuel and fooder, biomass, bamboo, cane, grasses, fibre, oil, tannin and dyes, gums, resins, medicinal plants, barks, leaves flowers, fruits, tubersl, mushrooms, seeds, mammals, birds, reptiles, fish and insects etc. The term minor forest produce clearly indicates that the produce was not of any great economic importance to merit serious consideration. However, recent facts and figures give altogether a different picture. NTFPs accounted for nearly "two fifths of forest department revenue and three fourths of net exporet earnings from forest produce. About 70% of the NTFPs are collected from the five states of Maharashtra, Madhya Pradesh, Bihar, Orissa and Andhra Pradesh (World bank, 1991). Sixty five per cent of India's tribgal population live in these five states.

It is estimated that employment opportunities through collection of NTFP can be increased from 0.8 million to 3.3 million persons/year. Again it is estimated that out of approximately 571.85 women days of women's employment generated in forest based enterprises, 90% is in small scale enterprises using NTFP as raw material. It is worth recalling here, the figures for NTFP have been derived from forests which are already degraded. With the improvement of the protection status of the forests through JFM it is expected that barring a few items like bidi leaves, production of most other items will increase significantly and the total turn over in terms of money will fare exceed timber. Consequent potential as well as the export earinings will also go up. Despite all this, adequate attention has not been paid to NTFP either at the national or at the state level. Sustainable extraction of NTFPs together with processing and marketing can generate significant income and economy. In fact, in terms of employment as well as income, NTFP in many instances have been found to give better return than commercial.

India is a country of vast diversity lying at the juncture of the biogeographic provinces of Afro-Eurasia and orient. Due to its wide ranging environmental regime and diverse biological communities, it has been recognised as one of the world's top twelve mega diversity nations. There are 3000 plant species in India which yield NTFPs. But only 126 have developed marketability. According to E.O.Wilson there may be 100 million species of plants and animals in tropical forests. It is estimated that about 1.7 million species, formally identified and classified represent only 5% of the total number of species now present on earth. Though extinction of species also has been a predictable feature of evolution since life appeared on each some 3.6 billion years ago byt man has been major cause in this extinction. Species which are of MFP value only have suffered more in this regard.

The scope of NWFPs is so wide and fruitful that if properly managed the return from these products can well outweigh the losses in the revenue due to the ban on felling of trees and can help as most powerful tool for poverty alleviation of rural masses. The royalty realised through the disposal of NWFPs extracted from government forests was over Rs. 100 crore in 1985—86, which has gone up during subsequent years. The contribution of NWFPs to the total value of forest based export is over 70 per cent. Similarly out of total employment of 2—3 million man years generated by forestry sector, employment of 1.6 million man years is available from NWFP, by way of collection, processing and sale. At present, only 0.32 million tonnes of NWFPs are being collected against the production of 1.25 million tonnes. In case arrangements to extract the totsal available NWFPs are made employment on this account shall go up to 4 million man years from the present 1.6 million man years. this will not only improve the economy of poor inhabitants living in and around forests but also boost the state revenue as well as export earning of the country. Management of NWFPs has therefore, gained renewed importance in India for sustainable development.For environment and ecological security restrictons, regulations and restraints are the fundamental requirements. But the socio—economic compulsion of the socially and economically less or unprivileged people with their exploding population necessitates and culminates into unrestricted, unrestrained and unregulated use of the forest ecosystem. Both these also these also need the resource to comprise a variety of floral and faunal richness. Just contrary to these, commercial and industrial economies are concerned with the bulk production of a few commercially and industrially relevant commodities to be produced in bulk and specific sizes.

Management perspectives with regard to forest have to accomodate these situations ina balancing way. For tree species there has been bias (at least) towards commercial and industrial economies. But NTFP have so far not been adequately and properly managed even for these economies. There is urgent need to develop proper management perspective for forests in general and NTFPs in particular. NTFPs can be harvested without damaging the forest ecosystem. It should be possible to develop a management system to meet demand of certain mix of products. The trio of tribal–forest–ecology needs an urgent change in the management approach.

The change should put the NTFP in forefront. First step is intimacy with the forest ecosystem and the people in and around. Optimum levels of interference patterns should be worked out. Forest ecosystem should include the resource base adiacent to forests. Assessment of what, where and how much in respect of NTFPs should be done. National, regional and local level lists of NTFPs should be prepared. Ecological, socio—economic, harvesting, storage, processing, value addition and marketing studies of listed items should be done. Forest working Plans should deal with NTFPs seperately and adequately. NTFP stock maps should be prepared.

In aerial photographs and satellite imageries layers below tree canopies should be interpreted. NTFP atlas of the country should be prepared. Management should be prescribed for species mix both horizontally and vertically. Canopy manipulations should be prescribed for yielding NTFPs. Fodder should be recognised as NTFP. Zoning based on the richness of particular NTFP should be done and maps prepared. Local and internal consumption should be recorded. Prevailing prices at different salepoints should be accurately surveyed.

The human population in India has increased from 361 million in 1951 to 844 million in 1991 and is likelyk to cross 1.18 billion by 2010. The danger of population pressure is lurking on unguarded forest and it may be totally wiped out if the present trend continues.

Similarly, the livestock population not only destroys forest ecosystem completely but stops its natural regeneration capacity. Unfortunately, livestock population has also shown a phenomenal rise over the years as it has increased from 155.3 million in 1951 to 429.60 million in 1987. The goat population has shown the maximum increase amongst all the livestock from 47.1 million in 1951 to 99.4 million in 1992. It is expected to cross 152.7 million by 2001 A.D. It is a widely accepted fact that goats disturb the forest ecosystem more seriouly than other animals. The other factor which has led to illegal felling of valuable timber from our forest ecosystem is primarily economic and its related market forces. The problem is of such a gigantic dimension that its impact would be felt in times to come, if it is not realised today. In Uttar Pradesh, the most populous state of India, approximately 5000 young poles of 0-10 cm. diameter class are cut illegally everyday. It is not only a serious problem from socio-economic angle but from silvicultural point of view also as the forest ecosystem is being depleted from natural regeneration and these forests are gradually turning out to be dead forest.

There are manifold causes for the loss of bio-diversity. Among these are the rapid expansion of industry, agriculture, urbanisation and large scale development of projects like dams, highways, mining and increased expansion and intensification of human activities. About 20 species are categorised as possibly extinct as these species have not been sighted during last 6 to 10 decades. Cheetah has become extinct during this century 0. The pressure on many mega-fauna like tiger, rihnos etc. is so intense that nothing could be estimated as yet about their future. Tiger census of 1993 has very clearly indicated a declining trend in their population. Similarly, 81 species of mammals, 47 birds, 15 reptiles, 3 amphibians and a large number of butterflies, moths and beetles, besides 1500 plant species are considered vulnerable and endangered. Unfortunately, illegal trade still continues in ivory, rhino's horns, bones of tigers and many other threatened plant species. There are many government programmes which are aiming at conservation of ecologically fragile forest ecosystem buyt their forceful implementation is lacking in the absence of forceful legislation. Biodiversity conservation was the focal point after Earth Summit held at Rio in 1992. A concrete Action Plan is the need of the hour.

Timber production

FAO estimates that in 1994, the world produced 3,419.9 mcum of round wood, out of which India's share was only 293.9 mcum (8.59%). Firewood and charcoal accounted for as much as 91.5% (269.2 mcum) of the Indian Production (FAO, 1994). Although only less than 10% of the total wood production in the country is used for industrial purpopses, industrial demand has been rising sharply. Projected demands for forest products show a 22 to 183% increase from 1990 to 2000. By a long—term trend analysis of forest products in India, Rao (1992) showed that production of almost all products except pulpwood and particles and veneer sheets registered an increase in the 1980s. Industrial use of wood has been growing at the rate of 3.5 per cent per annum, according to him.

The decade from 1975–76 to 1985–86, saw Indian production of wood and wood products recording an increase of 22 to 135%. However, statistics on timber production is less revealing, perhaps as incomplete as its demand itself. Timber is normally obtained from government forests, community and private forests and farm lands. While the timber extracted from the national forests is reported in the official statistics, the timber harvested from the other sources goes unreported in the official statistics. Therefore, the epithet 'recorded production', a gross underestimate of total production is fashionable among foresters.

According to FSI, consumption of firewood exceeded recorded production by a staggering 195 mcum in 1987. All existing projections show that there is a big gap between demand and supply of industrial timber too. Total sustained yield increment of existing forests is stated to be 35 million m^3 With an additional 4–5 million m^3 from private sources, it sums up to a grand total of 40 million m^3 (Campbell, 1987). To meet the industrial needs alone (64.4 mcum in 2000 AD, according to NCA, 1976), an additional sustained yield increment of 24 mcum will be needed. Furthermore, all indicators suggest that this gap is going to grow. Presumably this wide gap between demand and sup[ply is being met from unrecorded sources like farm lands and agroforestry and other privately owned sources.

Given this huge deficit in industrial timber availability in the country, we may probably have two options. The first, is to enhance the area under plantation forests and to improve their productivity. However, given a conservative average productivity of 0.3 cum/ha for long rotation timber and roundwood species, and 3–5 cum/ha for short rotation pulp wood, this would then mean at least 30 million ha of new plantations for timber species and two million ha for pulpwood–a total for 32 million ha for industrial needs alone (Campbell, 1987). Considering the poor productivity of forest plantations and the general inhability to expand area under plantation forestry, it is impossible to achieve such gargantuan targets through the plantation forestry route.

India's wastelands

The reclamation of wastelands is not an easy task and warrants careful approach with a defined methodology. This, in turn, requires survey and mapping of such lands in their natural environment. Such maps showing the localities of different categories of wastelands with soil and site characteristics, climate, land form, erosion, land use, etc. hould be prepared, because all these factors individually or in combination influence the growth of wasteland. Otherwise, any planning for the reclamation of the wastelands, which does not take into account the geographical aspects, may not bring about the desired result.

The basic requirement for the development of wastelands is the creation of a suitable vegetative cover which not only prevents further degradation but improves the environment. On wastelands, if a green cover with grasses, legumes, shrubs and trees is established and maintained and cutting and grazing are prohibited, the land may slowly recover on its own and may eventually even become productive. The choice of plant species for reclamation and afforestation of any type of wasteland should be such that it should suit the local conditions and grow normally with least attention.

Some of the important tree species suitable for the reclamation of degraded and wastelands are Acacia auriculaeformis, A. catechu, A. nilotica, Albizia lebbeck, Anacardium occidentale, Anogeissus latifolia, Zadirachta indica, Bambusa arundicacea, Bauhinia racemosa, Butea monosperma, Cassia siamea, Casuarina equisetifolia, Eucalyptus spp., Populus spp., Prosopis juliflora, Salix alba, Sesbania grandiflora, Syzygium cuminii, Tamarindus indica, Tamarix aphylla, Tectona grandis, Terminalia arjuna and Ziziphus mauritiana.

Many perenial grasses survive under adverse conditions and help in preventing soil erosion. Grass species such as Cenchrus ciliaris, Chrysopogon fulvus, Eulaliopsis binata, Imperata cylindrica (I. arundinacea), Panicum maximum, Panicum repens, Pennisetum pedicillatum, Vetiveriazianioides can be employed for reclaiming degraded and wastelands. Apart from the above mentioned grass species, many other herb and shrub species such as Calotropis spp, Datura spp, Tephrosia purpurea are good soil—binders and are helpful in controlling erosion and degradation.

Agro—forestry and social forestry provide an excellent basis of tree planting to prevent and reclaim soil from degradation. Agroforestry integrates agriculture and forestry on the same unit of land so as to meet the local demands of fooder, fuelwood,l timber and foodgrains and thus, further destruction of forests is stopped and a suitable ecological balance is maintained. Similarly, social forestry programme aims at growing the trees by utilising the land lying unused to meet the demand for fuel, fooder and timber, to check soil erosion and protect the ecology and environment.

Saline and alkali soils along with the acidic soils are the major problematic soils, the former often referred to as salt—affected soils.

Reclamation of alkali soils, basically, requires replacing of excess sodium on the soil exchange complex by calcium through amendments (gypsum being the cheapest and abundantly available) and leaching out of the exchanged sodium form the rootzone. For any lasting reclamation, provision of adequate drainage is important. Growing crops tolerant to alkalinity of soils such as barley, wheat, sunflower, etc. may ensure reasonable returns during the initial phases od reclamation. Similarly, management of waterlogged saline soils basically involves lowering of water—table below the root zone of crop and leaching of excess salts with good quality water. Acidic soils could be corrected by adding amendments such as lime to the soil.

Afforestation of wastelands through proper financial assitance by various agencies would provide income and employment opportunities to the poor and improve the quality of the environment. The government can play a facilitating role by removing obstacles and simplifying procedures. The lack of ground-level data has affected the afforestation programme, the author feels. The afforestation of wastelands has now emerged as an important feature in the present socio-economic and political scenario in India, which aims at solving the problems of scarcity of timber, firewood, fodder and other forest produce as well as reclamation of wastelands and degraded forests. India has vast tracts of wastelands, and these lands are mostly owned by government and village Panchayats and are highly degraded. Tree plantation is the socially optimum and ecologically-sound use of such lands. It may not be economically desirable for a farmer to plant trees on good lands which have a very high opportunity cost in terms of value of agricultural production forgone. However, tree planting may be profitable for a farmer in region prone to recurring drought and having unproductive soil which is not fit for growing agricultural crops.

Although the practice of planting trees is as old as cultivation of other crops, the need for government intervation to promote afforestation was articulated by the National Commission on Agriculture (NCA) in 1976. The government of India accepted the NCA's recommendation and subsequently various afforestation programmes like farm forestry, rehabilitation/ reforestation of degraded lands, formation of community woodlots and strip plantation were started in some States in the late seventies. Recent evidences from various parts of the country indicate that the success of afforestation programmes has been remarkable. In India, there is still a vast scope for implementing afforestation programmes in regions which are not yet brought within the fold of tree plantation schemes and in which there is acute shortage of firewood, timber and other forest produce.

In conjunction with technical guidance and financing, availability of wastelands for afforestation is the other crucial component of the wastelands development and afforestation programmes determing their success. There are many constraints which are hampering the implementation of afforestation programmes in various parts of the country. The non-availability of wastelands for afforestation programmes is one of them. In the absence of a comprehensive survey of land use, several estimates have been made about the extent of wastelands in India. One of the estimates of wastelands indicate that about 175 million hectares of (m ha) land fall in this category (Sigh et al, 1981). The other estimate by the Society for the Promotion of Wastelands Development (SPWD) puts it at 129 m ha-93 m ha in non-forest area and 36 m ha in forest area (SPWD, 1984). The National Wastelands Development Board (NWDB, 1989) estimates wastelands to the extent of 120 m ha with 40 m ha in forest lands and 80 m a in agricultural lands. According to Singh (1994), more than half of the geographical area of India consists of degraded lands. The estimates for wastelands range between 38.4 m ha (11.7% of total geographical area of the country, Directorate of Economics & Statistics, GOI, New Delhi 1978-79) to 175 m ha (53.2% of total geographical area of the country, Ministry of Agriculture & Co-operation, New Delhi, 1982) (Gautam and Narayan, 1988:96). However, Bentley (1984) has estimated that 200 m ha of land in India are partially degraded in terms of short-term productivity. According to Khan (1987), the wastelands which may ultimately be available for development would not be more than 80 m ha, bulk of which is degraded forests and marginal agriculatural lands. There are many other estimates of wastelands in India.

The information needed for assessing the potential of non-forest and cultivated lands, like ownership, extent and type of degradation, and present and future uses, has never been collected on a systematic basis for the entire country (Romm, 1981). Recently, some initiatives have been taken to improve the availability of grass roots level data for this purpose. The Government of India has already implemented a National Wastelands Identification Project to identify the extent and type of wastelands in 146 districts in 19 States.

One of the most serious problems threatening the country today is its population growth. Although the foodgrain production in the last few years has kept pace with the population increase, the daunting task of feeding each and everyone in the next century is the biggest challenge before us. In our attempts to meet such increasing demands, the improper and over—use of chemical inputs had deteriorated the agro—ecosystems to a considerable extent. Moreover, the pressure due to growing human and cattle population on the land has added to the deterioration of land status of the country. The increasing deterioration of land due to soil—erosion, injudicious use of chemical fertilizers, water logging, salinity/alkalinity, shifting cultivation, etc. necessitates a more scientific approach towards the utilisation of these lands, often termed as degraded or waste—lands. The growing awareness world over on the environment conservation and the emphasis on the concept of 'sustainability' has focussed on the area of 'wasteland utilization' as an important component of 'sustainable development.'

There are various aerial estimates of wastelands in the country varying from one—third to one half of the country's total area. The primary reason of the variation in such estimates could be ascribed to the fact that until recently, wastelands had neither been systematically defined nor identified. The first comprehensive attempt to map out such areas and categories them, was done by the National Commission on Agriculture (1976), which estimated different types of wastelands and suggested guidelines for reclaiming and developing such land. The

Commission had estimated the extent of wastelands in the country to be 175 million hectares which is more than half the total geographical area in he country. However, this estimate was not based on scientific data. As per an estimate by the Society for Promotion of Wastelands Development (1993), the area under wastelands is around 129 million hectares or about one—third of country's total geographical area.

According to the statistics presented, the state with the greatest expanse of wastelands in the country is Madhya Pradesh with 20.14 million ha very closely followed by Rajasthan with 19.93 million ha. The states with over 10 million ha of wastelands each are Andhra Pradesh and Maharashtra. Gujarat, Karnataka and Uttar Pradesh have each approximately 9 million ha of wastelands.

To a layman, wasteland is a piece of land which is lying uninhabited or uncultivated. These lands are also commonly perceived to produce much less than their potential. Despleted of the green cover and productivity, such lands are often in a critical condition. Boradly, wastelands may be defined as land where the production of biomass is less than its opotimum productivity. Wasteland also refers to lands which are economically unproductive, ecologically unstable and subject to environmental deterioration.

According to the Technical Task Group, constituted by the Planning Commisison and NWDB (National Wastelands Development Board), wasteland is defined as that land which is degraded and is presently lying unutilised except as current fallows due to different constraints.

Wastelands have been classified by NWDB into culturable and unculturable wastelands.

Land which is capable of or has the potential for the development of vegetative cover and is not being used due to different constraints of varying degree is termed as culturable wasteland. The culturable wastelands comprise the following categories:

— Gullied and/or ravinous land;

— Undulating upland with or without scrub;

— Surface–waterlogged lands and marsh;

— Salt–affected land;

— Shifting—cultivation area;

— Degraded forest—lands;

— Degraded pastures/grazing—lands;

— Degraded non forest—plantation land;

— Strip—land;

— Sands; and

— Mining/industrial wastelands.

Lands, which can not be developed for vegetative cover, are defined as unculturable wastelands. The unculturable wastelands comprise the following categories:

— Baren rocky/Stony wastes/Sheet–rock area;

— Steep–sloping area; and

— Snow–covered and/or glacial area.

Besides the above categories of wastelands, the following could also be included:

— Over cultivated soils leading to depletion of micro–nutrients;

— Acidic soils; and

— Land overgrown with aggressive weeds.

The major causes of land being rendered waste include—deforestation, overgrazing, faulty water management practices, extensive mining activities, etc. Deforestation and overgrazing distinctly hastens the process of soil erosion and land degradation. Faulty water managemnt practices lead to problems such as water logging, soil salinity/alkalinity, etc. Deforestation has often been described as the most primary reason of land degradation and the factors in deforestation are—conversion of forest land into agricultural land, the urban and industrial demand for forest products, indiscriminate quarrying for mineral resources, etc. Besides the above mentioned casuses, the environmental factors like slope, intensity of rainfall and the pedogenic characteristics of a particular area interact to increase the formation of wastelands.

An important feature of the SFP has been the raising of trees on the tank foreshore areas. The afforestation of the tank foreshores has been taken up with various objectives such as (a) to prevent the farmers adjacent to the tank-bed from encroaching; (b) to provide a source of income to the local government through sale of forest produce; (c) to provide a source of income to small farmers by giving a claim on forest produce raised on the tank foreshores; and (d) to reduce the pressure on the forest for firewood and small timber.

But our observation is that the scheme has failed not only to fulfil the above objectives but also has taken away several advantages hitherto enjoyed by the village community.

As the villagers do not possess any swimming pools and playgrounds, they were using the village tanks for playing when the tanks were empty and for swimming when the tanks were full of water. Such benefits have been taken away by planting the trees on the tank foreshores. Earlier, tanks were major component of the common property resources in many villages, which the villagers were using extensively for grazing of cattle during summer season. On several occasions, small and marginal farmers used to grow very profitable cash crops such as cucumber, watermelon and other vegetables. Because of plantation, they have lost a source of income.

Further, tanks were used as pathways for transporting manure to land and bringing the agricultural produce to the harvesting yards. The planting of trees has deprived the villagers of this infrastructural facility.

Afforestation on tank foreshores has badly affected fishing activity depriving the villagers of nutritous food in the form of fish. Besides, the raising of trees such as Acacia Nilotica on the tank foreshores has resulted in water pollution (on account of cumulative accumulation of leaves, flowers, thorns and pods on the tank-beds and their subsequent decomposition) making it difficult for the villagers to use iteither for drinking, bathing or washing purposes. One has to carefully examine these issues more scientifically.

Now we venture to make some suggestions to tackle the above mentioned problems relating to the Social Forestry Programme.

In order to make people participate actively in social forestry activities, efforts should be made to create proper awareness among them through door-to-door canvassing, training programmes, shows of documentaries, besides displaying eye-catching billboards at strategic places like local markets, shops, schools and so on. It is also important to make serious efforts to impress upon the people that common property resources belong to them and that it is their responsibility to maintain them for the collective good of the community.

VSFC should comprise such members as are enthusiastic and community-welfare oriented. Efforts shuld be made to convene meetings frequently to discuss issues concerning forestry Programme can also be given to selected VSFC members. Last but not least, a vast VSFC should be formed on an informal basis comprising villagers from different sectons of society, and not through election; for, elections may possibly politicize the functioning of VSFC.

Before selecting plots, the people should be consulted about the soil and environmental suitability of the sites. It will avoid any conflict which may arise between officials and local people at a later stage. Further, the plantation work should be carried out in phased manner as it would help the villagers graze their livestock in the implanted areas.

The fruit bearing and timber giving plants can be raised on common property resources. More incentives should be given to the private land owners who like to take up agro forestry on a large scale.

The success of social forestry activities depends on the co-operation of the people, but in the absence of social cohesiveness—due to excessive commercia-lization—the government and NGOs have an important role to play not only in the revival and management of common property resources but also to see that benefits of Social Forestry Programmes 'rickle down' to the common people as the social needs of the people for food, fooder, firewood and timber may not be met within the market framework.

While the government can take initiative in reviving and maintaining CPRs till such time as the process becomes community-based, NGOs can act as a catalyst in mobilizing people and creating awareness among them about CPRs.

It is also important that revival and maintenance of CPRs is viewed as a component of the overall development process through institutionalization of people's participation as it is well-known that there is a close relationship between forest, agriculture and 'sustainable development.'

India's indigenous communities

Degradation of forest land and denial of forest resources due to rigid local forest laws have seriously affected the local indigenous communities. Limited substitution possibilities or alternative sources of livelihood have added to their improverishment. Better management of forest resources by redefining their access to forest resources and clarifying their roles and responsibilities is the need of the hour. Their deprived status can be improved, if not fully restored, by involving them in decision-making regarding regeneration of forest wealth. The subject of environment and development has become a critical topic especially in the context of the modern race towards industrialization. As more and more of industrialization is taking place leading to sizeable increase in national income, the costs in terms of permanent loss of limited environmental resources is also being realized in most quarters. Experts across the world are searching for models which would yield 'industrialized development' which at the same time is 'environment-friendly'. The search is still on but the 'trade offs' in terms of destruction of environment has become continuous phenomena.

In the current development literature, there are at least four schools of thought on environment and development. The conventional or old school of thought is the 'exploitative school' which is preoccupied with maximum gain in terms of the present generation and takes a narrow view of 'development' as that of creating material assets. It propounds the view that natural resources like any other resources exist for the purpose of development and maximum effort should be made to maximize use of such resources for obtaining higher returns. In recent decades, this school has fallen from grace and three other schools have emerged which are propounding the theory of sustainable development, where the development needs to be sustained much beyond that of the present generation. Such schools emphasize on the fragility of environmental resources, the critical life-support system which environment provides and the permanent damages inflicted to environment as a result of development activity.

One such school is conservationist school which argues that any development activity needs to consider the 'trade off' in terms of environment and any such damage done to environment needs to be adequately compensated. Another school is the preservationist school which believes in having standards set and areas and zones of nature preserved from development activities. The environment is not meant for development and there has to be rules, regulations and standards for preserving nature. Still another school is the extreme school of sustainable development which believes in maximum ecological preservation where human beings are to live in harmony with nature. Hence, sustainable development has different dimensions contours depending on the school propunding it.

One of the most urgent and crucial tasks was the identification of the primitive tribal groups. The VI Plan emphasized the identification of these groups and then taking up unique programmes for each group relevant to its ecosystem. The Working Group on tribal development for the Sixth Plan admitted that in planning for tribal development, the basic handicap was the lack of basic statistical data relating to the Scheduled Tribes.

The Dhebar Commission also mentioned that many tribals in order to circumvent the provisions of the Act related to land, changed their names and adopted non-tribal names. Mundas changed to Mahadeo Pal because Mahadeo Pal is not a Scheduled Tribe. This change of name resulted in the parting of lands by the tribals.

In Darjeeling areas, the Bhutias took advantage of the Alienation Act and got lands from poorer sections of the tribals, i.e. Lepchas, at very nominal prices.

Article 350A of the Constitution lays down that adequate facilities for instruction in the mother tongue at the primary stage of education shall be endeavoured to be provided. To protect and promote tribal language and culture and to search out talent, tribal language must be promoted as medium of instruction at the primary level. The Central Institute of Indian Language, Mysore, NCERT, and State Tribal Research Institutes have been making their contributions in the preparation of textbooks and teaching aid and materials.

The Dhebar Commission also mentioned that the tribals and their leaders emphasized that the instruction in primary schools be imparted to them through their mother tongue. Teachers from amongst them, or tribal dialect-knowing teachers may be appointed. Boys and girls may be taught in their mother tongue up to the primary stage. In Sikkim, Lepcha language is being taught up to the primary stage.

A recent report of the Planning Commission also mentions that 'a policy decision had to be taken in regard to adoption of tribal language as medium of instruction at the primary stage', and suggested that the efforts of various agencies in this direction might be coordinated.

Another important aspect involving the improvement of life of the weaker tribe is education. While the overall situation in the field of tribal education improved as the literacy percentage went up from 11.3 in 1971 to 16.35 in 1981, and 23.03 in 1991, yet the general awareness of the tribal community to protect itself from economic and exploitative onslaught from outside has not improved much.

Formal and non-formal education, forest education, and vocational courses need to get due emphasis. Teacher should be recruited from amongst the tribals so as to engender confidence among the children and make the school functional, and minimize absenteeism among teachers. As the Christian missionaries have done for the spread of education in the north-eastern States, so should the voluntary organisations be encouraged to do among the tribal people.

A few years ago, the Ministry of Education at the Centre set up a committee consisting of social scientists, educationists and administrators et al to examine the relevance of educational curricula and contents to the tribal context and make appropriate recommendations. What happened to the Committee is not known. The committee should be revived to take up its work urgently.

The VII Plan emphasized that education in tribal areas be given highest priority; and scheduled Tribe boys in large number be placed on vocational courses; non-enrolment and drop-outs be reduced; low literacy areas and low literacy groups among Scheduled Tribes be identified; and residential schools be opened in such areas.

Surprisingly, an element of exploitation entered into the tribal areas through educational institutions permitted to be run by non-government outside agencies. Permission to such new schools to be opened may not be granted, no foreign funds be allowed to flow to educational institutions in these areas whether through foreign agencies or voluntary organizations within the country, unless a specific clearance had been obtained.

Hostel facilities at primary, middle and secondary levels both for boys and girls, sports facilities and encouragement to various aspects of tribal culture in the sphere of art, music, painting and dance be provided. Institutions like Lalit Kala Akademi, Sahitya Akademi, Sangeet Natak Akademi, besides, Tribal Research Institutes should undertake to encourage these. There is no end to the debate on environment and development. However, instances of the preservationist approach is to be found in the local indigenous communities living in and around forests. In real life, such communities have been seriously affected as a result of both degradation of forest land and their reduced accessibility to forest resources on account of strict forest laws. Degradation of surrounding environment and rigid forestlaws have adversely affected food accessibility, livelihood options and quality of life of local indigenous communities. Such degradation has often caused periodic phases of hunger and malnutrition in the absence of supportive means of livelihood for acquiring basic essentials of life.

Forest plantations of eucalyptus and other species no longer provide the rich biodiversity available earlier in natural forests. Common property resources, in which groups of local people have co-equal use rights, such as community pastures, community forests, wastelands, village ponds, rivers, etc have declined at a rapid pace. Such phenomenon has led to a diminished role of local natural resources which have traditionally constituted invaluable asset-base for meeting basic needs and livelihood requirements of indigenous communities.

Such relatively undisturbed lands include forests, grasslands, wetlands, water bodies, etc which constitue habitat for indigenous communities, plants and animal species and thus contribute to maintenance of human and biological diversity. Such lands perform important environmental functions and also constitute essential means of livelihood. As far as fragility of such ecosystems is concerned, the indigenous communities have traditionally presented little threat to sensitive ecological zones, because their production systems have been sustainable, scattered over a large area, and they have traditionally kept encroachers, poachers and others out of the area.

The benefits provided by forests, trees and common property resources are basic to such communities and amongst direct benefits, the following are included:

- food such as nuts, wild fruits, vegetables, leaves, flowers, roots, stems honey, wild animals insects, etc;
- habitat and shelter;
- raw materials like bamboo, canes, fibres, oils, bhabbar grass, waxes, resins, gums, dyes and wood for furniture and capital equipment for agriculture, artisanship, etc;
- wood for building, fencing, tool making, etc;
- firewood;
- medicines and drugs;
- fodder such as grass, branches, twigs and leaves, grazing sites;
- means of livelihood, both seasonal and annual;

- shade;
- ornaments, religious items and cultural symbols; and
- drought relief.

Apart from direct benefits, forests, trees and common property resources also provide indirect benefits, such as preventing erosion, conserving moisture, conserving water, recycling nutrient, preventing drought or reducing its impact, providing leaf manure, fixing nitrogen by leguminous trees, regulating climate and rainfall, providing greenery and beauty and reducing pollution.

In short, forests, trees and common property resources provide safety nets to the local indigenous communities. In the presence of spiraling prices, reduced wages in real terms, unemployment, sickness, reduced productivity from land, and recurring shortages, forests, trees and common property resources act as a kind of safety net for local communities, protecting them from the harshness of market forces. They come to the rescue by providing a safety net against food and livelihood insecurity, drought attacks, pest attacks, illness, pollution, high prices, high rents, etc. They play a dominant role in providing alternative sources of livelihood and in offering coping strategies to local communities.

The strategy for development of the Scheduled Tribes is based on the TSP (tribal sub-plan) approach which came into operation since 1974-75 (V Plan) in 16 States (now 18 States) and two Union territories. The main objective of the tribal sub-plan is to (i) raise the socio-economic condition of the tribal population and strengthen infrastructure in the tribal areas, and (ii) to protect and promote tribal interests through legal and administrative support.

The programmes are now being implemented

through (i) 194 Integrated Tribal Development Projects (ITDPs) comprising generally blocks/tehsils with 50 per cent or more Scheduled Tribe population; (ii) 277 pockets of tribal concentration (Modified Area Development Approach Projects) having a total population of 10,000 or more, and Scheduled Tribe population of 50 per cent or more; and (iii) 90 primitive tribe projects or micro-projects.

The tribal sub-plan has a two-fold thrust, viz (i) socio-economic development of the tribal areas, and (ii) socio-economic development of the tribal families.

It was expected that during the Seventh Plan period, there would be cent per cent coverage of Scheduled Tribe population under the tribal sub-plan. Benefits were also proposed to be extended to the scattered Scheduled Tribe population which was not covered by any specific project through family-oriented programmes. It may be mentioned that the tribal population coverage during the Sixth Plan period was only 75 per cent. During the Seventh Plan, the following were the objectives under tribal sub-plan approach: (i) taking up family beneficiary programme through raising productivity-level of the beneficiary families in the field of agriculture, horticulture, animal husbandry, small industry, etc. (ii) elimination of exploration of the tribals in the sphere of alienation of land, money-lending, debt bondage, forest, etc. (iii) human resource development through education and training programmes, (vi) infrastructure development, (v) development of vulnerable tribal areas and groups like, forest villagers, displaced tribes and tribal women; and (vi) upgradation of environment of tribal areas.

For the year 1985-86, the target of tribal families to be economically assisted was fixed at 8.35 lakh, and the achievement reported was 8.3 lakh families. For 1986-87, the target fixed was 8.35 lakh tribal families and for 1987-88, a tentative target of assisting 8.50 lakh tribal families had been kept.

Under tribal development, Special Central Assistance (SCA) is an additive to the State Plan efforts for Scheduled Tribes. The Eighth Plan had a target to cover 46.50 lakh families. Against this, 28.69 lakh families were covered during the first three years of the Plan (8.88 lakh in 1992-93; 10.42 lakh in 1993-94; and 9.39 lakh in 1994-95). This constituted 61.7 per cent of the target. To improve the literacy rate among tribal women, a new scheme was introduced since 1992-93, and is being implemented through non-governmental organizations in 48 districts with tribal concentration where female population is less than two per cent.

Financing tribal sub-plan: There are four sources for financing tribal sub-plan programmes: (i) Special Central Assistance (SCA) administered by Ministry of Welfare, (ii) State Plan funds, (iii) centrally-sponsored schemes, and (vi) institutional finance.

Since the V Plan period, with the launching of the tribal sub-plan approach, special programmes for extremely backward tribe groups had been taken up. These were micro-projects or projects for primitive tribal groups. These primitive tribal groups had three criteria for their identification: (i) almost stagnant population, or extremely low growth rate facing the danger of extinction, (ii) having are pre-agricultural level of technology, and (iii) extremely low level of literacy.

Another important factor was the ecosystem in which they lived. There were also other factors which entered into the situation of each of these tribal groups calling for a sensitive and in-depth study of each, precedent to enforcement of any action plan.

The Planning Commission also mentioned that particular care need to be taken of the small primitive tribal groups, some of which were on the verge of extinction.

The Dhebar Commission (1961) alluded to them as the 'lowest layer}, and listed 50 tribes in various States which were in an extremely underdeveloped state. During the V Plan period, the Ministry of Home Affairs identified 52 tribal communities as primitive, their estimated population being 10 lakhs. During the VI Plan period, an additional 20 tribal groups were identified raising their total number to 72 with an estimated population of 14 lakhs. Now the clusters of tribal concentration have gone up to 90.

There had been emphasis since the V Plan period on preparation of a project report for each of these groups relative to its situation. Nevertheless, there had been considerable neglect in this regard. Apart form the continued misery of conditions in which they lived, the risk of extinction of some of these tribes was also great.

Crop productivity and Indian agriculture

The second International Crop Science Congress, held in New Delhi from November 17 to 24, has displayed the International scientific community's will to solve the mankind's basic problem of hunger and to lay the foundation for a vibrant, yet ecologically sustainable, agriculture to meet future needs. The world's largest assembly of crop scientists, over 1500 from nearly 70 countries, emphasised that the modern biotechnology, coupled with traditional wisdom, can mould future to suit the interest of the human society. Though new challenges will keep cropping up, the science would perhaps not only be able to deal with them but might indeed convert them into opportunities for the good of humanity.

The optimism would, however, hold true only if it is matched by political will to raise farm productivity as also to distribute its gains equitably. New technology accompanied by appropriate marketing policies and international cooperation holds the key to ensuring foods security in the years to come.

Deliberations of the mega scientific event, organised jointly by the National Academy of Agricultural Sciences (NAAS) and the Indian Council of Agricultural research (ICAR), once again confirmed the widely held notion that while the scientists would be able to cope with humanity's needs they may become helpless to cope with its greed. The world renowned agricultural expert, Dr. M.S. Swaminathan, who chaired the Congress, did not mince words in passing on this message. He said: "Whether in agriculture or aquaculture, we must curb the greed revolution and promote an ever-green revolution capable of bringing about continuous advances in terrestrial and aquatic productivity without harm to the environmental capital stocks of land, water forests, biological diversity, oceans and climate upon which such advances depend."

The theme of the Congress, "Crop productivity and sustainability—shaping the future"—was highly appropriate and topical for several reasons. Despite phenomenal growth in food production, nearly one-fifth of the world population is still malnourished and hungry. The impact of the green revolution is waning and concerns of productivity decline in major crop production systems are being expressed globally, diminishing per capita availability of land and water resources, expanding biotic and abiotic stresses and natural resources, including land, forest and environment, are fast degrading. This calls for greater resolve to ensure synergism among productivity, profitability and sustainability of major cropping systems. Moreover, for safeguarding food and nutritional security at the household level, crop intensification and diversification are needed on an ecologically sustainable basis.

The Agricultural Development Projects (ADPs) with the assitance from the World Bank are being implemented in the states of Bihar, Rajasthan and Tamil Nadu to enhance the long term sustainability in agricultural development and to create necessary infrastructure in the rural areas. Besides, three on-going ADPs, a project for Assam has been recently negotiated and three ADP proposals in respect of Andhra Pradesh, Maharashtra and Haryana are in the pipeline and under active consideration.

UNDP/FAO supported 'Farm Centred Agricultural Resource Management (FARM) Programme' has been started in 1994. Five on-going watersheds of NWDPRA have been selected as demonstration sites for the programme.

The Government of Denmark initially launched one Integrated Watershed Development Project in the State of Karnataka in 1990-91 to cover an area of 41,032 hectare at an outlay of Rs. 11.25 crore for five and a half years. Keeping in view the successful implementation of this project DANIDA agreed for a phase-II project which has appraised in February 1995. The second project i.e. Comprehensive Watershed Development Project, Tirunelveli, Tamil Nadu, to cover an area of 18,000 hectare with an outlay of Rs. 6.25 crore for three and a half years is in operation since 1990-91. Second Phase of this project has been negotiated and the project has become operational from 1994.

Another DANIDA assisted Comprehensive Watershed Development Project is in operation from

1992-93 in Koraput district of Orissa to cover an area of 43,000 hectare at a cost of Rs. 13.25 crore. The fourth project i.e. Comprehensive Watershed Development Project in Tamil Nadu-Ramanathpuram has also become operational from 1994 to cover an area of 11,000 hectare at a cost of Rs. 13.03 crore. Appraisal of a Comprehensive Watershed Development Project in Madhya Pradesh was completed. Appraisal report of this project has been received.

European Economic Community (EEC) assisted Integrated Watershed Management Project namely, Doon Valley Integrated Watershed Management Project is in operation in Uttar Pradesh since April 1993 with an area of 1,72,155 hectare at a cost of Rs. 808.5 million for nine years. The major components are social forestry, livestock, horticulture, minor irrigation, agriculture, soil consevation, energy conservation, community participation, management and administration. South Bhagirathi (Phase II) Integrated Watershed Management Project, has started in 1989 for a period of seven years with an outlay of Rs. 141.75 million to cover an area of 48,915 hectare. Bhimtal Integrated Watershed Managment Project, UP was implemented from 1991 for a period of seven years to area of 21,582 hectare at a cost of Rs. 115 million. the major components are forestry, agriculture, soil conservation horticulture, minor irrigation, animal husbandary, pilot and administration activities.

Two KFW Germany assisted watershed development projets, one in Maharashtra at a cost of Rs. 550.75 million and another in Karnataka at a cost of 12 million DM are being implemented. During 1995-96, under Maharashtra Integrated Watershed Development Project monitoring of the progress under on-going micro-watershed project and appraisal of new micro-watershed projects will be carried out. Under Watershed

Organisation Trust (WOTR) Project training activity and identification of non-governmental organisations (NGOs) will be taken up. Under Karnataka Watershed Project field activities will be initiated.

The Project aims to develop five watershed in five districts of Karnataka (three agro-climatic zones of Karnataka state) in line of the ongoing Participatory Integrated Watershed Development Project (PIDOW). This project is to be taken up in the districts of Bidar, Gulbarga, Bijapur, Raichur and Chikmanglur of Karnataka covering a project area of 30,000 hectare (74,968 hectare of geographical area). The Project aims to develop the watershed with the active participation of the farmers by developing Sanghas as Self Help Groups with the active collaboration of NGOs in each of the district. The estimated cost of the Project is Rs. 20.73 crore for 1995 to 1998.

To have an overall idea about the extent of development in the field of agriculture in South Assam only a few indicators, namely creation and utilisation of irrigation potential, use of high yielding variety of seeds and consumption of fertilizer were taken into account for their analysis. It was found that upto 31st March, 1994 only 39,164 hectares of land were brought under irrigation in South Assam. There has been a very poor tendency of increase in the creation of irrigation potential for the last five years in this part of the state. Least irrigation potential has been created in the Hailakandi district. Karbi Anglong is the only fortunate district having both the minor and medium/majopr irrigational facilities. Surprisingly only 35.2% of the total irrigated area comes under the three plain districts as against 64.8% in the two hill districts.

As far as the utilisation of these potential is concerned there has been very poor response from the farmers in the area. A wide gap has been observed between the irrigation potential created and their utilisation. Excepting in Karbi Anglong, there has been more or less diminishing tendency in the utilisation of irrigation potential. This necessitates the importance of conducting an intensive study on the problem to identify the reasons and suggest the remedial measures. The study also reveals that the degree of utilisation of irrigation potential like its creation is found to be more in the hill districts than that of the plain districts,. Uniformly more weightage has been given to Kharif crops in the utilisation of irrigation potential in all the five districts. only a meagre 10% of the total irrigation potential has been utilised for the Rabi crops.

It is shocking to note that the area under high yielding variety (HYV)of paddy in South Assam has decreased from 1.4 lakh hectares in 1991—92 to 1.3 lakh hectares in 1993—94. This tendency is common to all the districts excepting hailakandi. More than 78% of the total area under HYV of paddy in this part of the state has been in the plain districts only. It is also observed that the farmers are using HYV seeds in three different seasons. Out of 1.3 lakh hectares of land brought under HYV, 73.4% and 24.7% of it have been devoted to winter and autumn paddy respectively and only a meagure of 1.9% to summer paddy and thus, keeping enough scope of utilising HYV seeds for producing summer paddy in these districts.

It is equally painful to note that consumption of fertiliser in agriculture is far from satisfactory. In 1993—94, more than 98% of the total fertiliser consumption was in the plain districts only. Moreover, there is an indication of insignificant increase in the consumption of fertiliser over the last five years. Besides, the use of fertiliser has been very poor in Rabi crops in comparison to Kharif crops.

In view of the above mentioned facts it is, thus felt necessary to state that there is a greater need on the part of the Government to take some bold steps to solve these chronic problems. There is an urgent need of increasing the literacy rate in South Assam and particularly in the Karbi Anglong district. Creation of more irrigational facilities is a must for the overall development of agriculture in south Assam in general and the plain districts in it in particular. There is a need to encourage the farmers to utilise the available irrigation potential to the maximum and paricularly steps be taken to see that rabi crops are not neglected in this regard. Since the area is very remote there is also a need for creating awareness among the farmers in the hill districts to use fertiliser and HYV seeds through some extension programmes.

High yielding variety programme

High Yielding Variety Programme was started in 1966-67 as a major plan of agriculture strategy for increasing production of foodgrains in the country. Cropwise details are shown in table 1. The programme is supported through a number of Centrally-sponsored schemes and thrust has been shifted from single crop to cropping system approach since 1994-95. Identifying potential areas, the country has been grouped in three major cereal based cropping systems viz., (i) Integrated Cereal Development Programme in Rice Based Cropping System Areas (ICDP-Rice); (ii) Integrated Cereal Development Programme in Wheat Based Cropping System Areas (ICDP-Wheat); and (iii) Integrated Cereal Development Programme in Coarse Cereal Based Cropping System Areas (ICDP-Coarse Cereal).

These thrust programmes are designed to increase the productivity and production of foodgrains through adoption of latest scientific production technology. Minikit demonstration programme aims at popularising

Table 1. Area under High Yielding Varieties Programme

(Lakh Hectare)

Crop	1966-67	1985-86	1986-87	1987-88	1988-89	1989-90	1990-91	1991-92	1992-93[1]	1993-94[1]	1994-95 *Target*
Paddy	8.9	234.7	240.3	222.5	254.1	261.6	273.9	279.5	274.8	288.5	310.0
Wheat	5.4	190.8	191.9	196.9	201.8	202.9	209.7	205.4	217.0	220.3	230.0
Jowar	1.9	60.8	55.00	60.6	61.1	68.7	70.6	67.8	69.2	67.6	90.0
Bajra	0.6	49.9	52.7	39.5	58.7	55.9	57.0	54.4	56.2	51.2	69.0
Maize	2.1	18.0	21.9	21.5	25.4	22.6	26.1	27.8	25.8	26.7	35.0
Ragi	—	—	—	—	—	—	12.5	12.2	11.0	11.8	11.0
Total	18.9	554.2	561.8	541.00	601.1	611.7	649.8	647.1	654.1	666.1	745.0

1. Anticipated achievemnet

newly released varietity and getting the newly released evolved varieties tested under field conditions. For this a large number of seed minikits containing 0.25 kg to 10 kg seed are distributed at a nominal cost to farmers. State level training programmes are being organised at agricultural universities and ICAR research institutes in collaboration with concerned state agriculture departments to disseminate the latest crop production technology to the district/block level extension officers.

About 990 lakh hecare area in the country is rainfed accounting for 70 per cent of the net sown area of 1,410.6 lakh hectare. Crops grown and cropping practices followed in these areas entirely depend on the rainfall which is often erratic and unpredictable. Bulk of the crops like rice, *jawar, bajara,* other millets, pulses, oilseeds and cotton are grown in this area under rainfed conditions. Farmers in these areas, particularly, small and marginal, are still practising subsistence farming and are in the vertex of vicious circle. Wide fluctuations in production occur in these areas year after year. Increasing and stabilising agricultural production in these areas is, therefore, of crucial importance.

Government has given high priority for the development of dryland areas and, therefore, several programmes and projects have been launched for utilisation of potential of these areas for: (i) realising the projected requirement of about 240 mt of annual food production by 2000 AD and to smoothen out fluctuation in annual production; (ii) reducing regional disparities between irrigated and vast rainfed areas; (iii) restoring ecological balance by greening rainfed areas through appropriate mixture of trees, shrubs and grasses; and (iv) generating employment for rural masses and reducing large-scale migration from rural areas to already congested cities and towns. Holistic approach for integrated farming system development on watershed basis in rainfed areas would be main pursuit of the development activities under the National Watershed Development Project for Rainfed Areas (NWDPRA) in the Eighth Plan.

The Governmental programmes have been oriented to promote the farm mechanisation and make the improved and modern agricultural machines available to the farmers throughout the country with a view to increasing the agricultural production and removing socio-economical disparity among the farmers. Farmers have been provided assistance for owning agricultural machinery including tractors. The infrastructure for human resource development on farm machinery has been expanded with a view to imparting training in the proper selection, operation, repair/maintenance and management of farm machinery. During these training programmes, emphasis has also been given on the energy conservation techniques in the use of agricultural machinery. Besides this, farm machines are tested with a view to evaluating their performance characteristics and upgrading their quality. However, despite a progressive increase in the use of agricultural machines, its sustainable benefits towards agricutural development have not been uniform in-as-much as only the improvement has mostly been in the northern states and in a few pockets/areas where irrigation facilities have been developed.

Although animal and human power continue to be the main power sources in agriculture, yet the power driven machines, namely tractors, power-tillers and combine harvestors continue to be in the frontline of farm machanisation. Fuel efficient tractors and better quality farm machines are now available in the country. Tractors are mostly sold in Haryana, Punjab, Uttar Pradesh and Madhya Pradesh and power tillers in

Assam, West Bengal, Karnataka, Tamil Nadu, Kerala and Maharashtra.

During the Eighth Plan, thrust has been given to popularise the improved animal/power driven implements and small tractors with the objectives of promotion of mechanisation and to reduce the drudgrey associated with the farm operations. Water management has also been given specific attention and the water saving devices *viz.,* sprinkler and drip irrigation system have been promoted through oilseeds, pulses and horticulture development programmes. Industrial designs, prototypes, jigs and fixtures have also been developed * . These schemes would give a fillip to the promotion of agricultural mechanisation in the country.

Farm Machinery Training and Testing Institutes set up a Budni (Madhya Pradesh), Hissar (Haryana), Garladinne (Andhra Pradesh) and Biswanath Chariali (Assam) impart on-the-job training in selection, operation, maintenance and management of farm machinery. These institutes also undertake testing of farm machinery to ascertain their performance characteristics and suggest improvement in their quality. So far over 43,000 personnel were trained and 1,160 test reports on farm machinery released. Two more institutes are likely to be set up in Rajasthan and Tamil Nadu. To suplement the efforts of these institutes five state agricultural universities have been identified for undertaking training on farm machinery and two agricultural universities for testing activities.

The Government of India and state government jointly established 17 state agro-industries corporations with the objective of streamlining input distribution and extending other agro-services to the farmers. These have significantly contributed to agricultral development, improvement of agro engineering services and promotion of agro-based industries during last two decades. Corporations in Gujarat, Haryana, Kerala, Maharashtra, Punjab and Madhya Pradesh earned estimated profits totalling Rs. 1,192.61 lakh during 1993-94. The National Productivity Performance Award for 1991-92 in the agro-industries sector was won by Punjab Agro-Industries Corporation Limited and Certificate of Merit for sustained productivity efforts was won by the Gujarat Agro-Industries Corporation Limited.

The Dangerous Machines (Regulation) Act, 1983 provides for the regulation of trade and commerce in production, supply, distribution and use of the products of any industry producing dangerous machines with a view to securing the welfare of labourers operating such machines, and for payment of compersation for the death or bodily injury suffered by any farmer/labourer while operating any such machines. The scope of the Act extends to the 'Dangerous Machines' intended to be used in agriculture and rural sectors. However, presently, only power thresher used in the agricultural production process has been brought under the purview of the Act.

The Government of India has adopted Integrated Pest Management (IPM) as a major thrust area and main plan of crop protection programme during Eighth plan. IPM approach is eco-friendly which aims at minimal use of hazardous chemical pesticides by employing all available alternate pest control methods and techniques such as cultural, mechanical and biological and bio-pesticides.

The Government of India has set up IPM Farmers Field Schools (FFS) for rice, cotton, sugarcane, vegetables, oilseeds and pulses etc., to impart training to farmers and extension workers. During, 1994-95, 844 farmers field schools were organised wherein 3,934 extension officers and 25,161 farmers have been trained. Besided 585 agricultural extension officers have been trained through season long training programme organised in rice, cotton and vegetables in various states.

The surveillance for pests and diseases on economically important crops was carried out by sample roving survey on an area of 5.55 lakh hectare and about 1,464 million parasites and predators were released for controlling identified pests on important crops during 1994. All the strategic areas in Thar desert were kept under continuous watch from April to October 1994 by conducting regular surveys and a few small concentration of locust hopper/adults of two grasshoppers species were detected and controlled over a total area of 327 hectare in Jaisalmer, Barmer and Jodhpur areas. As a result of timely operation swarm formation of locust has been effectively checked. To upgrade the skills of farmers and locust staff, two field training on locust control, one each at Bikaner and Palanpur were organised during November 1994.

The current legislation governing the plant quarantine rules entitled, 'The Plants, Fruits and Seeds (Regulation of Import into India) Order, 1989 (PFS Order 1989) came into force replacing the PFS Order 1984 in the wake of New Policy on Seed Development (NPSD) effective from 1 October 1988. The inspection procedure has been simplified in order to boost the export of floriculture and other agricultural commodities under NPSD.

The National Plant Protection Training Institute, Hyderabad continued to organise training programmes on various aspects of plant protection with special emphasis on IPM. It organised 30 training courses for master trainers in which 375 persons were trained. Beside special training course has been organised for technical personnel of fertilizer industry in Integrated Pest Management technology.

The Registration Committee constituted under the Section (5) of the Insecticides Act, 1968 received a total of 3,206 applications out of which 2193 registration certificates have been granted under various sections/ subsections of the Act. With a view to promote safer and non-chemical pesticides in IPM, biocides and plant origin pesticides like *Bacillus thuringiensis* and *Bacillus sphaericus* and need based pesticides have been provisionally registered and allowed commercialisation.

There is massive evidence to support the fact that appropriate legal protection acts as an incentive for productive research. The Uruguay Round, which was concluded in 1994, marked the beginning of a significant transformation in the global economic and trade environment. Annex 1c of the final Act deals with the agreement on Trade-Related Aspects of Intellectual Property Rights (TRIPs). Section 5 (Part II) of the annex pertains to "Patents" under article 27. With reference to agriculture, the text states, "Members shall provide for the protection of Plant Varieties by Patents or by an effective sui generis system or by any combination thereof'. Since the Indian Patents Act (1970) excluded to put into place a sui generis system by evolving a legislation on plant variety protection (PVP) by the year AD 2000.

The 1970 Act was also inadequate in terms of covering processes but not the product patents in food, medicine, drugs and substances provided by chemical processes. It now stands amended through a presidential ordinance (31/12/94), thus ushering in a new patents regime.

The TRIPs agreement has introduced profound changes which will influence competitiveness, generation and diffusion of technological innovations and ultimately the technological development prospects of developing countries (DCs) The impact of the changes can thus be far-reaching, though at this early stage it is difficult to assess the full implications of the agreement. An attempt is made here to consider, in a preliminary manner, some possible implications of the new regimes. IPRs constitute an important element of trade negotiations. The GATT accord on TRIPs has raised a whole lot of apprehensions and engaged the attention of intellectuals, politicians, farmers and media for quite sometime now. The legal dimensions of TRIPs make it difficult to understand, and vulnerable to a host of misgivings. Some discernible patterns can be identified in areas relating to limited duration, PBR and exclusions. By and large, the low income and lower-middle income countries do not accord PBR and have shorter protection periods. Pharmaceuticals and foodstuffs are the most commonly excluded products.

The debate on the implications of TRIPs began with reference to pharmaceuticals. Subsequently, myriad views have been expressed regarding the possible impact of TRIPs accord on Indian Agriculture.

Issues relating to germplasm and biotechnology are substantial and valid, but these are best pursued independently of the PBR debate. PBR is not a panacea, but can serve the farmers by increasing their access to improved seeds at reasonable prices by augmenting the efforts of public systems through private seed firms.

Research studies have pointed out a two—way relationship between education and other investments to improve agricultural productivity. Education—in the wide sense of the term primary education, literacy as well as extensional deucation and training—is a prerequisite qqqfor introducing modern methods of farming relying on fertilizers and new varieties of seeds.

Four basic stages of agricultural technology have

been identified by Maureen Woodhall in a book on Education and Development and they are: (a) traditional farming depending on father to son tradition; (b) use of a single modern input like fertilizer, seed; (c) Several complementary inputs simultaneously; and (d) full irrigation—based farming. Each stage calls for different levels of education to farmers commencing from literacy, maintenance skills, rudimentary knowledge of chemistry and biology and ability to calculate the effects of changes in crops, climate and so on.

It is through adequately qeqducated farmers who constitute local resources and by making available such local resources for improving agricultural productivity that the Ninth Plan target of 4.5 per cent rate of growth in agriculture can be achieved. In such an approach, requirements for improving agricultural productivity and rural development converge and it is this model of rural development through local resource mobilizaton which is the crying need of the hour. With the present level of educational backwardness, it may be difficult to achieve the agricultural growth target. But with adequate human resource development, it will be possible to achieve to goal.

Education appears to be a prerequisite to increase the yield from other types of agricultural investment, Formal education of farmers also improves the effectiveness of agricultural productivity. The extension services will become more effective if farmers have a basic level of education. This raises the question of whether the formal and non—formal education including agricultural extension are substitutes for each other.

Tamil Nadu experience: In this connnection, it is worth referring to Tamil Nadu's effort to raise productivty through investment in human resources. In 1994—95, a sum of Rs. 76 crore was allotted for human resource development to upgrade the knowledge and skill of the persons engaged in the development of agriculture, fisheries, agricultural engineering, forestry, etc. For agricultural productivity improvement through broad—based extension activities, Rs. 41.81 crore was set apart in the State budget.

There can be productivity and social change simultaneously in the rural sector. For gaining an insight into this aspect one can look at theories of social and institutional transformation as an integrated process of economic development as Schumpeter, Adam Smith, Veblen,Max Weber have advocated. Farmer education should be regarded as one link in an integrated system of generating and transferring knowledge. Other links are research and the production system like industry, services, etc. A good system of communication will serve as an intemediary.

For quite some time now Tamil Nadu has been following though not explicitly the above model. It has been called knowledge, attitude, performance and practice (KAPP) model resulting in considerable improvement in productivity in al crops (e.g. rice productivity improved from 1,306 Kg in the fifties to 3,116 Kg in the nineties).

The local needs can be carefully identified and resources can be mobilized both locally and from various sources. On the basis of the local needs a plan will have to be carefully drawn up for this purpose. There are income generating shcemes through self—employment and wage—employment and both of them should take note of the local resource endowment and the over all development strategy. At present, it is not done adequately because of the absence of local planning. Efforts should be made to get the best out of such schemes through the development of human resources and better linkage with all development schemes.

In agriculture, an Evergreen Revolution is called for, signifying the sustainable use of natural resources.As the eminent scientist Dr M.S. Swaminathan says the time has come to lay emphasis on knowledge-based inputs rather than on the physical inputs only (such as fertilizers and seeds) to derive the best from the land without depletng its inner strngth. A learning revolution is to be brought about. Fortunatley, icon–based computer technoloy shows that literacy need not be a barrier in bringing about a better awareness of theecofriendly methodsof cultivation. *It would beachallenge for the plannersto decentralize the knowledge based on agriculture to cover villages using computers and telecommunication links.* Modern ecofriendly practices such as biologicalpest control and post–harvest technologies) should find high priority on the S & T agenda.

It is heartening to note that the Ninth Plan approach has emphasized the importance of biocontrol agents and biogenic fertilizers.

The TRIPs agreement would require substantial changes in the patents regime of our country. Most developed countries, as they are members of the UPOV Conventions, accord protection to plant varieties. By contrast, only a handful of DCs have sui generis protection systems (e.g. Argentina, Chile, Kenya, the Republic of Korea, Uruguay and Zimbabwe). The PVP legislation proposed to be enacted is modelled on the basis of the International Union for the Protection of new Varieties of Plants (UPOV) guidelines. UPOV 1978 version allowed for the rights of plant breeders and farmers, whereas UPOV 1991 is more stringent in the sense that it disallows both. There is general consensus that we opt for UPOV 1978 and this option is available only till the UPOV 1991 is ratified by at least five member countries. But the...fourth International

Conference on Plant Genetic Resources, at Leipzig (Germany), has vindicated the state of the DCs. It succeeded in getting a global endorsement for farmers rights, paving the way for the member countries to enact PVP legislation in ways that best serve their respective national interests. The "World Intellectual Property Organization WIPO) model law for developing countries on inventions" can serve as a general outline for the proposed law on PVP.

Although, patent laws are inherently a national issue, it is time we join (albeit, selectively) various international conventions/treaties, so that cost of obtaining patents and international search reports can be reduced substantially. Also, keeping in view the distinct variations in cost of patenting across nations, there is a case for differential slabs of application fees for foreign applicants seeking patents in our country. Judicious provisions for compulsory licensing and non-voluntary license should be the feature of the proposed legislation to curb possible patent abuses. The proposed PVP has adequate safeguards to take care of farmers, researchers and environmental concerns. It is high time that the proposed legislation is enacted so that this unnecessary irritant in our trade relations, particularly with the DMEs is removed.

The TRIPs agreement aims at a certain minimum standard of IPR protection. Successful implementation of the TRIPs agreement has a number of prerequisites, the important ones being legal, administrative and institutional reforms, appropriate research investments, and first rate science and technology capability. Provided the IPR protection is adequate and effective (worldwide), the TRIPs accord can promote innovations, transfer of technology, foreign direct investment, use of genetic resources and environmental protection. The returns from the economic value of protection system far outweighs its costs. However, while legal protection may be a necessary condition for innovative activities and technology transfer, it is by no means a sufficient condition, given the importance of a host of other factors affecting research investment and the transfer and diffusion of technology in DCs and its ability to internalize benefits from the new rules of the game. The nation's capacity to move from technology importer to technology exporter will be the major determinant of its position in international hierarchy. Foresight demands towards quality and frontier areas.

Creation of a patent cell in the ICAR, is a step in the right direction. Having a clear-cut intellectual property policy and promoting patent literacy (similar to CSIR) among its scientists, must be the next logical step. A massive awareness programme needs to be undertaken to clear doubts regarding the process of patent application and registration, patent information services, inspection of files, determination of national need and the whole gamut of related issues.

To maximize opportunities, DCs must foster and reward entrepreneurship and evolve a regulatory environment conductive to technological innovation. An effective IP regime will provide the synergy between the private and public sector research institutions. This will then provide a basis for future growth and development, particularly in the case of India which has a large pool of scientific manpower.

Allied sectors

Apropos the sectors allied to agriculture, the strategies are as follows:

Attention is to be paid towards proper blending of technology, credit, scientific management, post—harvest infrastructure and marketing for higher growth. Steps will be taken to increase productivity of perennial fruits and spices, reduce losses at different stages of storage, grading, packing, etc (which amount to 20%—40%) by developing a sound post—harvest infrastructure.

Steps will be taken to increase productivity, accelerate replanting activities, expand this sector in non—traditional areas, improve packaging and enhance quality standards.

R & D activities for production of quality fish seeds and feed are to be intensified. to increase fish production and productivity, indiscriminate growth of brackish water farms is to be checked, overexploitation of coastal fisheries will be prevented, and the marketing infrastructure is to be developed.

This subsector will get greater attention in the Ninth Plan, for it has substantial employment generating avenues, particularly in the rainfed and drought—prone areas. Effective control of animal diseases, declaration of disease—free zones, scientific management of genetic stock resources, extension services, increasing production, productivity and profitability of livestock enterprises, etc will be areas of concern in this Plan. Priority will be given to improvement of breeding services, upgradation of health care services, fooder and feed activities, strengthening of training and research facilities, provision of adequate credit and marketing support, extension of processing facilities and measures for involving entrepreneurs, co-operative institutions and voluntary agencies.

Agro—exports are soght to be given fillip, in recognition of the valuable foreign exchange they bring, besides opening up new employment avenues. The strategies in this sphere are: development of markets and products, branch names and dissemination of information among exporters, improvement in quality and packaging, encouragement to export—oriented units and enhancing backward linkages with growers.

The role of co—operatives is to be enhanced—they are to be made more efficient, viable and competritive, through greater professionalism, diversification of activities, evolving effective recovery systems, technology upgradation, quality improvement, human resource development, etc.

Tea is India's traditional item of export besides being the most commonly consumed beverage. The domestic demand for tea has been rising faster than the expansion in its production, thus generating pressure on exportable surplus. Tea is a foreign exchange earner with negligible import content, besides being an important source of revenue to the Government. More than a million workers find employment in the tea industry. In 1995-96, 762.35 million Kgs. of tea was produced which was 34 per cent higher than preceding year's output of 737.4 million Kgs. Export of tea rose to 163.65 million Kgs. valued at Rs. 1191.19 crore in 1994-95. For 1996-97, a production target of 790 million Kgs. and an export target of 180 million Kgs. has been fixed.

Karnataka state dominated with 53 per cent of country's are under coffee. Arabica and Robusta are the two main varieties grown accounting for 49 per cent and 51 per cent of area respectively under coffee. In 1995-96, coffee output was 2.23 lakh tonnes, bulk of which (76 per cent) was exported. Apparently, coffee has emerged as an export oriented product. Coffee export during 1995-96 was 1.70 lakh tonnes valued at Rs. 1524 crore. In September, 1996, trade in coffee was totally deregulated. Growers are now free to sell their entire production in the domestic or export market without any quantitative restriction or compulsory routing through Coffee Board. Goverment also put decaffeinated/roasted coffee on OGL which allows free import in case of domestic scarcity. Country's demand for natural rubber is largely met by indigenous production, with only a small proportion (less than 5 per cent) met through imports. Production of natural rubber has increased from a modest 15,830 tonnes in 1995-51 to 3.3 lakh tonnes in 1990-91 and 5.07 lakh tonnes i 1995-96. Area under rubber has also gone up from 4.75 lakh hectares in 1990-91 to an estimated 5.22 lakh hectares in 1995-96. Kerala is the major rubber producing state and, together with Tamil Nadu, accounts for 86 per cent of the total area under rubber contributing over three fourth of total rubber production. Rest of the 14 per cent of area is located in Maharashtra, Tripura, Meghalaya, Mizoram, Manipur, Assam, Nagaland, Andaman and Nicobar Islands, Goa, Orissa etc. Most rubber plantations are small and the average size of holding is 0.5 hectare only. As against production and consumption during 1996-97 is 5.42 lakh tonnes and 5.56 lakh tonnes respectively. Import of natural rubber from time to time is necessary to bridge the gap between demand and supply. Yield per hectare has increased from 284 kg. in 1950-51 to 1130 kg. in 1991-92 and to 1422 kg. in 1995-96.

Immense agro-climatic diversity enables India to grow a large variety of horticulture crops which include fruits, vegetables, flowers, spices and plantation crops. From organised upland tea and coffee plantations to extensive and often dense coastal strips of coconut trees as also the subterranian tuber and root crops characterise the variegated nature ofthe potential in the country. The country holds the first position in global production of bananas, mangoes, coconut and cashew and is amongst the first ten in citrus, pineapple and apple production. India holds first position in global production of cauliflower and is amongst top ten in production of potato, tomato, onion and gree peas. Horticulture products-fruits, vegetables, flowers, cashew, spices etc. account for nearly 25 per cent of total agricultural exports. Floriculture—the production of flowers-has emerged as a promising area of high growth in recent years, particularly for its potential of export of cut flowers. In 1994-95 export of flowers was estimated at Rs. 30 crore. More than 200 export oriented units have been identified for accelerating export growth in this area.

Investment of Rs. 250 crore was allocated in the Eighth Plan period (1992-97) for encouraging the use of green houses, plastic mulches and drip irrigation, with Rs. 200 crore having been earmarked for drip irrigation alone. The earlier restriction of permitting assistance for 1 hectare per beneficiary for drip irrigation was removed during 1995-96 and assistance is now provided for the entire holding of the beneficiary for growing horticulture crops. During 1996-97, subsidy has been enhanced to 90 per cent of the total cost or Rs. 25000 per hectare, whichever is less for small and marginal farmers, SC/ST and women farmers, and 70 per cent of the total cost or Rs. 25000 per hectare whichever is less for other farmers. Low cost green houses are being encouraged not only for export oriented floriculture projects but also in cold arid regions like Ladakh for growing vegetables during the off season.

Due to lack of technology and poor ifrastructural support for handling, packing processing and preservation, substantial post harvest losses of fruits and vegetables still characterises the horticulture sector. Traditional mode of marketing fruits and vegetables currently results in an estimated loss of Rs. 3000 crore annually. National Horticulture Board (NHB) was provided Rs. 200 crore for implementing appropriate schemes (during Eighth Plan, 1992-97) for providing infrastructural support. The budgetary provision for 1996-97 is Rs. 41 crore.

In the hilly terrain of nagaland farmers have tilled land by constructing terraces. Traditionally terrace cultivation is termed as panikheti forests protect soil, they also regulate the rain water. the fertility of panikheti directly depends on the amount of land people can manage to keep under forests.

During the monsoons the fields are flooded. Rain water is used for irrigation, channelized through indigenous bamboo conduits. Young rice plants are transplanted to the panikhetis from the nurseries.

Through the months of August and September the paddy grows. During this time the paddy plants are bunched together and tied. This prevents them from being damaged by wind and reduces grain loss during harvest.

The Department of Agriculture in Nagaland has identified experts who in turn have guided farmers in other parts of the state in constructing panikhetis.

Erus provide an example of a traditional water management system still prevalent in Tamil Nadu. An ery is a reservoir of water formed by earthen embankments on three sides, with the fourth side open to the catchment to collect runoff water. Water distribution from each ery is managed by a water-users association, of which all cultivators of the area are members.

To combat the problem of water shortage, people of Rajasthan and of north-east India use traditional techniques based on low-cost technology and locally available resources. A wide range of such technologies are practices even today. The rain water harvesting tank of Ranisar in Jodhpur built by Maharani Jodha in AD 1500, and a wide range of kundis in the thar desert are some marvellous examples of traditional sustainable technologies.

The people of Ladakh, inhabitting the edge of the trans-Himalayan Tibetan plateau at an elevation of 4,000 m, trap the streams coming down from glaciers with the help of small channels. The water thus diverted from the streams, towards evening, is taken into small tanks locally known as zing. The stored glacier water is then used next day in the fields. Each village has a vast network of canals and zings.

The waters of the river Ganga sustan 37 per cent of the Indian population. Along its banks are pilgrim centres, industrial nuclei and large human settlements. As a consequence, the river is grossly polluted especially near the towns situated on its banks. The major sources of pollution are urban wasters, industrial effluents, surface runoff from waste dumps. To address these problems the Ganga Action Plan was formulated by the Government of India. A total of 261 schemes covering interception and diversion, sewage treatment plants, low-cost sanitation, river-front facilities etc. have been undertaken.

Van Panchayat is a democratically elected village level institution set up in Uttar Pradesh for the management of forests. It is responsible for the management of grazing, collection of fuelwood, fodder and timber, and protection of community forests. A Van Panchayat can be formed if one-third of the inhabitants of a village resolve to form one. At the village level, it is the sole arbitrator for the management of the Van Panchayat forests. It has linkages with the Forest Department of technical assistance and for the preparation of developmental plans.

To tackle the problems of providing rural areas with safe drinking water, the Government of India set up the National Drinking Water Mission in 1986. The objectives of the Mission are identification of new sources where there are none, better management of existing water resources using cost-effective and practical technologies, development of such technologies through existing scientific know-how, and ensuring sustained supply of safe drinking water to the community.

The Ministry of Agriculture is collaborating with the council of Scientific and Industrial Research, the Ministries of Science and Technology, Health and Family Welfare, Water Resources, and Environment and Forests, Defence R&D, Departments of Space and Atomic Energy and the state governments towards achieving this end. The Mission is focusing on conservation of water and recharging of aquifers, eradiction of guineaworm, control of fluorosis, desalination of water where it is brackish, and removal of excess iron. The Mission is also coordinating with various voluntary organizations to brig about people's participation of the government schemes.

In 1976 Anna Hazare, a retired army officer, returned to his village Ralegan siddhi in Maharashtra. A victim of recurring drought, the village was a picture of economic stagnation. Hazare resolved to change things. He felt water was the key and so studied the topography of the village and initiated steps to conserve rain water. Next, soil conservation was taken up under the state government's Comprehensive Wasteland Development Programme. Massive tree plantation was taken up, with a survival rate of 90 per cent as compared to 50-60 per cent in official programmes. Biogas plants and smokeless chulhas were installed. Today the village has proved its capability to withstand drought and has been selected by the Government as an Urja Gram (Energy Village) and is entitled to technical and financial assistance.

The Forest Conservation Act of 1980 is a unique piece of legislation to ensure the examination in depth of the diversion of forest land for non forest uses. It has been instrumental in slowing down such diversion while ensuring that developmental needs are married with environmental considerations.

The Forest Policy of 1988 is another landmark, wide ranging in its coverage and focusing on conservation efforts in Indian forestry coupled with sustainable utilization and people's participation.

In the thar desert rainfall levels fluctuate drastically from year to year. People therefore rely heavily on animal husbandry for survival. This in turn demands wise management of fodder resources.

The Thar desert has three excellent sources of fodder-a grass called sewan (Lesirius— Sindicus), a bush called jharberi (Zizyphus mummularia) and a tree called khejdi (Prosopis cineraria).

Sewan is an extremely nutritious grass which grows in clumps. It can grow fast even with little rainfall.

The *jharberi* and the *khejdi* provide excellent fodder during the dry months when no fodder is available. When the rains are inadequate and crops wither, with farmers are still assured fodder from these grasses and bushes.

Similarly, farmers do not cut the khejdi tree. Though rarely planted, the tree grows through natural regeneration. the density of the khejdi tree in the 300 mm to 500 mm rainfall zone of the Thar desert is about 40 to 100 trees per hectare, and this gives agricultural fields the appearance of an open woodland.

In the 1970s Sukhomajri near the Shivalik hills was like most Indian villages—impoverished. It came into prominence when 70 per cent of the Sukhna lake at Chandigarh was found filled up with silt from the denuded Shivalik hills. Soil conservationists initially attempted to deal with the denudation problem through technical soil conservation measures. However, it soon became evident that the problem lay in the poverty of the villagers and not in the hills. Initiating a dialogue with the villagers resulted in an earthen water—harvesting dam being built in the hills for irrigation of fields. A system of equitable distribution of water through the villagers' own organization, Hill resource Management Society, was instituted. With the resulting three-fold increase in crop production, the villagers could stop grazing their cattle in the hills. 'Social fencing' resulted in dramatic regeneration in the hills, providing increaed fodder and fibre grasses to the villagers through hand harvesting. Sukhomajri is now capable of withstanding the severest drought.

Unprotected land or land degraded due to extensive soil erosion, salinity, desertification etc. is termed as wastland. The Government on India set up the National Wastelands Development Board (NWDB) with the principal aim of reclaiming wastelands in the country through a massive programme of afforestation and other appropriate measures. While doing so it is expected to restore the disturbed ecological balance and provide employment opportunities in rural areas. The thrust in the Board's methodology is to secure people's active involvement in afforesting government as well as private wastelands.

To mitigate the energy crisis by developing technologies to harness non-conventional sources, the Department of Non-Conventional Energy Sources was set up in 1982. New and renewable sources of energy are being explored. In this effort entrepreneurial activity and industrial production are based entirely on indigenously developed technology. In the fields of biogas, improved chulhas and solar energy, India is leading in technology development and application. Over 1.2 million biogas plants have been installed all over the country. These plants are capable of producing 1,488 million cubic metres of gas, the fuel value of which is equivalent to 4.38 million tonnes of firewood. In addition, these plants produce high quality enriched manure.

The forest wealth in many partsof India has undergone a serious degeneration due to continuous jhum or shifting cultivation, heavy exploitation and maltreatment by burning and lumbering and ths has made a large area of land degradable. As shifting cultivation is generally practised as a food production system, we must think of a sustainable livelihood to the concerned people while suggesting alternatives to shifting cultivaton. As a mixed land—use system, agri—horti—silvipastoral system of land–use has often been suggested. The system comprises agricultural land use towards the foothills, horticulture in the mid portion of the hill slope and silvipastoral land use, towards the top of the hill. Contour bunding and bench terracing are the common conservation measures required for treatment of such lands. Subsidiary sources of income such as fish—production units should be promoted.

Other degraded lands having special disabilities also can be reclaimed by appropriate available technologies, so that these could be made suitable for bio—mass production. For example, aerial seeding techniques could be employed for regenerating/revegetating difficult and inaccessible areas like ravines, hills/mountains, desert areas, etc.

Realising the central importance of the utilisation of wastelands and an imminent ecological and socio—economic crisis due to continuing deforestation, the Government established the National Wastelands Development Board (NWDB) in May, 1985 with the principle aim of bringing the wastelands under productive use through a massive programme of afforestation and tree planting. The NWDB has taken up a number of schemes and activities since then and perceptions of wastelands as a problem and various strategies needed to develop them have evolved, as a result of better diagnosis. Various voluntary agencies/ NGOs have also lent their helping hands in the field of aforestation and wastelands development. The NWDB has also been working in close collaboration with Indian Council of Agricultural Research (ICAR), Council of Scientific and Industrial Research (CSIR) and specialised research institutions for the development of suitable technologies for development and utilisation of wastelands.

Land in the country available for productive use in limited and with the ever increasing population, the per capita cultivated land has dwindled further. As is mentioned earlier, a large area of the country (one third to one—half as per different estimates) is considered degraded in some form or the other. It is estimated that by the year 2000, the requirement of foodgrains would be around 240 million tonnes to feed about a bilion population. In addition, the large population of livestock will also add to the deterioration of lands. In such a situation, it has become imperative not only to halt any further deterioration of land but also to reclaim, properly develop and utilise the already degraded land for sunstainable development. This would also improve the environment and restore ecological balance.

India is recognized as a country uniquely rich in all aspects of biodiversity—ecosystem, species and genetic. For any one country in the world, it has perhaps the largest array of environmental situations by virtue of its tropical location, vaired physical features and climatic types. India has the widest variety of biomes, and attribute further enhanced by the meeting of three major biogeographic realms, namely Indo—Malayan (the richest in the world), the Eurasian and the Afro-tropical. India owes its unique biodiversity to this unmatched interspersion of biogeographic and environmental values. It is estimated that over 75,000 species of fauna and 45,000 of flora are found in India.

Over the centuries people in India have had a fascination and respect for this natural heritage. These sentiments were expressed in the Ishopanishad which dates back to over 2000 years.

(All in this manifested world, consisting of moving and non-moving, area covered by the Lord. Use its resources with restraint. Do not grab the property of others—distant and yet to come.)

It is seldom realized that the world's first recorded conservation measures, especially for wildlife, were enacted in India during the third century BC. Emperor Ashoka's benevolence extended to all living beings he set up hospitals and reserves for wild animals and birds, and extended his protection to many species. Some of his decres engraved in stone have survived to this day.

But it was not only the rulers of India who protected and preserved this heritage. Common people were as involved. An example is that of the Bishnoi faith, founded by a saint towards the end of the fifteenth century. Bishnois emphasize non-violence and respect for all living things. They actively protect wildlife and do not permit hunting or felling of trees in their areas. In 1730 the Maharaja of Jodhpur ordered his men to fetch timber from a Bishnoi area. The Bishnois hugged the trees to save them from the axemen, and over 360 of them, mostly women and children, were hacked to death before the kings men gave up. Even today the Bishnoi lands stand apart as oases in the vastness of the desert of Rajasthan.

The tradition continues. The Chipko movement, active since 1973 was one of the most successful examples of people-oriented environmental restoration. The brave method of hugging trees to save them was adopted. This movement, in which women played a key role, led to the cancellation of tree-felling programmes in parts of the Himalaya. Today the Chipko movement is not confined to tree protection or plantation but concerns itself with the safety and preservation of the environment, as also with achieving social justice and equality. Such restoration is now being carried out in many parts of India, where local people have fully participated in its planning and implementation. Like the Chipko movement, the Appiko movement was launched to save the tropical forests of the Western Ghats. This simple, non-violent action became popular and people have joined this movement spontaneously.

Sacred groves are another unique tradition which have been responsible for preserving pockets of biodiversity in various parts of the country. Usually a part of temple land, sacred groves are areas which are important as they represent the original flora of the locality, preserved in its natural form without outside disturbance. These patches of vegetation, and sometimes the fauna within, for example snakes and monkeys, are considered sacred and are worshipped by people. Such groves occur mainly in the Western Ghats and north-eastern India.

According to a recent clasification done by the Wildlife Institute of India, the country has 10 biogeographic zones :

— Trans-Himalayan

— Himalayan

— Indian Desert

— Semi-arid

— Western Ghats

— Deccan Peninsula

— Gangetic Plain

— North-east India

— Islands

— Coastal India

The Trans-Himalayan region with its sparse vegetation has the richest wild sheep and goat community in the world. The Snow Leopard (Panthera Uncia) is found here, as is the migratory Blacknecked Crane (Grus nigricollis). The Himalaya, the highest mountain range in the world, is located at the boundary of many boigeographical regions and is therefore one of the richest areas of India in terms of habitat and species diversity.

In the north west is the desert region with extensive grasslands. The Great Indian Bustard (Ardeotis nigriceps), a highly endangered bird, is found here. Adjoining the desert is the semi-arid region, a transitional zone between the desert and the denser forests of the Western Ghats. Beyond the ghats is the Deccan plateau, which is also a semi-arid region lying in the rain shadow of the Western Ghata.

In the north is the Gangetic plain extending up to the Himalayan foothills.

North-east India is one of the richest regions of biodiversity in the country. It has several species of orchids, bamboos, ferns and other plants. This region is also one of the early centres of domestication of cultivated plants such as banana, mango, citrus and jute.

India has two major groups of islands, Lakshadweep in the Arabian Sea, and Andaman and Nicobar Islands in the Bay of Bengal. The Andaman and Nicobar Island have some of the best preserved evergreen forests of India. Several species of plants and animals are endemic to these islands. India has a very long coastline extending over 5,500 kms. mangrove vegetation is characteristic of the estuarine tracts along the coast.

All the ecosystems are under pressure. Agriculture has largely replaced natural vegetation in most of the Gangetic plain and in extensive parts of the Deccan. Over the past century, tea and coffee plantations have come up in large tracts of what used to be the most forested regions of the Western Ghats, and in the north-east. the ever-shortening rotational cycles of shifting cultivation have also been a major cause of forest loss in the north-east.

Besides agriculture, industries and large-scale felling for wood, forests have been under pressure from river-valley projects, irrigation and mining. This pressure is particularly high as most mineral wealth and some of the best sites for water impoundment lie in areas which have high biodiversity. Replacement of natural forests by plantations of teak, eucalyptus, Prosopis juliflora etc., have done nothing to stem this loss of biodiversity. In the desert and semi-arid areas where vegetation is relatively sparse, requirements of fodder and of fuelwood have led to loss of vegetation. While there is pressure on all ecosystems, the more fragile ones such as mangroves, wetlands and coral reefs are particularly vulnerable to human activity.

The creation of protected areas in recent times started with the establishment of the Corbett National Park in 1936 in the foothills of the Himalaya. With the setting up of the Indian Board of Wildlife in 1952, growing consciousness about wildlife preservation and the enactment of the Wildlife Protection Act in 1972 the number of national parks and wildlife sanctuaries grew rapidly. As of 1992 there are 75 national parks and 419 sanctuaries covering about 138,000 sq kms or about 4 per cent of India's land area. These protected areas, from marine national parks to desert parks, cover a wide range of ecosystems—from wetland areas to mountain ecosystems.

It is also widely recognized today that preservation of habitats must extend beyond protectd areas. The biosphere reserve concept which is being developed in 14 potential sites extends the conservation initiatives beyond national parks and sanctuaries through developing an overall planning strategy for the area.

National parks and sanctuaries are managed by the forest departments of the state governments. However, the initiative for the creation of protected areas has not been confined to the Forest Department but has also been taken by individuals and NGOs. The declaration of Silent Valley in Kerala as a national park is an example of people's action leading to the declaration of an areas as protected. Similarly the World Wide Found for Nature (WWF) played an important catalytic role in the establishment of 'Project Tiger' an effort which not only aimed at saving the tiger but doing so through protecting entire ecosystems which form its habitat.

There is now widespread acceptance that our management strategies for protected areas should actively elicit the participation of local people for the sustainable utilization of natural resources and the effective conservation of biodiversity. Buffer—zone development programmes which balance the conservation requirement with the resource needs of the people are being initiated by forest departments as well as NGOs. In addition, public awareness programmes for people in the buffer zones, and interpretation programmes for visitors have also been initiated.

The Zoological Survey of India, the Botanical Survey of India and the Forest Survey of India have been studying and documenting the plant and animal diversity of the country. Of the estimated 45,000 plants species, about 15,000 species of flowering plants have been described. Estimates of other plant taxa include 5,000 species of algae, 1,600 lichens, 20,000 fungi, 2,700 bryophytes and 600 pteridophytes. there are about 75,000 species of animals including 50,000 insects, 4,000 molluscs, 2,000 fishes, 140 amphibians, 420 reptiles, 1,200 birds and 340 mammals, and other invertebrates.

A very large number of the species described are endemic to India. Among the larger animals 79 species of mammals, 44 of birds, 15 or reptiles, and three of amphibians are threatened. Nearly 1,500 plant species are considered endangered.

The main strategy for the conservation of species is the protection of viable habitats in representative ecosystems. In addition, specific measures have been taken to prevent poaching and trade in wildlife products. Special steps to check illegal trade in ivory, rhino horns, furs, skins, musk and peacock feathers have also been taken. India is also a signatory to the Convention on International Trade in Endangered Species of wild fauna and flora (CITES).

Certain species have been identified as needing a concerted and specfically directed protection effort. Projects such as Project Tiger, 'Save the Barasingha' campaign, and more recently a project on the Asiatic Elephant, have been initiated. A citrus sanctuary has been set up in Meghalaya. These programmes, though focused on single species, have a wider impact as they conserve habitats and a variety of other species.

Ex situ conservation is another thrust in conservation efforts. The Indian Botanical Garden in Howrah (West Bengal) is over 200 years old. Other important botanical gardens include those in Bangalore and Lucknow. Whereas zoological parks have been looked upon essentially as centres for education and recreation, they have also played an important role in the conservation of species such as the Manipur Thamin Deer (Cervus eldi eldi) and the Whitewinged Wood Duck (Cairina scutlata). Notable examples of successful captive breeding are those of the Gangetic Gharial (Gavialis gangeticus), turtles and the white tiger.

A great deal of research needs to be done on the conservation of genetic diversity in India. Sanctuaries and national parks have isolated populations of wild animals thereby decreasing chances of one group breeding with another. Experiments are under way in creating corridors between parks and integrating different parks into larger protected zones in order to broaden the genetic base.

India has a long tradition of breeding domestic animals for specific qualities. These include cattle, goats, pigs and sheep, as well as horses and pigeons for sport. With the focus on increasing milk yields through cross-breeding, some of the original cattle breeds are in danger of becoming extinct. efforts for the maintenance of pure breeds of native animals need to be considerably strengthened.

A good deal of attention has been paid to the genetic conservation of domesticated plants. Both in situ and ex situ conservation methods have been put into practice. However, as in the case of cattle, hybrid varieties of crops are rapidly replacing the land races.

Out of an estimated 50,000 varieties of rice in India, the country may be dependent on just 300 in the next decade.

Numerous locally adapted varieties which performed well under low or no input conditions are being replaced by a few high yielding strains dependent on large quantities of inputs. Such replacement, in large contiguous areas, presents the danger of the spread of serious diseases capable of wiping out entire crops.

Ex situ collection and preservation of genetic resources is done through the National Bureau of Plant Genetic Resources (NBPGR), New Delhi, for wild relatives of crop plants, the National Bureau of Animal Genetic Resources at Karnal in Haryana, for domesticated animals, and the National Bureau of Fish Genetic Resources, Lucknow. The NBPGE is the nodal agency for providing germplasm on request to scientific and research institutions both within and outside India. The Department of Biotechnology, established by the Government of India in 1986, aims to guide, supervise and develop biotechnology programes in the country and to establish infrastructural support for them.

The Government of India established the National Bureau of Plant Genetic Resources (NBPGR) to act as the nodal agency for the collection, introduction, evaluation, documentation, conservation and exchange of the genetic wealth of crop plants and their wild relatives, NBPGR has its head office in New Delhi and field centres all over the country. The bureau is also a repository for in vitro cultures of agricultural crops. The NBPGR works through regional stations and base centres, and has linkages with crop institutes and projects in India and 40 other countries.

The National Bureau of animal Genetic Resources and the national Institute of Animal Genetics at Karnal

(Haryana), are the main national agencies for conserving the genetic resources of indigenous livestock and poultry. They maintain a data bank on indigenous breeds of cattle and poultry. the institute has initiated measures to conserve local breeds which are facing extinction in the near future.

The National Research Centre on Equines is the premier institute for conserving the native heritage of horses and donkeys. The centre conducts basic research on equine health and undertakes outreach programmes for effective transfer of technology.

The Ministry of Environment & Forest has the mandate for the conservation of ecologically fragile regions and biological diversity in India. The Ministry implements the following schemes/programmes on this:

- Biosphere Reserves.
- Integrated Action Oriented Research Demonstration and Projects for Himalayan Regions.
- Association of Scheduled Tribes and Rural Poor in the Region of degraded Forest.
- Modern Forest Fire Control Methods.
- Development of National Parks and Sanctuaries.
- Project Tiger.
- Beneficiaries Oriented Scheme for Tribal Villages of Project Areas, National Parks and Wildlife Sanctuaries.
- Eco-Development around National Parks including Tiger reserves.
- Project Elephant.
- National Afforestation & Eco-Development Board NAEB.

There are many schemes in NAEB with the mandate of conservation of ecologically fragile areas. They are :

- Integrated Afforestation and Eco-Development Project.
- Fuelwood and Fooder Project.
- Aerial Seedling.
- Non-Timber Forest Produce, including medicinal plants.

All the above schemes are supposed to address basic issues of conservation of degraded forest areas.

The State Governments have also many programmes which help conservation of ecologically fragile region. Some of the important schemes of State Plan are:

(a) Afforestation and regeneration of degraded forests.

(b) Greening of rural and urban areas.

(c) Social forestry.

(d) Development and conservation of minor forest produce

(e) Development of National Parks and Sanctuaries.

(f) Regeneration of Sal and Oak forest.

(g) Rehabilitation of common lands in Aravalli hills.

(h) Western Ghat forestry project.

Agroforestry and private forestry (industrial and non–industrial) constitute the second option in this regard. There exists a vast potential for using agriculturtal lands as sources of timber and for meeting the wood requirements of the society. Agricultural lands (net area sown) make up as much as 43.5% of the total geopraphical area of the country, while forests (including degraded) occupy only about 20%. Moreover, many of our traditional land use practices are examples of integrated, intensive farming systems/practices that blend trees with various other life forms. Trees including perennial horticultural crops have traditionally formed an integral component of our agricultural landscape. Growing trees of various kinds is part of the tradition in India. Most people also perceive the economic, social and cultural benefits of trees as a source of fruits, fuelwood, fooder and timber. The Kerala homegardens form a spectacular example in this regard. Homegardens create a forest-like multi–storey canopy structure and is also a source of tremndous agrobiodiversity.

Plantation agriculture, is another important land use activity in many parts of the country. Examples include palms, rubber and many fruit trees. Other salient traditonal agroforestry systems include, growing multipurpose trees (trees that yield fruits, vegetables, fooder, fuelwood, timber etc.) either on the farm boundaries or as scattered trees on the farm fields, growing commercial crops (tea, coffee, pepper etc.) under planted shade trees and/or trained on to them, growing commercial crops (nutmeg, clove, cacao etc.) under the shade of planted commerical tree crops (coconut, arecanut etc.) growing commerical crops (cardamom) under the shade of trees in natural forests, commercial woodlots, live fences, silvopastoralism, grazing in natural forests and shelterbelts.

A wide spectrum of trees and shrubs is often encountered in all these land use systems. The floristic elements, however, vary from region to region and depending on size of holdings, socio—economic factors and the socio-cultural background of farmers. Wood productivity in agroforestry is also correspondingly diverse. Predise macro-level data are, however, not available concerning availability and/or standing stock of wood from agricultural lands. Available microlevel studies, although limited, indicate that standing stock of commercial timber from the Kerala homesteads, is between 6.6 and 50.8 m^3 ha^{-1} (Kumar et al 1994). In another study Krishnankutty (1990)assessed the wood harvested from rubber plantatons of Kerala in 1987 at 0.999 mcum. To enhance timber productivity from the traditional land use systems, therefore, concerted efforts are necessary with respect to selection of better genotypes/provenances/clones of multipurpose trees, making available quality planting stock and evolving appropriate technological packages on tree management.

Private industrial forestry, nevertheless, is a recent phenomenon. It involves growing high value timber species such as teak and other fast growing tree species (e.g. teak, eucalyptus, popular, mangium and many soft wood species) under short rotation intensive cultural systems (SRIC) on private lands. Nonetheless, such practices are in vogue in many developed and less developed nation-states including China New Zealand etc. In the Indian context also, there are many examples where the farmers' initiative has been effectively harnessed by the wood based industries for raw material production. Examples include tree planting programmes sponsored by industrial houses such as South India Viscose Ltd., ITC Bhadrachalam Paper Boards Ltd. and WIMCO. Such industrial establishments in general supply planting stock and technology packages to the farmers besides, reaching 'buy back' agreements with them on purchase of produce. Private forestry assumes significance in view of the shrinking forest resource base and its ability to ese pressure on shrinking forest resource base. Perhaps with little over 2% of the total geographical area of the world and about 15% of its human and livestock population, India already expereinces a critical imbalance in its natural resource base. The National FOrest Policy 1988 also highlights the importance of the wood based industries producing their own raw materials.

There are, however, institutional, technological and socio—economic factors acting either separately or in unison, which constrain or obstruct the spread and diffusion on tree farming in India. Restrictions on tree felling, non–availability of quality planting stock, lack of appropriate technology packages especially for polycultural systems and the absence of public policy support hamper adoption of tree farming by private entrepreneurs. For fear of interspecific competition, many small farmers are also reluctant to grow timber and fuel wood species in association with woody perennial plantation agricultural species. Furthermore, as agroforestry extension and communication networks are choked, credit and other facilities are limited.

Agroforestry has tremendous potential to convert India into the 'wood basket' of world. Implicit in agroforestry and tree farming are two fundamental themes: ecological security and generation of income and employment. Quite apart the indirect ecological benefits, tree farming is an economically viable land use option. Demand for timber land other forest products is expanding at a very rapid rate. Incokrporation of tree growing as part of the farm system technology can make significant contribution to the supply of wood based products. However, a paradigm shift in our planning and development thinking is imperative to make it operational. Evolving appropriate technology packages for tree farming (SRIC systems) and provision of inputs are central to this.

Lack of an apropriate public policy support and absence of technological packages too are critical constraints in this regard. Agroforestry extension is particularly weak. At present, enither the Forest Department nor the Agriculture Department considers integrated land use systems such as agroforestry important. Presumably they act as water-tight compartments, although agroforestry is a mixture of agriculture and forestry. Suitable corrective mechanisms are indispensable in this regard. This includes amendment to the restrictive provisions of laws, providing public policy and credit support to the tree farming enterprises, evolving improved post harvest processing techniques, removal of hidden subsidies to the wood based industries, strengthening agroforestry extension and encouraging farmers' initiative in rural afforestation and raw material production for wood based industries.

Analysing the performance of the Social Forestry scheme in Karnataka vis-a-vis the objectives set, the authors suggest some effective steps tomake the programme a success. Inclusionof politician in thevillage Social Forestry Committes, belated formation of the committees, the indifferent attitude of the members and the lack of awareness among the people have affected the effective management of the scheme,. Serious effort are to be made to impress upon the people that the common property resources belong to them and that it is their responsibility to maintain them for the collective good. Forests are significant segment in a country's economy. In fact, they acan be considered as the very 'lifeline' of the economy, for apart from meeting the basic social needs of the people such as fodder, firewood and small timber, they also play an important role in earning foreign exchange. Indirectly also, their role is significant in retaining soil moisture, preventing soil erosion, building soil fertility and keeping the environment clean.

Of late, the tremendous increase in human and

animal population, concomitant rise in the number of landless labourers and small landholders, and growing instances of enroachment of forests and other common property resources (CPRs) have led to unviable agriculture. This disturbing situation is reflected in the fact that while the cultivated land in India is more than half of its geographical area, in other developing countries like Pakistan, Sri Lanka, and the Philippines, the ratio is much lower. Besides, the cost per unit of output has increased substantially in recent years indicating strains on sustainability of agriculture (Nadkarni, 1988).

A recent estimate by the satellite shows that only about 19 per cent of the land is covered by forests; it means that per capita availability of forest area is now barely 0.1 hectare as against the international average of 1.1 ha. The situation in Karnataka is no different either. The area under forest was about 18.82 per cent of the total geographical area in 1973; this proportion rose to 20 per cent during 1993-94 (according to the Forest Department data). However, the recent satellite imagery data (estimates) show that the actual forest area in the State accounts for just about 14 per cent of the total geographical area which means the per below the availablity of forest area is 0.08 ha much below the international (1.1 ha) and the national (0.1 ha) levels. Ironically, due to excessive biotic interference, even the surviving forests are getting increasingly denuded, thereby accentuating the fears about the greenhouse effect, floods, frequent droughts and loss of top soils.

New Scheme to Revive Forests: Realizing the importance of forests, steps were taken in recent years for controlling the denudation and reviving forests. One such measures was the introduction of the Social Forestry Programme (SFP) in different States.

In Karnataka, this scheme was launched in 1983-84 with the financial assistance from the World Bank and Overseas Development Administration of Britain. A total outlay of Rs 55.23 crore was earmarked for the purpose. Of which, 47.7 per cent were provided by the World Bank, 46.6 per cent by Overseas Development Administration and the remaining 11.7 per cent were met by both the Central and State governments. This scheme came to an end in 1991-92. However, the State government continued the programme as a part of Zilla Parishads (now known as Zilla Panchayats).

The basic idea of the scheme was to convert the wasteland around the villages into economically productive lands or plantations, with the specific objective of providing basic needs like firewood, small timber, food and fodder to the rural people, bamboos for cottage industries and seedlings free of cost to farmers for raising plantations on private holdings.

The scheme has been in operation for the last 11 years. This paper tries to analyse the performance of the SFP in relation to the objectives set and to suggest some measures for effective implementation of the programme. The analysis is based on secondary data gathered from the Forest Department as well as from the findings of a research study conducted at the Institute for Social and Economic Change, Bangalore, during 1989-90 and general observations of the authors.

Agroforestry connotes land use systems where woody perennials (trees and shrubs) are deliberately grown with field crops and/or livestock, either simultaneously or sequentially, on the same land management unit. It implies a combination of agriculture and forestry aiming at diversified and sustainable production. Agroforestry practices frequently include tree/pasture systems, tree/speciality crop systems, alley cropping, windbreaks, living fences, etc. riparian buffers, stream band bioengineering, wildlife habitat and some other vegetation management systems also have been lately included under it. Such diverse land use systems encompassed by the generic concept of 'agroforestry', broadly falls under agrisilviculture, silvopasture, agrisilvipasture and other (miscellaneous) systems.

The basic philosophy of all agroforestry, however, is two-fold: (1) to optimise the combined production of woody perennials and agricultural crops and (2) to conserve and improve the site. Agroforestry, thus aims at ecological security, increased productivity and above all, sustainability. It is a prominent example of the traditional ecotechnological aproaches adapted by tropical farmers ('Ecotechnology' denotes technology rooted in the principles of ecology, economics and equity).

Multiplicity of goods and services is a unique feature of agroforestry. Agroforestry systems in general, are capable of producing timber, fuel, fooder and green leaf manure besides, performing various ecological functions such as reducing wind speed, checking soil erosion and causing microclimatic modifications. Production of wood, however, is a dominant function of agroforestry. This is further exemplified by the fact that homesteads, a prominent agroforestry system in Kerala, contribute as much as 74.4 to 83.6% of its effective wood demand (14.645 mcum in 1987-88) and about 67.2–75% of its firewood requirement (Krishanankutty, 1990).

Estimates on timber requirements vary widely in the Indian context. Different agencies voice digressing figures. Statistics on wood requirements and availability, therefore, presents a hazy picture. Precise studies have not been conducted to assess the timber requirement in our country. Furthermore, demand for timber in the unorganised sector has been grossly ignored. The 1988

National Forest Policy also laments about the poor data environment in this regard. It states succinctly, "inadequacy of data regarding forest resources is a matter of great concern...."

Regarding India's industrial timber requirement at the turn of the century, the oft cited National Commission on Agriculture Report (NCA, 1976) indicates a ranges of 47.1 to 64.4 million cubic metres (mcum), depending on production, growth and economic development. Wood requirement of any society, is presumably a function of the size of populaltion, level of development, availability, price ad the like. The higher estimate of NCA pre–supposes a high growth rate and consumption. Of the 64.4 mcum of wood required by India in the year 2000 AD, approximately 30 million for pulp and paper and 13 million for round wood (NCA, 1976).

Inventories made by Forest Survey (FSI, 1987) on demand for woood (other than firewood), however, puts India's total industrial wood requirement at 27.58 mcum and supply at 12 mcum. The Interministerial Group on Wood Substitution, estimate it as 24.88 million m (Singh, 1992). Demand projections of industrial round wood by Rai et al (1983) using a compound growth rate equation and transcendental production function had given figures such as 30 mcum and 11 mcum respectively for the year 1995. In another study, Kalla (1988), estimated that demand for industrial roundwood in Indian in 1990 would be 24.07 mcum.

To generate knowledge of the extent and distribution of different soils for planning rational land use, National Bureau of Soil Survey and Land Use Planning (NBSS and LUP) and state soil survey units have taken up Soil Map of India Project. The soil resources and land-use maps of West Bengal, Haryana,

Pondicherry, Punjab, Bihar, Orissa, Tamil Nadu and Gujarat have been prepared in 1:250,000 scale and released for users and planners. Training courses are being conducted by the Bureau to train state and agricultural university officials in the area of soil survey, soil correlation and land-use planning.

Intensive and high-yielding cropping systems suitable for irrigated areas and involving major crops have been indentified for different agroecological zones. These systems are capable of producing over 10 tonnes of grain per hectare. Cropping systems for rainfed and problem areas such as Wastel land and diara land etc., have also been evolved and watershed programmes are being advocated for sustained productivity. A number of seedling machines have been fabricated for uniform and timely saving. For effective utilisation of soil and other natural resources suitable agroforestry systems have been developed for marginal and non-forest areas.

Technologies have been generated to control soil erosion from different soils and agro-ecological regions by using biological and mechanical measures. Attempts have also been made to stabilize the areas prone to landslides and restore and revegetate the degraded areas. Alternate permanent agricultural systems have been developed to wean away the farmers from shifting cultivation (jhumming) in the north-east region. Technologies are availabe for arresting the sand movement in the desert areas by planting shelter belts and stabilising the shifting sand dunes with the help of vegetation. Improving productivity of the sandy soil through arid horticulture and introduction of multi-purpose tree species and grasses have been highly remunerative to farmers. The Central Soil and Water Conservation Research and Training Institute (CS and WCR and TI), Dehradun runs a five and a half month training course on soil conservation and watershed planning for state officials.

The use of micro-nutrients has helped to increase the production in specific nutrient-deficient situations and it maintains the soil health. Water management programmes aim at developing technologies for efficient use of available water with minimum degradation of soil. The methods and frequency of water application have been worked out for major cropping systems to increase the water-use efficiency and improve the productivity on the one hand and saving large quantities of water on the other. For judicious use of water, adoption of sprinkler/ drip irrigation is being advocated.

The contribution of research in the field of agricultural engineering since Indpendence can be gauged from the fact that India is presently self-sufficient in production of improved farm machinery used by the farmers. All this has been possible because of the sustained research and extension work carried out by the ICAR's Central Institute of Agricultural Engineering, Bhopal, agricultural universities under ICAR research system and commercial production of machines undertaken by Indian farm industries.

Efforts have been continued to develop improved agricultural implements for ensuring timeliness of operation with available power sources. An improved animal drawn blade harrow, high ground clearance self-propelled sprayer, improved multicrop thresher, groundnut pod stripper and yarn testing device have been developed. Studies have indicated possibility of adoption of self-propelled vertical conveyer reaper in the State of Kerala.

A small capacity boiler for treating sunflower seed with steam at rural level, scaled-up of cassava peeling knife, grain flour separator, technology for production of protein hydrolysate from soyabean meal using Bacilus subtillis cells, preparation of citric acid from soywheg have been developed. Blends of solution of lac shellac and poly (vinyl acetol)/vinylacetale) has been found to possess higher tracking index valves and resistance towards humadity. A pigmented (red-coloured) lack shellac-based insulating varnish has been developed with superior quality than imported varnish used in railway traction motors. A substituted cournerin derivative compound usable in perfumery and artificial flavouring has been developed from jailoric acid (major constituent acid from lac resin) which possess antibacterial and antifungal properties. Laminated and non-laminated corrugated boxes for packaging of fruits have been prepared using kraft paper made out of cotton plant stalk. Technology for production of particle board from cotton, plant stalk has been transferred for commercial exploitation. A noval fancy yarn has been developed out of jute yarn and viscous multifilament yarn and has potential for use as weft in handloom industry for weaving of decorative fabircs. Adhesive bonded jute and jute-polypropylene blended non-woven prepared with phosphate-based fire retardent chemicals have shown significant fire retardency. Several end products viz., geo-textiles, filter-media, floor covering reinforced plastics were developed by cross-laid, needle-punched non-wovens prepared out of jute and its blends.

In the energy sector, a rice husk gasifier, improved animal yoke, assessment of draftability of donkey for field operations have been developed/undertaken.

Application of sub-surface drainage technology in Andhra Pradesh have resulted in maximum leaching of 648 kg of salt per hectare-centimeter of water drained from crop root zone for rice cultivation. This improved the paddy yield between 16-36 per cent and betal vine crop by 28 per ent in farmer's field.

The Indian Council of Agricultural Research discharges the frontline extension education responsibilities through a network of 261 Krishi Vigyan Kendras (Farm Science Centres) in the country. The KVK functions on the principles of collaborative participation of scientists, subject matte specialists, extension workers and farmers. The KVKs are implemented through state agricultural universities, ICAR institutes, registered reputed NGOs having experience in agriculture and rural development and state governments. The mandate of the Krishi Vigyan Kendras are; (i) collaborate with the subject-matter specialists of the state agricultural universities/scientists of the Regional Research Station, NAEP and the State Extension Personnel in 'On farm testing', refining and documenting technologies for developing region-specific sustainable land use system; (ii) organise training to update the Extension Personnel within the area of operation with emerging advances in agricultural research on regular basis; (iii) organise long-term vocational training course in agriculture and allied vocations for the rural youths with emphasis on 'learning by doing' for generating self-employment through institutional financing; and (iv) organise front-line demonstrations in various crops to generate production data and feedback information. Based on the mandates, four major functions viz., on farm research, inservice training, vocational training for farmers, farm-women and rural youth ad frontline demonstrations have been identified for the KVKs. Under 'on farm research' adaptive trials are conducted on farmers' fields on technologies ranging from new varieties to new agronomic practices and plant protection measures. These trails conducted by the farmers with the support from scientists/subject matter specialists. These trials are conducted to generate scientific data on the performance of new technologies and provide feed-back to the research system. In-service training of grass-root level extension workers is conducted to up-date the knowledge of these functionaries. These trainings are arranged in collaboration with the State Department of Agriculture, Horticulture, Fisheries etc. Vocational training for farmers, farm-women, rural youth and school drop-outs are conducted so that the training results in self-employment income generating enterprises. Frontline demonstratins are organised to aim at demonstrating the production potentialities of newly released and pre-released production technologies of cereals, pulses and oilseeds on farmers' fields.

The KVK network gest technical support from regional research stations of the state agricultural universities and ICAR research institutes located in the country. The eight trainers' training centres established in eight specialised areas of agriculture give a back-up support to these KVKs. The monitoring and evaluation of KVK activities are done at three levels viz., KVK level, zonal level and central level. Strong monitoring and evaluation mechanism have been developed for this purpose including performance evaluation by Quin-quinniel Review Teams (QRT). Periodic workshops and training programmes are organised at state level and at zonal level.The eight zonal coordiantors located in eight zones monitor the activities of KVKs. Thus the KVK is one of the potential first-line transfer of technology institution at the district level which has to act as a light house of knowledge in the district.

Keeping in view the importance of women in agriculture, a National Research Centre for women in agriculture has been established at Bhubaneswar in Orissa. This Centre will be responsible to generate women's specific technical information and refine the same in order to make them appropriate for the women in various parts of the country.

One of the objectives ICAR is to act as a clearing house of research and general information relating to agriculture, animal husbandry, home science and allied sicences and fisheries matters through its publications and information system. The publications and information division publishes nine journals and a range of publications in Engligh and Hindi for the benefit of scientists, policy makers, scholars and the public. The publications in English comprise four research journals. In additions to these journals, the Division brings out scientific bulletins, reports, directories and other miscellaneous publications. The science popularisation unit releases features to the print and broadcast media.

The ICAR also operates an Agricultural Research Information Centre (ARIC) which is an integral part and a constituent unit of the publications and information division. ARIC brings out directories of agricultural personnel, research workers in India, research schemes, etc. Besides these, exhibitions and film shows are organised for disseminating agricultural technologies to the farmers.

Cottage and agro industries

The meaning attached to the term "Cottage Industries" has undergone changes with the progress in technology and its definition no longer restricts it to industries using manual labour and simple tools only. The use of power and machines has been admitted in the definition of the term. The basic implications which differentiate the cottage industries from large scale and heavy industries are: (1) the small scale of production, and (2) usually the worker works on his own, although the employment of wage-paid labour is not ruled out. Attempts to define the term very precisely have not been quite successful. With technological progress the concept behind cottage industries has been undergoing modifications. However, the sense in which the term is employed is commonly well understood. (Some of the definitions are given in an Appendix to this chapter).

Cottage industries may be divided into four broad classes, viz., handicrafts, home industries, small-scale industries and village industries. The dexterity of human hands and mainly their use in making the final product are the characteristics of handicrafts. Handicrafts, as the name indicates, always represent the best type of art for the art produced by hand can hardly be excelled.

In home industries, hand or power driven machinery may be used. But the chief characteristics of home industries is that raw materials are procurable locally and labour consists normally of family members. If there are any outsiders they are employed only as apprentices. The industry thus gets the most careful attention of the master.

Small industries are distinguishable by the place of work, the amount of capital invested and equipment used. They are carried on either in the house of the artisan or in a small workshop run by the entrepreneur. The capital invested may be theoretically large as is the case with ivory carving. But generally the capital is limited and this places restrictions on the employment of labour, the use of machinery, etc.

Hired labour may be employed both in the small-scale and village industries; but the village industries have necessarily to be located in the villages, while the small industries may even be located in the urban or semi-urban areas. The number or employees in the small industries should also not be large and may not exceed nine persons.

The importance of village and cottage industries is emphasised by the fact that India, in spite of considerable progress towards urbanisation in the recent past, still lives in villages and her national economy is predominantly agricultural. Her agriculture, even when the required degree of intensity of cultivation is achieved through the development of irrigation, use of fertilizers and above all with the assistance of an all-pervading extension service, by its very seasonal nature and overcrowding in it, would not be able to free itself from the disguised unemployment and underemployment.

The industrial development, with its concentration in towns, is no solution to the problem of unemployment in villages. The small enterprises employed about 20 million workers as against about five million workers in the factory establishments in 1966. There has been a great rise in building and other construction activities and people have found new employment opportunities in them. But this is so only during the transitional stage of economic development and the tempo of construction programmes may slow down. Therefore a more stable source of employment has to be looked for. Rural industries provide great promise in this respect.

The greatest advantage of small and cottage industries is that employment is provided in the natural setting of the workers' own place with numerous physical, moral and other benefits that go with such employment. It helps them to develop inherent talents and aptitudes in occupations congenial to them. Another important reason for employment to be found in the villages and not outside is that agriculture may not provide full employment, yet a larger labour force has to remain in villages at certain periods to provide the needed labour for cultivation, weeding, harvesting and other operations. Mechanised agriculture, to any appreciable extent, does not seem to be a practical proposition for many years to come. The introduction and encouragement of well-chosen village industries in each region of India, on grounds of availability of raw material, local talent, the ability of the industry to fit in with and adjust within a limit with the peak labour demand in agriculture, should add to rural welfare in many ways.

- It will reduce considerably unemployment and underemployment in many regions.
- It will provide useful outlet for many of the raw materials and waste material of agriculture, the transport of which, for reasons of their bulk and low value, is not economical over long distances. Such raw material will be converted into national wealth.
- The farmer and his family members will get an additional source of income which is so needed to raise their standard of living and help them tide over difficulties caused by the failure of crops.
- The country is facing an extreme shortage of foreign exchange. The restrictions on imports does not help very much to ease the problem. An all-out effort required to encourage exports. The produce of cottage industries hae fairly reasonable prospects of commanding foreign markets where there is great demand for them. The opening of cottage industries emporia in some of the European countries has already brought to light the potentialities of these products as earners of foreign exchange.

  Phulkaris of Punjab, shawls, wood work and art pieces of Kashmir, are but a few items, which are much in demand in other countries and promise to fetch prices commensurate with the labour put in the production of these commodities.
- The products of small industries which employ local

raw materials and talent do not call for any heavy capital investment. This suits our austere economy.

- There need not be any clash between the large and small industries. If properly organised, small industries will provide employment opportunities to enable India to achieve her cherished goal of full employment, but also act as feeders to large industries.
- A developing economy depending upon deficit financing has to face a time lag between the commencement and completion of big projects particularly when the country lacks technical know-how and equipment. During this period, the available consumption goods cannot keep pace with the rise in the purchasing power. Products of cottage and small-scale industries would come in very handy under these circumstances. In addition to making available a variety of consumer goods, they will to a great extent be free from the distribution problem. Transportation over long distances would not be necessary and a major portion of the products would be consumed near the producing centres. These readily available goods will help to mop up the newly released purchasing power and fill the necessary gap, till the investment on capital good strats producing consumer goods.
- India is wedded to a democratic form of government and is committed to a socialistic pattern of society. Like peasant farming in agriculture, cottage and small industries in the industrial sector strengthen the foundation of democracy and socialist structure of society. For this reason also, cottage and small industries have to get a place in the national economy to usher in economic democracy and the desired social order.

In view of the benefits conferred on the national economy and increase in rural welfare, cottage and small scale industries have a very strong case for rehabilitation and development. The power projects completed and nearing completion under the Five Year Plans are adding to the supply of total electricity in the country at reasonable costs. The Government have already taken up the programmes of rural electrification. This should give further impetus to development of small industries in villages. This favourable development in the availability of cheap power in rural areas can greatly help to remove the stigma attached to cottage industries of being sweated ones with low returns. As technological progress in the form of the steam engine gave a staggering blow to the small scale production in the 19th century, the change from steam power to electric power, particularly in countries where the electric power can be produced cheaply, can help in reversing the process from large scale to small scale production in the case of a number of products on economic grounds, considerations of rural welfare and decentraliisation of economy in the interest of a democratic socialistic set up. It is just not a theoretical deducation but is in actual practice in countries like Japan and Switzerland. The various forms of help needed by the small scale industries are described below:

- An organised extension service of technical guidance to the cottage workers in designing, use of tools and machines and production of quality goods or goods according to demand.
- The extension service has to be supported with appropriate research institutions at central, regional and state levels.
- Development of industrial cooperatives for supplies, services, finance, and marketing of products and in

some instances even for production. If farming can be run on cooperative lines, there appears no reason why it cannot be done in the production of goods in certain cottage or village industries as well. For an understanding of the causes of failure of cooperative societies in the past, the findings of Sri Vishwanathan Vekumalla who surveyed some of the representative industrial cooperatives in Andhra would be of interest. These are:

— Lack of adequate capital. Societies do not have enough capital either to give full time work to members or to enable them to manage until the products are sold. Consequently the members are obliged to produce for the local market or for the local sahukar.

— Lack of good faith among the members. The limited benefits conferred by the societies make the members disloyal. The artisans distrust one another.

— Personal interest of office-bearers. Some influential members as office beares utilise the societies' funds to further their own personal ends.

— Low purchasing capacity. The consumer, majority of whom have low incomes, care more for cheap goods rather than for quality. The member artisans face keen competition from non-members who under-sell by producing inferior stuff for the market.

— Lack of cooperation among departmental and non-official staff. Instead of obtaining the cooperation of the supervising officials, the office bearers of some societies actually betray their own cause by hoodwinking them.

With cooperative education, proper training and supervision, these difficulties can be overcome but it must be clearly realised that efforts on a cooperative basis in all possible directions are necessary for the development of handicrafts and cottage industries. It is only through cooperation that these industries can reduce their costs of production and marketing.

- There should be adequate and institutional credit made available to the cottage workers for meeting the financial needs of their business.
- The State should help develop home and foreign markets for cottage goods.
- A system of quality control must be imposed on the cottage products.
- Government should give preference to cottage products in buying their requirements.

Nobody quite knows who first propounded the thesis that India could stamp out poverty by setting up agro-industries in a big way. The term came into vogue no more than a decade ago. But since then it has become highly fashionable. Almost everything ranging from a giant nuclear power reactor to cellophane packing is now sought to be justified on the ground that it is necessary to promote agro-industries. Most of the big business houses have already diversified into the field and others want to do so.

For the new entrepreneurs it is not merely a matter of keeping up with the established industrial Joneses. The opportunities are vast and highly attractive, considering the governmental incentives on offer. The authorities in their anxiety to industrialise the countryside have decided to extend the benefits to a large number of industries whose link agriculture is remote if at all one exists. The 155-point list of "agro-industries" issued by the Commissioner of Small-Scale Industries, for instance, includes refrigeration plants for milk and factories for the canning of fish.

The Planning Commission goes even further. It says that any enterprise which processes farm produce, supplies chemical inputs to agriculture (fertilizers, insecticides, etc.), manufactures improved agricultural equipment (hoes, bullock cart tyres, tractors, etc.), or helps raise farm output is an agro-industry. This means that the term not only covers the nation's biggest industry—cotton textiles—but also the whole range of plantations like tea, coffee and cashewnut and of course, jute.

Going only by statistics the result is somewhat ironical. They show that a much bigger segment of the Indian industry was agro-based at the time of Independence than has been the case in recent years. In 1951 agro-industries accounted for 75 per cent of the total productive capital employed and 78 per cent of all value added by manufacturing in the organised sector. By 1963, however, these percentage had fallen respectively to 34 and 53. The steep decline in these figures does not mean that agro-industries are on their way out. But it does indicate that their growth has been slow in comparison with the phenomenal expansion of other industries like steel, oil refining or electronics.

The word "agro-industries" broadly means industries manufacturing "input" for agriculture, or processing agricultural "output." Agencies supporting agriculture by designing and manufacturing inputs are termed as "agro-industrials" and those supported by agricultural products are classed as "agro-based industries."

Generally most of the industries use agricultural output as basic raw material. But the concept of agro-based industries leave out of account "industrial product". It is confined to those industries that are engaged in processing the agricultural produce either for consumption or for the use of industry. They include wheat milling, rice milling, dal-making, oil crushing, cotton ginning, khandsari, fruit beverages, and so on. Thus, the agro-industries serve at both the ends of farming.

In the first instance agro-industrials provide the essential input and in the second phase agro-based industries function as an outlet for agricultural output. The purpose of helping these industries is to make farming a profitable and commercially viable proposition; since agro-industrials directly influence the cost structure of farming and agro-based industries, they have their impact on the receipts of the farmer. Agro-industries also serve as a means for providing better employment opportunities to the labour during off season.

The concept of agro-industrial is not new. Formerly the village smith, the carpenter and cobbler used to prepare and repair the various traditional types of agricultural tools and implements. These industries were, and in some regions still are, the part and parcel of rural life. The agricultural implements are exchanged for a share in the harvest.

Likewise in its refined form modern agro-industrial manufacture, process and supply agriculture inputs either on cash basis or realise the value in instalments. The distribution of fertilizers and seeds has been taken over by the cooperatives for quite a long time now. The various agro-industrial corporations in the states seek to supply agriculture machinery on cash, credit and hire-purchase system.

The idea of "in—kind" assistance has been mooted from the simple fact that outright cash grant to the farmer for production is often misused and misdirected in consumption. Even those genuinely interested in buy..ng implements and machinery, have faced numerous problems in purchasing them at reasonable prices. The farmer who is detached from urban life takes time in locating the supplier and picking up the operating technique. Because of "scarcity" of modern machinery, is said that a "black market" has also grown in agricultural inputs.

The purpose of establishing the agro-industrial corporations, therefore, is not only to equip the farmer with modern implements but also to train him in the operation of machines—so essential at the early stages of mechanisation* , ensure proper use of funds and protect the farmer from the difficulties involved in purchasing right type of machinery and implements suitable for cultivation in his region. In India, the soil and climate conditions so sharply differ from one region to another that only regional corporations could take a better view and mould the tools according to regional requirements.

Although there has been an impressive development of large-scale industries during the two decades of planned development, India still remains predominantly a country of villages and small industries. About two crore persons are engaged in these industries, of whom nearly 90 lakhs work in the handloom industries, i.e., more than the total number of persons employed in the organised industries and mining put together.

The small-scale and village industries sector covers a wide range of traditional and modern 'small-scale industries including handloom, khadi, powerloom, sericulture, coir, handicrafts, village industries and mechanised small-scale industries.

This sector consists broadly of (i) traditional cottage and household industries (viz., handloom, khadi & village industries, handicrafts, sericulture and coir industry), and (ii) modern small scale industries (defined as those having investment of up to Rs. 10 lakhs in plant and machinery and Rs. 15 lakhs in the case of ancillary industries). As distinguished from modern small scale industries, the traditional cottage and household industries are located mostly in rural and semi-urban areas. A large number of these traditional industries do not use power-operated appliances and equipment. These also involve relatively lower levels of investment and technology and provide largely part-time employment. A very large number of the persons dependent on traditional industries belong to the poorer sections of the society and live below the poverty line. However, a number of these industries produce certain essential articles required by the masses and also some other items which are exported. The number of persons employed in principal traditional industries is estimated at 140 lakhs, including about 57 lakhs in the handloom industry and about 36 lakhs in sericulture. Much of this employment is neither full-time nor well remunerative. Modern small scale industries are estimated to provide full-time employment to about 28 lakh persons.

The Industrial Policy Resolution of the Government of India, 1948 recognised cottage and small scale industries as an important sector of our economy. The Cottage Industries Board and the Cottage Industries Directorate were accordingly set up. Since each of these industries have their own complexities and problems, separate Boards were also created to look after individual industries such as coir, silk and handicrafts. The Small Scale Industries Organisation was also created to take care of those small enterprises which were outside the orbit of all such Boards. For purposes of definition, it was decided that a unit which has an investment of less than Rs. 5 lakhs and employs less than 50 persons could be classed as small scale. The limit on employment has been removed since then.

In spite of the awareness of the importance of cottage and small scale industries and initiative of the organisational measures as mentioned above nothing much could be achieved during the First Plan period. Some protection was given to handloom and three or four other village industries. But a large number of the cottage industries faced strong competition from mill—and factory-made goods.

In order to review the problems and programmes of such industries, a Village and Small Industries Committee was set up in 1955 under the chairmanship of Prof. D.G. Karve. The recommendations of the Committee deal with the following three objectives:

- Further technological unemployment such as occurs in traditional village industries should be avoided as far as possible.
- Employment opportunities for as large a number as possible should be created through different village and small industries.
- The basis should be prepared for an essentially decentralised society and also for progressive economic development at a fairly rapid rate.

With these objectives in view, the Committee considered that the progressive expansion and modernisation of rural industry could be best brought about by the establishment of small industries units, along with the necessary services in large villages and small towns located all over the country. Industrial expansion on the periphery of large towns could scarcely be said to reduce the concentration of industry. What was needed, therefore, was a pattern of industrial activity in which a group of villages converging on their natural industrial and urban centre, form a unit, what the Committee called "a pyramid of industry broad-based on a progressive rural economy."

The Committee also visualised the introduction of technical improvement even in the traditional village industries. It was recommended that for the future there should be a regular programme of gradual transition to better techniques.

Necessitated by the acceptance of a socialist pattern of society as the national objective and to meet the requirement of the planned economic development, a fresh statement of industrial policy was made on April 30, 1956. "The Resolution accepted the policy of supporting cottage as well as village and small scale industries by restricting the volume of production in the large scale sector by differential taxation or direct subsidies. The aim of state policy was declared as that of ensuring a decentralised sector acquiring sufficient vitality to be self-supporting and integrating its development with that of the large scale industry. The state was thus to concentrate on measures designed to improve the competitive strength of the small scale producer."

The second Five Year Plan could then take bolder steps for the development of small scale and cottage industries, as a means of achieving dispersed industrial growth on the one hand and provide better employment opportunities on the other. The Development Commissioner's Organisation for Small Scale Industries was set up at the Centre as the apex administrative machinery which has since then rendered technical assistance through a network of 15 State Institutions, Branch Institues and 36 Extension Centres already established for this purpose all over the country.

Intensive area and marketing schemes for khadi and village industries were introduced. The scheme aimed at the integrated economic development of selected contiguous areas with a population ranging between

20,000 to 30,000 with a view to developing village industries as an integral part of the rural economy. The number of such intensive areas was increased from 35 in 1955-56 to 200 at the end of the Second Plan.

A provision of Rs. 10 crores was also made for setting up industrial estates. The object was to provide conditions favourable to working efficiency, maintenance of uniform standards in production and economic utilisation of materials and equipment. This was intended to enable the small scale units to have the advantage of common services and other facilities such as good site, electricity, water, gas, steam, compressed air, railway sidings, watch and ward, etc.

It was felt in 1959 that the impact of the small industries programme was more confined to the cities and towns or to areas within close proximity of the headquarters of the Institutes and Extension Centres and had not permeated the countryside. Little advance had been made by this programme into rural areas. The objective of regional and dispersed development of industries as conceived by the Second Plan had not been achieved.

In order to carry the programme to the underdeveloped areas and make the people interested in the development of small industry, an intensive development campaign programme was chalked out.

The programme was primarily to be launched in such areas (districts), which though underdeveloped, offered maximum potentialities for the development of small industries. Closest cooperation was also intended to be provided among the Central Small Industries Organisation including the Small Industries Service Insitute, the State Directorates of Industries, National Small Industries Corporation (P) Ltd. and other official and non-official institutions and agencies. The underlying idea of the campaign was to carry the development programme to the very doors of the potential entrepreneurs and apprise them of the benefits that were likely to accrue to them from taking up small scale industries.

At the end of September 1960 the scheme was in operation in 65 intensive and 18 preintensive areas. The basic unit for working out the scheme was a selected areas comprising 30-40 villages with a population of about 20,000. Warrangal district in Andhra Pradesh and Pali as well as Bhilwara districts in Rajasthan were the first to receive the benefit of this programme.

The work of forestry research is supervised by the Indian Council of Forestry Research and Education (ICFRE). The Council has six research institutes under it. The major activities carried out currently are:

— Development of suitable technological methods for storage of seeds.

— Clonal variation study on the basis of length, leaf area index and lead number.

— Vegetative propagation studies of Eucalyptus, Casurina, etc.

— Studies to control pests of Bambusa and Dalbergia spp.

— Study mechanical and physical properties of several important commercial species etc.

— Tissue culture technology.

— Bio-diversity conservation etc.

The major problem area in the research activities carried out by ICFRE is not the research content but linkages with the state forest departments. Today, what is happening in ICFRE is not being translated into action at the field level. Unfortunatley, the State forest departments have neither inherited a strong research base nor tried to institutionalise Research and development (R&D).

The main emphasis of 1894 Forest Policy was management of forest to promote the general well—being of the country. It is further observed that maintenance of adequate forest is dictated primarily for the preservation of climatic and physical condition of the country and secondly to fulfill the demands of the people. However, the above mentioned two objectives were subject to:

— Permanent cultivation should come before forestry.

— Satisfaction of the needs of local population should override all consideration of revenue.

— After fulfilment of the above conditions, the realisation of maximum revenue would be the guiding factor in the management of forest.

The forest policy of 1952 emphasised the need of forests in balanced and complementary land use system. It also realised the need of forests for checking soil erosion and denudation in the mountainous regions, invasion of sea sands on coastal terrain, and shifting sand dunes. The Policy also emphasised on planting and establishing trees for amelioration of physical and climatic conditions and increasing supply of large quantities of small wood and firewood for local population. The value of forests was recognised not only in the physical fields, such conservation of moisture and prevention of erosion, but also in economic fields like development of agriculture, industry and communication by supply of timber to railways, defence, industries etc.

The forest policy of 1952 proposed classfication of forests on functional basis into protected forests, National forests, village forests and tree lands. The policy also laid down that it would be the duty of foresters to awaken interest of people for development, extension and establishment of tree lands or woodlands wherever possible. The policy laid stress on

— weaning the tribal people away from shiftng cultivation particularly in the North-Eastern states, Andhra Pradesh, Orissa, etc.

— increasing the efficiency of forest administration to maintain adequate forest lands and giving requisite training to staff.

— providing adequae facilities for conducting research in the field of forestry.

— controlling grazing, etc.

Over the years, forests in the country have suffered serious depletion. To overcome these problems the National Forest Policy was revised in 1988.

The principal aim of National Forest Policy is to ensure environmental stability and maintenance of ecological balance. The main features of this Policy are as under:

— The existing forests and forest lands should be fully protected and their productivity should be improved.

— Forest cover should be increased rapidly on hilly slopes, in the catchment areas of rivers, lakes reservoirs and on the semi-arid and desert tracts.

— There is a need for the establishment of National parks, sanctuaries and biosphere reserves and protected areas for the conservation of total biological diversity.

— The country should have a minimum of 33 per cent of total area under forest cover. Hilly and mountainous regions should have 2/3 of the area under forest cover to prevent erosion and land degradation.

— A massive need based and time bound programme of afforestation should be undertaken with particular emphasis on fuelwood and fooder development.

— The rights and concessions including grazing should remain related to carrying capacity of the forests.

— The forestry activities should be designed in such a way that they could work as levers for improvement of the socio-economic conditions of the rural poor and tribal communities.

— Division of forest land for any non-forest purpose should be subject to most careful examination and with stringent conditions.

— The damage to forests from encroachment, fire, grazing, shifting cultivation, etc. needs to be checked.

— Good agriculture land should not be diverted for raising plantations/afforestation.

— The need for more attention for forestry research, personnel management, adequate data base and infrastructure in the field of forestry is realised and recommended.

5

Environmental Impact Assessment

Environmental Impact Assessment (EIA) is one of the tools used to achieve sustainable development. At present EIA is mandatory for 29 specific activities. EIA is also required for some of the activities to be taken up in identified areas like Coastal Zone, Murad-Janjira, Doonvalley, Dahanu, Aravalli and Numaligarh.

Over the years the Ministry has evolved a procedure for examining the impact of different activities such as Industry and Mining, Irrigation and Power, Ports and Harbours, Airports, Roads, Hotels, Beach resorts and Tourism projects. These include providing requisite information as per questionnaire, preparation of EIA report, holding of public hearing wherever necessary and examination by a duly constituted Expert Committee (EC).

Status of appraisal of projects

During the year, the ECs were reconstituted, Following are the details of the committee and the number of meetings held by them.

Besides the above, an EC has been constituted to examine the mining projects falling under the purview of Aravalli notification. This committee has met twice during the year and considered 63 projects.

S. No.	Name of the Committee	No. of meetings held
1.	Industry	5
2.	Mining	4
3.	Thermal Power	6
4.	River Valley and Hydroelectric	4
5.	Infrastructure and Miscellaneous	4

Monitoring

Since the initiation of EIA procedure, a number of steps have been taken to monitor the implementation of conditions stipulated while according environmental clearance. Six Regional Offices of the Ministry at Bangalore, Bhopal, Bhubaneswar, Chandigarh, Lucknow and Shillong scrutinise the monitoring reports received from the project authorities, review the implementation of the conditions and if necessary make a site visit to ensure that conditions are being implemented and if not bring it to the attention of the project authorities. To streamline the monitoring process a one day workshop was organized in September 1998, in which representatives of Central Pollution Control Board (CPCB), State Pollution Control Boards (SPCBs)/ Committees, Officials of the Ministry and Regional Offices participated.

Constitution of authorities

Coastal zone authority

During the year, Coastal Zone Authorities have been set up both at National and State/Union Territory levels. The objective of these authorities is to take 'Measures for protecting and improving the quality of coastal environment and preventing, abating and controlling environmental pollution in coastal areas.

Aquaculture authority

The authority which has been constituted under Environment (Protection) Act, 1986 is being administered by Ministry of Agriculture and Co-operatives. Since its constitution, the authority has met nine times and has formulated guidelines for aquaculture farms, procedure for considering the application for setting up of aquaculture farms, training etc.

Dahanu taluka environment protection authority

During the year, this authority continued its work. The major activity undertaken by the authority includes matters regarding setting up of a port at Vahavan, Maharashtra. It also monitored the activities of the thermal power plant at Dahanu and implementation of Dahanu Regional Plan.

Central ground water authority

This authority was also constituted under the provisions of Environment Protection Act, 1986. 'Me authority, which was under Ministry of Water Resources, has now initiated action regarding registration for ground water abstraction. It has identified areas vulnerable to ground water pollution/ depletion. It has also initiated mass awareness programmes,

Notification on pachmarhi

A draft notification was issued in September 1998 notifying Pachmarhi region in Madhya Pradesh as an Eco sensitive zone. The notification has been issued with the intention of regulating industrial mining and tourism activities in the area and conserve the natural and man-made heritage. The notification applies to Pachmarhi Town and its immediate environs. The notification also provides for the preparation of a Zonal Development Plan and constitution of a High Level Monitoring Committee.

ADB project

The Ministry of Environment and Forests has taken up a project on Strengthening Environment Impact Assessment and Environmental Legislation with the assistance of Asian Development Bank. The project involves preparation of EIA manual for appraisal and training of technical personnel in the use of the manual. Besides the project will provide input to strengthening of Environmental Legislation and Institutions based on international experience by preparing a report detailing the environmental legislation and institutional structure of two industrialised countries. The project is expected to be completed by April 1999.

Studies sponsored

The first phase of the following studies have been completed :

1. Sustainable development plan for Environment Protection of Kutch district in Gujarat State.
2. Evaluation and Characterisation of natural and alternate sand resources in selected zone in Andaman and Nicobar Islands.
3. Carrying Capacity based Developmental Planning for Tinnakara Island, Lakshadweep.

The progress of these studies is being monitored regularly.

Constitution of specified committees

The Ministry has constituted a committee to identify abandoned mines in two specific areas so as to prepare an action plan for restoration of these areas, review the mining strategy and technology adopted and prepare short/long term plans.

A committee has been constituted under the Chairmanship of Director General of Hydrocarbons,

Ministry of Petroleum and Natural Gas to formulate guidelines for management of wastes emanating during offshore drilling.

In order that the environmental concerns are integrated in the initial stage itself, the Ministry is associating itself in the selection of sites for Mega power projects.

Carrying capacity based regional planning studies

All development projects utilise natural resources in one form or the other and also generate wastes. It is necessary to develop alternate strategies for sustainable development in the context of a developing country like India. Carrying Capacity based regional planning takes into account the environmental quality of the ecosystem also so that the welfare of human beings is not impaired. To demonstrate the viability of the carrying capacity based planning process, studies have been taken up in selected areas considered to be representative of similar problematic areas in the country. The regions selected for such studies are:

— Ecologically fragile Doon Valley

— Environmentally critical National Capital Region

— Industrially and/environmentally sensitive Tapi Estuary

— Industrialised and Resource - Rich Damodar River Basin

— Coastal area with multi-scetoral development, Greater Kochi

Carrying capacity based planning approach

During the period under reporting, the final reports for two carrying capacity studies, which were earlier completed, namely, Doon Vallley and National Capital

Region have been prepared. Copies of these reports have been sent to the concerned agencies for interaction and necessary follow up.

Review Meetings were held to discuss the progress in the Carrying Capacity Studies for Damodar River Basin. Tapi Estuary and Greater Kochi Region. The draft reports on Damodar River Basin and Tapi Estuary have been received and reviewed. Suggestions based on these discussions are being incorporated in-the final report.

Three meetings were held to discuss the progress on the carrying capacity study for Greater Kochi Region. Collection of secondary data for this study is complete and based on the primary data which is under compilation, various development scenarios are being worked out for the future development of the region.

6

Plans and Programmes

The Central Ganga Authority (CGA) was set up in 1985 to oversee the implementation of the Ganga Action Plan drawn up for cleaning polluted stretches of the river Ganga. A Steering Committee has identified different schemes to be taken up in Uttar Pradesh, Bihar and West Bengal through which the rive runs and a Monitoring Committee monitors the progress of the schemes and their impact on the river quality.

The Ganga Action Plan proposes to divert the sewage flowing into the river to other locations for treatment and conversion into valuable energy sources. Schemes identified for this purpose include: renovation of existing trunk rivers and outfalls to prevent overflow of sewage into the Ganga, construction of interceptions to divert the flow of sewage and other liquid wastes into the river and renovation and construction of pumping stations and sewage treatment plants to recover maximum possible resources. Smaller schemes such as construction of community toilets, conversion of dry toilets to flush toilets, construction of electric crematoria, development of river Ghats and modernisation of solid waste management system, have also been taken up to reduce domestic waste load on the Ganga. As against the target of creating infrastructure capable of intercepting, diverting and treating 873 million litres per day (mld) of domestic waste, infrastructure capable of intercepting and diverting 628 mld and treating 431 mild of municipal sewage has been created. Out of 261 schemes sanctioned, 237 have been completed and almost all low-cost sanitation schemes and construction of electric crematoria have been completed leading to significant reduction in the polluction load of the river Ganga.

The second phase of the Ganga Action Plan is proposed to be taken up as a Centrally-sponsored scheme with equal contribution from the Centre and the concerned state governments and Yamuna and Gomati Action Plan have been approved under the phase at an estimated cost of Rs. 421 crore.

An approach Paper on the National River Action Plan (NRAP) has been approved at an estimated outlay of Rs. 1,000 crore spread oover a period of 10 years. The NRAP includes grossly polluted stretches of those rivers of the country not covered under both the phases of the Ganga action Plan. The NRAP is to be renamed as the National River Conservation Plan (NRCP).

India's most sacred river, the Ganga, which orginates from the snow-caps of the Himalaya, is one of the most polluted rivers of the country. To address these pollution problems, the Central Ganga Authority (CGA) was constituted to oversee and guide the implementation of a programme for restoring the quality of the river. In addition to carrying out treatment measures, the CGA also conducts awareness programmes for the general masses. Commissioning of the Howrah Sewage Treatment Plant and of electric crematoria in West Bengal are positive steps taken by the Government to help in the cleaning of the Ganga. The Damodar Valley Corporation (DVC) has initiated efforts to clean the river Damodar.

A recent scheme of the Government of India provides for the award of a label known as ECOMARK to environment friendly household and other consumer products. These products will have to meet specified environmental criteria along with the quality requirements laid down by the Bureau of Indian Standards. Criteria have so far been notified in the case of soaps and detergents. Criteria for paints, paper, plastic, aerosols, packing materials and wood substitutes are under consideration. It is hoped that the ECOMARK scheme will motivate the manufacture, use and disposal of commonly used consumer products in a way that would cause less harm to the environment than at present.

The National Environmental Engineering Research Institute, Nagpur, is concerned with issues of quality control in respect of air and water, and disposal of waste water and solids. Its activites include development of analytical capabilities to improve monitoring of pollutants, waste recycling, urban and industrial solid waste management, environmental impact analysis, development of appropriate processes for water treatment and environmental support programmes for integrated rural development to minimize health hazards.

The Housing and Urban Development Corporation (HUDCO) was set up in 1970 as a government owned company to finance or undertake housing or urban development programmes, develop new or satellite towns, set up building materials industries, and extend consultancy assistance for projects in India and abroad. In addition, the State Housing Ministries and Boards along with the Municipal Corporations and Metropolitan Development Authorities also work for the upgradation of urban areas.

To generate public involvement in environmental protection, the Government has decided that the amount paid by a taxpayer to any association or institution for programmes of conservation of natural resources will be exempt from income tax. A depreciation allowance at 50 per cent on devices and systems installed for minimizing pollution or for conservation of natural resources was introduced in 1982. An investment allowance at the rate of 35 per cent, as against the general rate of 25 per cent of the actual cost of new machineery or plant which assists in the control of pollution or protection of environment is also allowed. To encourage industries to shift from urban areas, capital gains arising from transfer of buildings or lands used for the purpose of business are exempt from tax on capital gains if these are used for capital investments for the purpose of business at the new place.

The Water Cess Act 1977, provides for the levy of a cess on water consumed by certain industries and by local authorities. If any of these bodies install plants for the treatment of sewage or effluent, they are entitled to a rebate on the cess.

The Central Pollution Control Board was constituted under the Water (Prevention and Control of Pollution) Act, 1974. All states have their own Pollution Control Boards. The main function of the Boards is to promote cleanliness of different water bodies, to improve the quality of air and to control air pollution in the country. The Environment Protection Act of 1986 has further widened the scope of these Boards. They have also been entrusted with teh additional responsibility of air pollution control under the Air (Prevention and Control of Pollution) Act, 1981.

The Industrial Toxicological Research Centre, Lucknow, is a pioneering institute dealing with effects of industrial and environmental pollutants on environment and human health. Studies on the role of various factors like age, sex, physiological status, nutritional status and genetic make-up in morbidity, hitherto largely unexplored in the Indian context, are being taken up. It also takes up occupational health related studies and environmental monitoring of pollutants.

Ground water depletion and watershed development

The situation has become more serious in states like Haryana and Punjab. The annual ground-water depletion rate in some districts of these states is over 30 cms. As the water-table goes down, the farmers have to take their pumping sets to a higher depth for increasing the delivery of water and this involves much cost. Generally, the pumping set depth is increased once in five years.

The problem of water shortage because of sinking tube-wells has become so acute in some areas like Kurukshetra district of Haryana that the resource-rich farmers have started getting more and more submersible pumps installed which is a very costly affair. The cost involved in installation of one submersible pump is more than Rs. 1.25 lakh. These pumps fetch water from different depths. But there is limit to the depth from which even a submersible pump can tap water. If the water-table goes beyond this limit, the pump can no longer exploit ground water. It was with the introduction of high-yielding genotypes of wheat and rice in mid-sixties that India ushered in the era of what is commonly referred to as 'Green Revolution'. Our country has since made spectacular achievements in the field of agriculture. It is evidence by the fact that we are today not only self-sufficient in matter of food but also in a position to export food grains and other agricultural products, in addition to having comfortable food reserve to meet unforeseen exigencies. We have emerged as the largest producer of fruits and the second largest producer of vegetables in the world. But unfortunately, the efforts made during the last thirty years have not been confined to constructive measures and useful results. Frightful damage has been wrought to the basic natural assets, particularly soil, water and genetic (plant and animal) resources on which agriculture is dependent. Although some of the damage is irreparable, the wide spread growing realization of the disastrous consequences that thoughtless exploitation of nature leads to justify hope for the future. It is a happy situation that the whole world today has become very much concerned about healing the wounds inflicted by the errors committed in the wake of modernization.

Our country is today faced with serous problems of falling ground-water-table in tube-well/pump-set irrigated areas and rising water-table in canal irrigated areas. Although our policy makers, planners, administrators and agricultural scientists are very much aware of these problems, the situation is getting alarming year after year. The remedial measures taken so far do not seem to have touched even the fringe of the problems. The situation demands time-bound aggressive measures to overcome the problems which have cropped up over the years.

"The water-table in much of the country is steadily sinking. The fall in a little over a decade has been two to four metres in many states. Delhi and the surrounding states are worse, the decline being four to eight metres in the decade after 1971, with a further fall in a decade after."

India is one of the countries affected by serious and vast land desertification in the world. Such areas are characterised by severe ecological degradation with denuded forests and poor protective vegetative cover causing soil erosion and decline in the productivity of the land. The water table is receding thus causing shortage of water for irrigation as well as drinking purposes. The increase in human and cattle populaltion has only added to the immense pressue on the already fragile ecosystems.

Signs of reclamation of degraded areas of late have become visible in some parts of the country such as Ralegon Sidhi and Adgaon in Maharashtra, Kabbernala and Mittemari in Karnataka, Jhansi in Uttar Pradesh and Jhabua in Madhya Pradesh. The development of these areas which until recently epitomised poverty, resourceslessness, is characterised by the adoption of watershed based development of the area and active involvement of voluntary organisations in facilitating the participation of local community.

Watershed is a geo-hydrological unit and drains at a common point. It has been accepted the world over as a scientific unit for area development. The long-term objective of watershed development is the rational utilisation of natural resources of soil, water and vegetation for increasing and stabilising the productivity of land on a sustainable basis. The benefits that would flow from the development of watersheds would include increase in sub-soil water regime, recharge of wells along the down stream of watershed and augmentation of drinking water availability. The agricultural production would be enhanced and there will be greater availability of fooder, fuelwood, small timber and raw materials for rural industries. In the process, some intangible benefits like institution building, as people get together to manage the watersheds, and increased bio-diversity of the watershed can also be expected.

Constitution of two High-Powered Committees by Government of India recently, first headed b;y Prof. C.H. Hanumantha Rao and second chaired by Shri Mohan Dharia on drought prone, desert and wastelands development can aptly be termed as turning points in the whole perception of and approach towards area development planning in the country. Both these committees have diagnosed the problem of degradation of land, water and vegetation resources and have recommended in unequivocal terms that waershed as the over—arching principle of area development will have to be adopted by all the concerned departments if 175 million hectares of drought peone, desert and wastelands are to be brought to reasonable level of productivity and ecological balance is to be restored in these areas.

It has been clearly pointed out that without taking into account the local communities' outlook and development builds upon traditional soil and water conservation measures and farming systems, any area development programme is bound to fail.

Watershed approach is currently being followed with different thrusts by different Ministries. Ministry of Agriculture through its National Watershed Development Programme for Rainfed Areas (NWDPRA) seeks to enhance agricultural production in the rainfed areas. Ministry of Environment & Forests has used it for regeneration of vast degraded forests especially in hilly and sloppy regions. Ministry of Rural Areas & Employment h;as gone further in recognising the watershed based developmental planning in its broader sense and has used it as a tool for overall economic development of rural areas by launching the Watershed Development Programme from 1st April, 1995 for implementing Drought Prone Areas Programme (DPAP). Desert Development Programme (DDP), Integrated Wastelands Development Assurance Scheme (EAS). As a result, the flow of funds for development of land, water and vegetative resources is no more a constraint. According to an estimate, approximately Rs. 5000 crore is annually available from various government sponsored development programmes for this purpose. But, co-ordinated efforts to establish longterm strategies that are coherent at all levels would need to be made to achieve the desired objectives.

The submersible pumps extract water from such high depths that they may render shallow tube-wells of other farmers around useless. "The situation is so alarming in some of surveyed villages in Kurukshetra district (Haryana) that small and marginal farmers whose shallow tubewells have dried due to ground water depletion and can not afford submersible tube-wells are getting converted as farm labour by subletting their land to those farmers who have submersible tube-wells." Even those fetching water from wells and hand pumps for drinking and other purposes fall victims to the few haves having submersible pumps around them. Thus, reckless installation of particularly submersible pumps is highly detrimental and unjustified even from the view point of equity and social justice. This is why there is so much cry about the urgency and immediacy of effective measures not only to arrest the depletion of ground water but also to replenish it. Even the Supreme Court has taken cognizance of the problem of continuously dropping water-table. "The continuous ground water exploitation led to another serious problem which is brackish/alkaline water in Haryana. The exploitation of such water spoils not only good quality of water/canal water but it also destroys the soil fertility."

Ground water must be viewed as a national, rather than regional or local, resource and an optimum-use model should be designed for irrigation, drinking and other purposes with due consideration of the interests of all the users. "Even if water is scarce in a region, through more efficient planned use, it is possible to increase the overall benefits to everyone there... To use water properly, you must look at all the trade-offs to all significant users, not must a few and not just one time."

The steady fall of ground water-table is seriously impairing the original productive power of nature. It is highly disastrous for stable and sustainable agriculture.

The results of over exploitation of ground water is hazardous to even public health. In Calcutta and the rest of the state, "the exploitation has upset the geological balance, with arsenic from the bed rock flowing into the water. In a third of West Bengal's districts, the government admitted in Parliament earlier this year (1996), drinking water has more arsenic than the maximum limit prescribed by the world Health Organisation."

"The affected area is growing by 20 per cent every year. As for the metropolis of Calcutta, heavily dependent on tube-well water, a city university study says, it is on the brink of an arsenic bomb."

The problems caused by excessive use of ground water are visible every where. "In Delhi, for instance, though most residents are blissfully unaware, the level of fluorides in the water, which can have a crippling effect over time, is well above the safe limit in a number of localities. Some places have increasing salinity problems, some have other contamination and many have a mix of all these."

The water supply department of the metropolis of Delhi pumps out 65 million gallons of ground water every day for municipal supply as a result of which water table is continuously dropping.

The pressure on ground water has tremendously increased over the last thirty years because of high-yielding varieties, intensive cultivation involving water-loving crops and dominance of such crops in the cropping patterns which require much water, on one hand and wane of traditional sources and methods of irrigation, on the other. The yield potential of high-yielding varieties in general can not be exploited without adequate and timely irrigation water obviously increases with increase in cropping intensity. Some crops require much water. Paddy is number one among such crops. It requires a very high amount of water. Dominance of crops like paddy and wheat in the cropping patterns necessitates increased use of ground water. Sustainability of agriculture underlines the need for diversion of area from the crops demanding more water, particularly paddy, to the crops requiring less water. Emphasis has to be laid on selecting such crop verities which give equivalent yields with less moisture and are of short duration. Even in respect of crop varieties, cropping patterns and cropping intensity, we must go back to the past and seek in traditional agriculture some solution to the present-day problems.

National Watershed Development Project for Rainfed Areas (NWDPRA) was launched in 1990-91 and to cover 25 states and two union territories. The objective of the project is restoration of ecological balance in rainfed areas and sustainable bio-mass production. It focuses on: (i) Conservation, upgradation and utilisation of natural endowments in integrated manner with low cost replicable technology and (ii) generating employment opportunities for the poverty striken rural masses in the rainfed areas through directly involving the farmers and watershed beneficiaries in planning, execution of all project works in the watershed by developing Self Help Groups of Mitra Krishak Mandals. The farming systems approach on watershed management principles has been adopted in order to conserve rainwater and top soils with people's participation. Animal husbandry, agroforestry, horticulture, fisheries development, sericulture, agro-processing etc., are some of the diverse activities which are also being taken up.

Under this project the target is of treating an area of 28 lakh hectare at a cost of Rs. 1,100 crore. Taking into consideration the project criterion of covering all the blocks where arable areas under assured means of irrigation is less than 30 per cent, 2,621 blocks have been identified in which a micro watershed of 500 to 5,000 hectare has been taken up for treatment. In all 2,497 micro-watershed with an area of 38.41 lakh have been sanctioned by the state governments at an estimated cost of Rs. 1,128.50 crore. So far 1,407 composite, 1,343 Kisan/ Mihila Mandal and 199 government-owned nurseries have been established. The project currently in operation in 25 states and two UTs covering 115 agro-climatic zones, is expected to saturate by the end of the Eighth Plan period.

Salient achievements in the field of integrated watershed development are: (i) unified command approach of multi-disciplinary team has proved to be an effective organisational set up for implementing the watershed managemet development programme; (ii) contour farming in both black and red soil regions has shown encouraging results in increasing the yields of different crops; (iii) different farming systems based on contour vegetative barriers in watershed development programme has shown substantial in situ moisture conservation and yield increase; (iv) cropping intensity has increased significatly following the integrated approach of farming and (v) people's participation has shown encouraging results.

The Integrated Watershed Development Project (Hills) has been in operation from 1991-92 within the states of Haryana, Himachal Pradesh, Jammu and Kashmir and Punjab. The main objectives of the project are to slow down and reverse degradation of natural environment through use of appropriate soil and moisture conservation technology and improve production potential of the area. The duration of the project is seven years. Under this project, an area of 2.30 lakh hectare will be treated with an estimated cost of US dollar 125.6 million. Integrated Watershed Development Project (Plains) has been taken up in the states of Gujarat, Orissa and Rajasthan with a total cost of US dollar 91.8 million to cover an area of 2.65 lakh hectare in a period of seven years from February 1991. The main objectives of this project are to slow down and reverse ecological degradation in a variety of agri-ecological zones by promoting sustainable and replicable production system.

Among the various factors responsible for steady ground water depletion is growing dependence on tube-wells/pumping sets. In fact, it is not be because of tube-wells/pumping sets as such but because of excessive exploitation of ground water through these artificial methods of irrigation that water-table is continuously dropping. There is no recharge of ground water. In order that ground water depletion is checked and effective measures taken for its replenishment, it is imperative to restrict reckless and indiscriminate installation of tube-wells/pumping sets. The number of tube-wells/pumping sets to be installed in an area should be determined considering how many of them can be sustained by ground water reservoirs. It calls for strict legislation with respect to the spacing, the depth and the quantity of the quality of pumped water to prevent its contamination. If fact, mere legislation won't do. More important is forceful implementation of the legislation. Perhaps only three states and one union territory have presently some legislation to regulate ground water exploitation.

In view of fast declining ground water resource, unavailability of adequate energy to tap it by pumping is, in a way, blessing in disguise. Had adequate energy been available, the ground water situation would have become most alarming.

While inadequacy of energy restricts the use of ground water, "the major and medium irrigation system's inefficiency is a big contributor to the ground water recharge. It would indeed be a very costly way of recharging the ground water. Further, the water recharged this way is turning a great extent of the area saline."

"The ultimate source of all water is precipitation, that is snow and rainfall. The precipitation that falls on the ground is dispersed in several ways and ultimately appears in the form of surface and ground water resources."

It is unfortunate that in our zeal and enthusiasm for modernisation, we have become oblivious of the centuries old time-tested system of irrigation where in our farmers depended mostly on surface rain water. As the situation stands today, the dependence on rainfall has drastically reduced because of increasing use of tube-wells/pumping sets and canal. In the traditional systems of irrigation, in-situ conservation of rainfall by way of such practices as bunding, terracing were very common. The excess run-off was stored at appropriate sets in tanks, ponds and natural reservoirs for future use. We had a network of such reservoirs scattered throughout the length and breadth of the country. The impounded water was used for irrigation directly or indirectly through recharge where also used ground water for irrigation and other pursposes, digging wells without adversely affecting the ground water reserve. Numerous references to wells, tanks, ponds and natural reservoirs are found in the Vedas.

When the run-off is stored in widely scattered tanks, ponds and other reservoirs, a sizable portion of the water that infiltrates into the soil percolates deeply and adds to the ground water. So far as rain water is concerned, it has been estimated that approximately 54 per cent of the total amount infiltrates into the soil of which about 23 per cent is added to the ground water. By adopting some simple low-cost measures, it is possible to conserve upto about 65 to 70 per cent of the total rainfall.

The fast declining ground water must be recharged and the best way it can be done is In-situ conservaton of the rain water and storage of excess run-off at appropriate sites by following the age-old traditional practices which have stood the test of time. We wish and hope that decisive steps will soon be taken to revive these practices which is a must for stable and sustainable agriculture.

A key to successful implementation of watershed management is appropriate planning and selection of activities followed by an efficient monitoring and objective evaluation.

The efficient planning for watershed management would require efforts at both policy and implementation levels supported byan effective information analysis system.

Some requisite changes have to be brought in at the policy level so as to remove or, at least, lessen the constraints in the effective watershed management. These are as follows:

Through regularisation of genuine encroachments following a politically suitable and socially accpetable criteria so that people can undertake ecologically sound activities like agro-forestry without fear of being evicted.

Although the needs of local people as well as their management efforts is gradually being recognised as desirable and even essential, their involvement in the process of conceptualising these efforts in a cohesive manner is still only marginal. The local population's aspirations are as important—as a potential benefit or as a potential constraint—as those of the government and, therefore, should find accommodation in the development process through appropriate policy measures.

At the district level various develkopment activities are carried out by different Departments of Central and State Governments in a watershed areas with very little cohesion. Optimum benefits can be obtained by creating a Watershed Mission at the district level which would pool resources and technical expertise and take up the watershed treatment in a comprehensive manner.

It should be appropriately amended to rehabilitate oustees from illegally occupied forest uplands. They should also be given priority in employment under various employment programmes.

The development activities under watershed development being primarily land based, the area development programmes tend to benefit the land owners more than the landless. Though the landless people may benefit to a small extent in terms of wage labour and greater availaability of drinking water, fuelwood, grasses or forest based usufructs from the village common lands, the landed class would be benefitted substantially by way of greater availability of water for irrigation, development of their lands and the improved cropping patterns. This inequity is bound to cause social tensions between the already polarised rual community into the rich and the poor. Any developmental endeavour with such overtones of social inequities would be socially unacceptable and thus would not be able to sustain for long.

An apropriate mechanism with adequate legal and institutional support will have to be devised to provide adequate income generating opportunities to the landless and assetless in the watershed area. This may involve among others. allotment of land to the landless and granting of rights over trees and other usufructs.

Policies in Non-farm sector: these have to be redesigned to diversify the rural economy and provide full benefit of the value addition to the local inhabitants. For example, establishment of wool processing units, tanneries, food processing and other agro-based industries in such areas will raise employment and income for local people. This would also supplement the income generating avenues for the landless.

Following measures may be taken at the implementation level:

It should get greater attention as the degradation of uplands has far reaching ecological consequences especially for low land people. People inhabitating uplands should be given some incentive for not taking up intensive agriculture.

Under the Integrated watershed management, close cooperation and assistance form various government agencies is reqauired, like the Ministries of Rural Areas & Employment, Agriculture and Cooperation, FOrests and Environment, Education and Commerce (for export of agricultural and forest priduce).

Greater productivity from developed watersheds would demand a better and extended marketing facility for the forest and agriculture produce which must be created by appropriate institutional and economic measures.

Target groups for training would be policy planners, administrators, technical experts, extension agents, village leaders and workers. Sufficient books and extension materials should be printed in the local language and made available for trainees.

Awareness raising including dissemination of relevant information to the field functionaries and the community is of prime importance and should be taken up on a regular and continuous basis by a district level task Force drawing persons from amongst technical experts, fold artists and social motivators.

Since watershed management planning would require the collection, storage and analysis of a wide range of physiographic as well as socio-economic data both spatially and temporally, an efficient and state-of-the-art information system is required to be incorporated in the very concept of watershed management. An essential component of planning is to make projections of future situaations under different sets of conditions. A Geographical Information System (GIS) being capable of such simulations can be a valuable tool for planning for watershed management. Recently, Integrated Mission for Sustainable Development (IMSD) launched by the National Remote Sensing Agency (NRSA) of the Department of Space, Government of India, using remote sensing and GIS techniques, has developed treatment plans for comprehensive development of watersheds in a few selected blocks of the country. The scope of the project should be widened to cover more areas so that scientific and technically sound development plans are readily available with the field level agencies. But, the scientific and technical inputs from space imageries and aerial photographs in the planning and implementation of the wateshed development programmes need to be supported by Rapid Rural Appraisal (RRA) and Participatory Rural Appraisal (PRA) involving local people for collection and appraisal of field level data.

Soil and water conservation

Soil and water conservation measures are one of the essential inputs for increasing agricultural ouput in the country. These programmes were first launched during the First Plan. From the very beginning, emphasis has been on development of technology for problem identification, enactment of appropriate legislation and constitution of policy coordination bodies. While conceptual framework of soil and water conservation activities has not changed, concept of programmes has undergone considerable revision during successive Five Year Plans.

Till the end of 1993-94, an area of 2.91 million hectare out of the total treatable area of 17.59 million hectare in the catchments of River Valley Project has been treated, which comes to 16.50 per cent of the treatable area. Similarly in the case of Flood Prone River scheme till the end of the 1993-94, an area of 0.61 million hectare out of the treatable are of 4.37 million hectare has been treated, which comes to about 13.96 per cent of the treatable area.

A Centrally-sponsored scheme for reclamation of alkali (usar) soils initiated during the Seventh Five Year Plan is continuing in Haryana, Punjab and Uttar Pradesh. The major components of the scheme include assured irrigation water on farm development works like land levelling, deep ploughing, community drainage system, application of soils amendment, organic manure, etc. It is a 50:50 funding between the Centre and the concerned state on identified components. Since the inception of the scheme, an area of 3.36 lakh hectare of land has been reclaimed with Central investment of Rs. 41.78 crore upto 1993-94. During 1994-95, it is expected to reclaim 60,000 hectare of land with Central investment of Rs. 7.88 crore.

The scheme for control of shifting cultivation (CSC) was implemented with cent per cent special Central assistance in all the north-eastern states, Andhra Pradesh and Orissa till 1990-91 wherein 26,532 families were selected (out of which 18,842 families in the north-eastern states) for rehabilitation. However, in pursuance of the decision taken in the NDC meeting held in October 1990 the scheme was transferred to the state sector * ture of Rs. 61.72 crore has been reported till 1991-92 against a release of Rs. 55.67 crore.

The Planning Commission has approved for the revival of the scheme only for the north-eastern states from 1994-95. An outlay of Rs. 15 crore has been provided for this purpose. The Scheme for Watershed Development Project in Shifting Cultivation Areas (WDPSCA) of North-Eastern States is to be implemented in accordance with the guidelines of the ongoing Centrally-sponsored scheme for National Watershed Development Project in the Rainfed Areas (NWDPRA). An outlay of Rs. 16 crore has been provided for 1995-96 for this purpose.

In order to make the watershed development programme effective and sustainable efficient monitoring and evaluation oare as crucial as its implementation. Monitoring provides a mechanism to supervose, direct and control the sequence of actions so that the implementation of the programme could be guided to achieve the desired objectives. An effective monitoring helps to detect the shortcomings, if any, in planning and implementation of the Programme and thus makes possible mid-course corrections simultaneously. Similarly, evaluation of the programme helps in assessing the achievements and impact and also identifying the possibilities and constraints which work as incentives or obstructions to successful and speedy implementation of the programme.

In case of watershed management with complex networking of different activities and its implementation as a people's programme, an elaborate monitoring and evaluation system will have to be evolved right through its grounding stage to the implementation phase and post-project period. Important criteria for monitoring the successful grounding of the programme could be the following:

— Institutional framework with adequate people's participation for effective delivery system.

— The existence of the legal and regulatory framework to ensure the protection of rights of different sections of society with special emphasis on the assetless and women.

— Regular and continuous technical support to the programme.

—• The presence of inter-sectoral linkages kfor effective integration and dovetailing of resources.

—• An efficient mechanism for release of funds to the field implementing agencies.

The tools for monitoring the implementation phase of the programme would include:

— Physical and financial achievements through periodical progress reports from the field level implementing agencies.

— Field visits to get a first hand information about the quality of the implementation through interaction with the field functoinaries and the beneficiaries.

— Seminars and workshops to get feedback on the field level difficulties and suggestions for improvement.

— Revies meeting to examine broad policy issues.

Similarly, important indicators for an objective impact evaluation of programme could be:

— Economic indicators such as income level,

purchasing capacity of the inhabitants of the project area and the trend of migration.

— Changes in land use cropping pattern as a result of land development and various water conservation measures taken up in the watershed area.

— Improvement in the geohydrological regime by way of recharge of ground water and surface water bodies and enhancement of sub-soil moisture.

— Capacity building of non-governmental organisations and local community as a result of participatory working.

As the Watershed Development Programmes primarily concentrate on dry regions such as drought prone, desert, wasteland infested and sloppy areas their success would not only bring about improvement in the productivity of land and water resources and restoration of ecological balances but would also help in correcting the regional imbalances caused by the Green Revolution of 60s and 70s between the irrigated and rainfed areas. Moreover, as the Watershed Management is based on the sound principles of sustainability, the enhancement in agricultural production as a result of watershed development is not likely to be acckompanied by such harmful practices as overuse of fertilisers and pesticides, over exploitation of ground water resources and intensive farming resulting in depletion of soil nutrients. We have sufficient funds, technical expertise, instutional infrastructure and policy-framework in the form of well formulated guidelines to treat and develop our vast degraded lands. But what is required is a proper orientation of implementing agencies towards adoption of watershed based planned and integrated aproach and willingness to involve the local people in the right earnestin the whole process. This concerted endeavour by all only would help in realising the dual goals of conserving the legendry splendour and munificence of our natural resources and making of a drought free country with food for all.

Fragile ecosystems

The Government of India started the Crocodile Breeding and Management project in 1976 with FAO/UNDP assistance to save all the three endangered crocodilian species, namely, the freshwater crocodile (crocodylus palustris), saltwater crocodile (C. porosus) and the rare gharial (Gavivalis gangeticus). The project surveyed the remaining crocodile habitats and facilitated their protection through declaration of sanctuaries and national parks. Captive breeding and reintroduction or restocking programmes cover regimented collection of eggs from the wild. Research and training necessary for all these activities are also undertaken. Till 1980, 11 sanctuaries had been declared especially for crocodile protection, including the tri state National Chambal Sanctuary in Madhya Pradesh, one of the largest in India. By then thousands of crocodiles of all three species had been reared at 16 centres. several thousands of these had been released in the wild. This project has thus secured conservation of crocodilians on a long-term basis.

Special initiatives are being taken for the conservation of fragile ecosystems such as wetlands, mangroves and coral reefs. A National Wetland Management Committee has been constituted which has identified 16 wetlands for conservation and management on a priority basis. Steering committees have been set up by the concerned state governmetns in which representatives of the State Government, universities and research institutions are included. A number of research projects on various aspects of wetlands are also being taken up. Notable research on wetlands and waterfowl has been conducted by the Bombay Natural History Society. This effort is strengthened by the new Salim Ali Centre for Ornithology and Natural History, recently set up in Coimbatore (Tamil Nadu). A National Mangrove Committee has been set up which has identified 15 mangrove areas for immediate attention. similarly, four coral areas have been identified for conservation programmes and concerned state governments are preparing management action plans for these. The National Institute of Oceanography, Goa, has undertaken a project to prepare a status report on corals of the Andaman and Nicobar Islands and the Gulf of Kachchh.

An all-India tiger census conducted in 1972 revealed that there were only 1,872 tigers (Panthera tigris) in the country as compared to an estimated 40,000 at the turn of the century. Taking this as an indication of the deteriorating health of India's wilderness, the Government of India launched Project Tiger in 1973 with the support of WWF International. Launching the Project, Prime Minister Indira Gandhi said, "The tiger cannot be preserved in isolation. It is at the apex of a large and complex biotope. Its habitat, threatened by human intrusion, commercial forestry and cattle grazing, must first be made inviolate."

Today there are 18 tiger reserves, comprising an area of 28,017 sq. km, of which the core segment is 12,634 sq. km. Fire protection and habitat development activities have increased the vegetation and improved the water regimes of the reserves.

By 1989 the tiger population had more than doubled to an estimated 4,200. The tiger has not been the only beneficiary. A number of other endangered species such as the swap deer, elephant, rhino and wild buffalo have received protection. The floral diversity of the tiger reserves has also shown a significant improvement. This programme has thus had a direct impact on conservation of biodiversity.

The enhanced programmes introduced in the second phase or Project Tiger include establishment of guidelines for tourism in the tiger reserves, management of buffer areas, integration of local population through ecodevelopment programmes, and establishment of nature interpretation centres.

Biodiversity

Research is the foundation of an effective conservation strategy for the preservation of biodiversity. NGOs in India have played a key role in enhancing knowledge and understanding of the ecology of the country.

The Bombay Natural History Society (BNHS) founded in 1883, is recognized as one of the foremost conservation research organizations in the world. It has undertaken a wide range of projects in conjunction with both local and overseas counterpart organizations on birds, reptiles, mammals, natural history, and of late, on the impact of development programmes on wildlife. BNHS is represented on the Indian Board of Wildlife, and on many State Wildlife Advisory Boards.

The World Wide Fund for Nature—India, was established in 1969 as a charitable trust and with a network of 18 state and divisional offices is the country's largest conservation NGO. WWF—India started as a wildlife conservation organization and has, over the years, broadened the scope of its policy work and field programmes to encompass conservation of ecosystems and support to the management of the country's protected areas network.

The centre for Ecological Sciences at the Indian Institute of Science is supported by the Ministry of Environment and Forests under the Centres of Excellence

Scheme. Its mandate is to focus on the ecological problems of the Western Ghats. It has played an important role in the setting up of the Nilgiri Biosphere Reserve.

The Bombay Natural History Society (BNHS) was formed in 1883 as a forum for exchanging information on natural history. Over the years its members and scientists have helped document India's diversity of wildlife.

The Botanical Survey of India (BSI) was established in 1890 with the objective of surveying and identifying the plant resources of the country and to undertake studies on selected critical and fragile ecosystems. The Survey has nine circles located in different phytogeographical regions of the country. It is headquartered in Calcutta and has several regional offices. It studies coastal vegetation, flora of protected areas, and ecology of endangered species. It s industrial section displays about 15,000 specimens to create appreciation and public awareness of the importance of plants in our daily life and the value of conservation. BSI is also trying to conserve threatened plant species in national parks. Surveys of areas affected by irrigation dams, hydroelectric projects, canals etc., with reference to their impact on the flora, are also undertaken by BSI.

The Zoological Survey of India (ZSI) established in 1916 was assigned the task and responsibility of exploring and determining the faunal wealth of the country. ZSI has been studying the rich and diverse faunal wealth of the country in almost all areas, with respect to taxonomy status, bio-ecological features, bio-geographical pattern of distribution etc.

The inclusion of ZSI under the Minsitry of Environment and Forests in 1981 has enlarged the sphere of its activities, especially in the areas of conservation and protection of rare and endangered animals, the assessment of environmental degradation from the biological viewpoint, and the management of natural resources.

ZSI has conducted studies on wildlife of different regions, sanctuaries and national parks, and population and status surveys of a number of species. It has initiated ecological and environment research to collect baseline data on the characteristic fauna of a biosphere reserve and to gain insight into overall protection and management.

The Forest Survey of India (FSI) came into existence in 1981 as a successor to the Preinvestment Survey of Forest Resources which was established in 1965 with the limited objective of assessing wood and bamboo availability in certain selected industrial catchments. FSI has made several independent assessments of the forest cover in the country by visual interpretation of Landsat imagery. The ground inventories give an indication of the potential productivity of the forests of the country. A digital cartography system installed at the National Forest Data Management Centre, Dehra Dun, facilitates digital processing of remote sensing data.

The barasingha (Cervus duvauceli) was once plentiful in central, northern and eastern India. In 1970 only 66 were left in and around Kanha, in central India. These 66 were the last of their kind, wild or capative. The major reason for this was the progressive reduction in their grassland habitat due to heavy cattle grazing, cultivation and poaching. Fortunately at this point the precarious situation of the Barasingha was realized. In 1969 the Government of Madhya Pradesh, supported by the Government of India, launched the 'Save the Barasingh' campaign. The broad strategy was to regenerate the grasslands and to limit the other factors. Reclaiming areas which were once Barasingha habitat was the first priority. The villages inside were relocated outside the park and cattle grazing was stopped in the park. Later, water bodies wer constructed, which helped to reduce the grazing pressure of other wild herbivores on the Kanha meadows. The tiger baiting sites of Kanha where most of the Barasingha habitat existed were shifted in 1969, and in 1979 tiger baiting was given up altogether.

Anti-poaching measures were also taken up. A 28—hectare enclosure was constructed around a typical Barasingha habitat to ensure the survival of at least a small population of Barasingha in their natural habitat, though in captivity. All these measures proved to be highly satisfactory and the number of Barasingha rose from 66 in 1970 to 547 in 1988.

—The Wildlife Institute of India (WII) is an autonomous institute devoted to the development of wildlife science and to suggesting wildlife management in the field. It trains wildlife biologists through a Master's—programme and also in service foresters at the post graduate diploma level. Its short courses provide conservation orientation to others concerned with land use and management.

Wildlife Institue of India has major research programmes which cover biological management and human aspects of wildlife and biodiversity conservation. The topics and sites conform to national priorities so that findings are helpful in improving management. A notable contribution is by way of a detailed biogeographic classification, an examination of the existing network of protected areas, with suggestions for additional sites in order to fill in the gaps in representative biogeographic coverage. It has a rapidly growing wildlife database which includes information on protected areas, status of major habitat types and main species.

New initiatives include development of landscape level integrated management strategies in areas harbouring protected area clusters, and training in planning of ecodevelopment measures around protected areas. Its training programmes show an upward trend in utilization by countries of the region.

Although the first protected areas in this century were set up in the mid thirties their numbers went up susbtantially in the fifties. The onslaught on natural areas in the fifties and sixties led to gazetting of a large number of new areas in the seventies and eighties. The number reached 75 national parks and 419 sanctuaries, covering 138,000 sq km in 1992.

The need for systematic coverage of the full spectrum of the country's biological diversity in the protected area network was, however, strongly felt. In 1988 the Wildlife Institute of India came up with a biogeographic classification system recognizing 10 zones divided into 25 provinces in which over three hundred landforms were identified. The existing network was then tested for its representativeness vis-a-vis the classification system. Sites were identified to fill the gaps and the suggested network now recommends 148 national parks and 503 sanctuaries covering an area of 151,000 sq km or about 4.6 per cent of the country's geographic area. These suggestions have found extensive support and already the present network covers 75 national parks and 419 sanctuaries, equivalent to about 4 per cent of India's land area.

Tourism is now recognised as an industry generating a number of social and economic benefits. It promotes national integration and international understanding, creates employment opportunities and augments foreign exchange earnings. Tourism also gives support to local handicrats and cultural activities.

International tourism in India has grown substantially over the last three decades. Foreign tourist arrivals including the nationals of Pakistan and Bangladesh during 1994 were 18,86,433 as compared to 17,64,830 during 1993, registering an increase of 6.9 per cent. India's share in the world tourist market at the beginning of the Seventh Plan was 0.39 per cent, and it remained almost the same by the end of the Plan. Foreign exchange earnings from tourism during 1993-94 were provisionally estimated at Rs. 6,509 crore and for 1994-95 at Rs. 7,449 crore. Thus, tourism has become one of the largest foreign exchange earner of the country. With the increase in income levels and emergence of powerful middle class, the potential for domestic tourism has grown substantially during the last few years.

In order to further accelerate the development of tourism in the country, the thrust during the Eighth Five Year Plan on various activities are enumerated as under: (a) development of selected tourist places/areas; (b) diversification from culture-oriented tourism to holiday and leisure tourism; (c) development of trekking, winter sports, wildlife and beach resort tourism; (d) exploring new source markets in regions and countries having cultural affinity; (e) restoration of national heritage projects; (f) launching of national image building and marketing plans in key markets; (g) providing inexpensive accommodation in different tourist centres; (h) improving service efficiency in public sector corporations; and (i) streamlining of facilitation procedures at airports.

The organisations involved in the development of tourism at the Centre are Department of Tourism, Indian Institute of Tourism and Travel Management, National Council for Hotel Management and Catering Technology and Indian Tourism Development Corporation Limited.

The Department of Tourism under the Ministry of Civil Aviation and Tourism is responsible for the formulation and implementation of policies and programmes for the development of tourism within the country and for attracting foreign tourists to India by way of developing tourist infrastructure, publicity and promotion overseas, dissemination of information on tourist places, coordination and supervision of activities of various segments of industry and travel trade such as hotels, trave agencies, tour operators, etc.

There are 20 tourist offices in India, which include four regional offices located at New Delhi, Bombay, Calcutta and Madras. These offices supervise the functioning of other offices at Aurangabad, Goa, Khajuraho, Jaipur, Varanasi, Agra, Patna, Bhubeneswar, Bangalore, Hyderabad, Cochin and Port Blair. there is also a sub-regional tourist office in the north eastern region at Guawahati which supervises the work of tourist offices at Shillong, Imphal and Itanagar. Tourist offices in India and abroad handle tourist equiries, diseeminate tourist information, undertake promotion by means of advertising and publicity, maintain liasion with trade and press. Tourist offices abroad also counter the adverse publicity by the foreign media in respect of various events taking place in India. The feed-back which is received from tourist offices abroad helps in determining the overseas marketing policy of the Government. With the objective of achieving optimum impact, the Department of Tourism and Air India under the operational scheme are engaged in joint promotional efforts in Europe, UK, America, East Asia, West Asia and Australia through 18 tourist offices located in various parts of the world.

The India Tourism Development Corporation (ITDC), a public sector undertaking, was established in October 1966. The activities of the Corporation include:

(a) construction, management and marketing of hotels, restaurants, travellers lodges for tourist at various places in the country; (b) provision of tourist transport facilities; (c) production, distribution and sale of tourist publicity materials; (d) provision of entertainment facilities such as light and sound shows, music concerts, etc; (e) provision of shopping facilities including duty free shops; and (f) provision of consultancy-cum-managerial service in India and aborad.

The Indian Institute of Tourism and Travel Management is an autonomous body set up to impart post-graduate level education in Tourism and Travel Management to meet the demands of professionally trained personnel in the tourism industry. It also organises executive development programmes, seminars and workships relating to tourism and travel management. The Institute has also assisted several universities for running courses at the post-graduate level. The Department of Tourism has accorded high priority to the development of manpower to meet the growing needs of hotels, restaurants and other tourism industries. For this purpose, the Department has set up 31 intitutes of hotel management and catering technology and food crafts in the country. These institutes conduct diploma courses in the fields of hotel management, catering technology and applied nutrition and craft courses in food and beverage services. Food craft institutes conduct craft courses for a duration ranging from six months to one year for operational staff.

In order to encourage adventure tourism, the Department of Tourism has set up a National Institute of Water Spots at Goa and the IISM at Gulmarg. The Indain Institutes of Skiing and Mountaineering conducted five courses at Auli, Patnitop, Gulmarg and Kulu and trained 330 persons during 1994-95. The National Institute of Water Sports conducted 15 courses for 166 participants in various activities, sailing, scuba diving, water skiing, etc. The institutes act as a nodal institute for adventure and sports oriented tourism activities in the country. These assist the state governments in building up tourism infrastructure in water sports and winter sports activities.

Development of tourism is primarily the responsibility of the state governments. However, the Central Department of Tourism extends financial assistance for the augmentation of tourism infrastructural facilities like yatri niwas, tourist lodges, wayside facilities, restaurants, cafeterias, tourist bungalows, etc. In addition, financial assistance is extended for adventure sports activities, tourist transport, tented accommodation, etc. To consolidate the development of tourism infrastructure, 17 circuits/areas have been identified for intensive development. It has been decided to take up five focus centres as 'special tourism areas' for integrated development.

The hotel sector from one of the most important segments of the tourism industry with high potential for employment generation and foreign exchange earnings. To give impetus to this sector, the Government provides tax benefits and other incentives to encourage the hotel industry. The Industrial Policy has now placed the hotels and tourism related activities as a priority industry. Foreign investmet and collaborations are now facilitated under the new economic policy. Upto 51 per cent foreign equity is now granted automatically. Non-resident Indians are allowed cent per cent investment.

Tourism promotion

In recent years, the Indian Railways have shown an interest in assisting and promoting the country's rich tourism industry. A beginning in this direction was made with the introduction of the Palace on Wheels trains on the Rajasthan sector. Now special trains are run to centres of both tourism and pilgrimage. Lately, the private sector has also been invited to aid the tourism efforts of the Indian Railways.

With the Government deciding to open up the economy in a big way, the private sector has been invited to assist the Indian Railways. Two major schemes are "own your wagon" and "build, operate lease and transfer (BOLT)" schemes.

Not every effort of the Indian Railways in improving its performance has been successful. For instance, there continues to be concern over the failure to lure back sufficient goods traffic from the road transport sector. Despite all the measures, the safety record of Indian Railways is not examplary. The woes of ordinary passengers hve not declined to any considerable extent. Despite its excellent work, the research and development activity also need to do better to meet newer callanges. On its own part, the Ministry of Railways continues to pine for higher budgetary support which has dropped to 15 per cent from a high of 75 per cent in the Third Plan, while some of its actions are seen as reckless by economists.

The Indian Railways, however, feel confident of meeting the needs of the 21st century. Its Corporate Plan, for the year 1985-2000 A.D., has outlined seven broad strategies: Optimise investment and improve productivity of assets; upgrade technology; bring down costs by reducing fuel consumption, material costs etc.; adopt cost-based tarrif policy; rehabilitate and maintain assets, particularly track and rolling stock; develop human resource and divest auxiliary activities. Perhaps a pursuit of this strategy might ensure a better ride for the Indian Railways in the next century.

India also started taking part in international tourism events like annual meetings of Pacific Asia

Travel Association, the American Society of Travel Agents, the International Tourism Exchange in Berlin and trade marts. Besides, Indian delegations participating in international conferences on a wide range of disciplines invited these bodies to hold their future meetings in India thereby giving an exposure to the manifold facets of the Indian tourism product.

Until the 70s the accent had been on cultural tourism. It still remains a major draw. At the same time, the need was felt to respond to global trends in tourism preferences by diversifing the roduct. The preferences varied according to age groups, origin of the market and the economic opportunites available at different places. Thus new attractions like beach holidays, wild life viewing, adventure travel and special interest tours were developed. Northern Europe shivering in winter sees a great exodus of holiday makers in search of sun and sand. Most of them used to go to the Mediterranean coast or islands off northern Africa or the Caribbean. For the first time, the Indian beaches at Kovalam, Goa, Mammalapuram, and Puri were marketed. These places used to receive only an occasional visitor from abroad until new facilitations were introduced and publicised. A measure of the progress of beach tourism is that charter flights by the dozen are operating every week to Goa and Kovalam (Kerala). New beaches have also been developed at Bekal, also in Kerala, Diu and Ahmed Mandvi on the Gujarat coast and quite a few resorts in Orissa in the Konark-Puri area.

For the more adventurous, trekking in the mountains as well as river rafting, kayaking and canoeing, skiing and hang gliding are being popularised and these find ever increasing stream of annual visitors. So much so, a section of the travel trade today finds it a profitable business to concentrate on this segment only. In promoting mountains and beaches a new accent is being laid on preservation of environment. And tourists are encouraged only to the limits of carrying capacity of these places. Still, happily the country is so extensively endowed with natural assets that it could welcome many more thousands of nature lovers is another thrust area fast being promoted in hills, islands and other remote areas.

In the wake of economic reforms yet another market segment has been enlarged. This is corporate travel. Investment and other business opportunities presented by the opening up of the Indian economy have set thousands of travellers in industrialised countries on their journey to India. A visible evidence of the spurt in business travel is the high occupancy rate in the classy hotels of metro cities—Delhi, Mumbai, Calcutta, Chennai and Bangalore. There has been an acute shortage of rooms in these places where in the last fifty years since Independence the accommodation sector has grown five hundred times. The position today is that the country is short of 65,000 rooms to reach a goal of 125,000 rooms just four years away when the number of international arrivals is targeted to reach a still modest figure of five million—a far cry from the officially listed 17,000 at the time of Independence.

Arrivals are going up gradually while there is phenomenal expansion in domestic travel. With increase in numbers of people having disposable income, change in life style, holiday outing is becoming a part of life. Destinations for the domestic visitor are no longer limited to pilgrim centres and hill stations. They go to other vacation spots with their families as far away as the Andamans and the Lakshadweep. The introduction of leave travel allowance for millions of employees of the Central and State governments as well as public sector undertakings and also holiday schemes in the private sector have added incentives for leisure time journeys.

To meet the demands of this vast movement of people a series of steps have been taken by the Union Ministry of Tourism as well as State governments. Incidentally, tourism remains a State subject. To encourage investment by entrepreneurs at least 22 States have declared tourism an industry entitling promoters to various tax concessions and other incentives. These are Andra Pradesh, Assam, Bihar, Haryana, Himachal Pradesh, Jammu & Kashmir, Kerala, Madhya Pradesh, Tamil Nadu, Tripura, Karnataka, Uttar Pradesh, Pondicherry, Maharashtra, Mizoram, Arunachal Pradesh, Andaman & Nicobar Islands, Rajasthan, Lakshadweep, Orissa, Chandigarh and West Bengal. The other states too are offering a range of incentives. New destinations are being developed as in Himachal to take the pressure off from places like Shimla and Manali. New products are also being developed like house boats in Kerala backwaters which have become an instant hit with both domestic and foreign tourists.

A National Action Plan for tourism was unfolded in 1992 to cover the development of infra-structure projects as well as promotion. In a follow up, a strategy paper has also been formulated calling for investment in different segments of infrastructure from approach roads to airport development. The private sector will be the major player in this exercise involving an estimated outlay of Rs. 31,000 crore. To promote international tourism new marketing strategies are being studied and enforced as also more international airlines are allowed to operate through India. Most of these carriers see a great future in the Indian market and for that reason want more frequencies and landing rights.

Thus, tourism has come into its own in India. International agencies forecast the Asia-Pacific region as the centerpiece of tomorrow's tourism and India is part of it. It opens up new challenges and opportunities. As part of the ongoing economic liberalisation, foreign investment from 51 to 100 per cent has been allowed in tourism related projects. Nonetheless, for such expanding multidimensional activity new directions and fresh initiatives are constantly called for particularly for up gradation of the product. A central tourism authority with powers to coordinate policy decisions by a multiplicity of agencies at the centre and in the States is called for. Strong political will and commitment is also an imperative for the tourism sector to fulfil the expectations from it.

Sectoral programmes

Both at the central and state level, the Government has initiated and supports many efforts towards capacity-building. The major thrust of development is on the implementation of sectoral programmes, particularly those related to agriculture and allied sectors. Programmes such as the National Rural Employment Programmes (NREP), Rural Landless Employment Guarantee Programme* (IRDP) aim to alleviate rural poverty. Programmes such as Hill Area Development are designed to tackle hostile environmental factors which affect development of certain areas. In the Drought-Prone Areas Programme (DPAP) and Desert Development Programme (DDP), the emphasis is on water and moisture conservation.

India has sovereign rights and jurisdiction in the economic zone extending 200 nautical miles from the coastline. The Government has established a wide-ranging network of legislative and institutional frameworks for protecting and preserving the marine environment.

The programme of the Department of Ocean Development and associated organizations include Development of Coastal Zones and Islands, Monitoring and modelling of the Marine Environment, Control of Marine Pollution, Wave Power Generation, Ocean Modelling, Sea Level Monitoring and Modelling, and Coastal Mapping.

Marine Satellite Information Secvice centres and a multi-institutional Marine Pollution Coastal Ocean Monitoring and Predictive System have been established.

The National Environmental Awareness Campaign (NEAC), which began in 1986, is a major programme of the Ministry of Environment and forests. The programme seeks to increase environmental awareness through the involvement of governmental and non-governmental organizations. Activities under the NEAC include seminars, workshops, rallies, teacher training, eco-clubs, environmental campus etc.

The Ministry of Environment and Forests set up the Environmental Information System (ENVIS) in 1982 as a decentralized system using a network of databases to ensure integration of national efforts in collecting information related to environment. ENVIS has ten centres working in diverse areas such as pollution control, coastal ecology, environmentally sound and appropriate technology etc. It has a documentation service and processes queries from national and international useres. A quarterly abstracting journal Paryavaran Abstracts is published after scanning nearlv five hundred scientific journals. ENVIS maintians a close liaison with other national information systems like National Information System on Science and Technology (NISSAT) and Biotechnology Information System (BTIS).

The Central Arid Zone Research Institute (CAZRI) was set up at Jodhpur in Rajasthan by the Government of India to undertake studies on land, soil water and vegetation resources of arid and semi-arid areas. The Institute carries out studies on precipitation, the regional dynamics of the landscape and the impact of climatic conditions and man-animal activities on it in order to determind the optimal natural plant community of major environments, and to optimize the use of water and land. CAZRI is also involved in transfer of technology, publicity and extension work to create awareness about the desertification process, and to achieve public participation in the development programmes of arid and semi-arid regions.

In the area of formal education, the National Policy on Education (1986) stresses the paramount need to create consciousness about the environment. This must permeate all ages and sections of the society, beginning with the child. The Policy gives unqualified priority to universalization of elementary eduction and substantial improvement in the quality of education. Detailed school mapping exercises have been planned under a master plan for universal provision of facilities for environment education. The National Council of Educational Research and Training (NCERT) has been assigned the responsibility of developing model syllabi and instructional packages in ten core cureicular ares, of which protection of environment is one.

The Ministry of Human Resource Development (MHRD) has taken a major initiative in the field of environment education through the launching of the Environment Orientation to School Education scheme. Under this scheme special cells have been created in the state departments of education. Support is also extended to NGOs to facilitate the development of locale-specific programmes and materials.

The Ministry of Environment and Forests supports two centres of excellence in the area of environmental educationl. These are the Centre for Environment Education, Ahmedabad, and the CPR Environmental

Education Centre, Madras. The Centre for Environment Education, Ahmedabad, is involved in developing innovative programmes and materials to increase awareness about the environment.

The National Museum of Natural History (NMNH), New Delhi, is a unique facility which provides people an opportunity to acquire a direct understanding of the world of nature, the inter relationships among plants, animals, and the environment, and the need to develop a new approach and ethic towards the natural environment. NMNH also has centres at Mysore, Bhubaneshwar and Bhopal.

The Government of India supports research projects for the study of ecosystems and the causes of their degradation. In this regard, two committees—the Environmental Research Committee (ERC) and Man and the Biosphere (MAB) Research Committee function as advisory bodies under the Ministry of Environment and Forests. The research is followed up by formulation of action plans for optimal utilistion of resources leading to sustainable development.

Man and the Biosphere programme is an inter-disciplinary programme of research and training which emphasized and ecological approach to the study of inter-relationships between humans and their environment. The programme aims to provide scientific basis to solve practical problems of resource management through understanding the environmental problems in the ecosystem context.

The Environmental Research Committee addresses problems of chemical, engineering and technological aspects of environmental management, and promotes research in all subjexts concerned with the human environment that are not covered by the MAB programme. ERCs thrust areas include environmental aspects of rural and urban settlemens, resource management, environmental degradation, planning, training and education. It promotes integrated action-oriented programmes which deal not only with research but also its demonstration and extension. Such action-oriented research has been taken up in the Himalayan region, and in the Western and Eastern Ghats, besides multinational project of integrated studies on the Kaveri river.

The Ministry of Environment and Forests has so far supported about 500 environmental research projects in different parts of the country. Of these, about 300 had been completed by March 1990.

The findings of the research projects are published in a departmental publication and also in scientific journals and the popular press. Some of the findings have direct applicability while others contribute to the data base for environmental planning and management.

Various other research organizations set up by the Government and other agencies are concerned with different aspects of evnironment. The physical Research Laboratory (PRL) Ahmedabad, is a premier national centre for research in space and allied sciences; the Indian Institute of Remote Sensing (IIRS), Hyderabad, imparts training in remote sensing techniques and promotes research in areas like thematic mapping of land.

The functions of the Council of Scientific and Industrial Research (CSIR) include institutional financing, awarding fellowships, collecting and disseminating information on research and industrial matters. It has a chain of 39 laboratories and about 80 field centres. From aeronautical products to oceanography, and from drugs to salt and marine chemicals research, CSIR is involved in helping the country enter frontier areas of research. Its centres include the Central Drug Research Institute, Lucknow; National Environmental Engineering Research Institute, Nagpur; Indian National Scientific Documentation Centre, New Delhi; National Chemical laboratory, Pune; Central Institute of Medicinal and Aromatic Plants, Lucknow; Industrial Toxicology Research Centre, Lucknow; Indian Institute of Chemical Technology, Hyderabad; and Central Food Technology Research Institute, Mysore.

Council for Advencement of People's Action and Rural Technology (CAPART), set up in 1986 is the central agency for funding rural development projects of voluntary agencies. It assists voluntary efforts which aim to implement locale-specific rural development projects. Funding for projects coming under several government programmes like the Drought Prone Area programme, Integrated Rural Development Programme etc., are disbursed through CAPART.

CAPART gives financial assistance to registered voluntary organization. Up to 80 per cent of the project expenditure is made available and the remaining has to be raised by the organization for other sources.

The Department of Science and Technology, Government of India, is involved in research and development related to several environmental issues throuhg its institutions.

The Indian Institute of Tropical Meteorology, Pune, is involved in studies of atmospheric ozone, effect of aerosols on climate change, effect of stratospheric changes and anthropogenic activities on climate change, carbon dioxide studies etc.

The Birbal Sahni Institute of Paleobotany, Lucknow, is engaged in paleobotanical research which aims to build up an evlutionary sequence charting the history of modern vegetation. It is also involved in investigating past climates.

The Wadia Institute of Himalayan Geology, Dehra Dun, has been studying various aspects of the chemistry of Himalayan glaciers. It has also conducted studies on the impact of growing human population on the Himalayan ecology.

The Indian institute of Astrophysics, Bangalore, studies solar activity while the Indian Institute of Geomagnetism, Bombay, has a programme for the study of atmospheric and solar terrestrial weather relationships.

The Survey of India, Dehra Dun, is responsible, among other things, for tide gauge observations along the Indian coastline and for the study of anticipated problems of sea-level rise and impact on coastal environment.

The Centre for Atmospheric Studies at the Indian Institute of Technology, New Delhi, studies the effect of aerosols on climate change, air pollution over India, and other related issues.

The Department of Science and Technology is also actively involved in the national efforts of the International Geosphere-Biosphere programme.

The practice of scientific forestry in India dates back to over 120 years. Systamatic research and trainign in foresting commenced nearly 70 years ago. Research and forestry education now come under the purview of the Indian Council of Forestry Research and Education, which conducts its programmes through six regional institutions and a number of universitites and other organizations. Its six regional institutions, including the Forest Research Institute at Dehra Dun which is a premier institution in forestry, carry out extensive field and laboratory research. The Indian Institute of Forest

Management (IIFM) Bhopal, was established in 1982 to meet the growing need for managerial expertise in forestry and allied sectors. The institute also runs management development programmes for in—service managers of forest departments, forest development corporations, forest based industries, financial institutions and voluntary organizations. In addition, the Institute is involved in applied research and provides consultancy service.

Forest management in the field is planned and implemented by the Indian Forest Service (IFS). Two year postgraduate training in forestry is imparted to IFS officers at the Indira Gandhi National Forest Academy, Dehra Dun. There are also three regional State Forest Service colleges and numerous rangers' colleges for training middle level and field professionals.

NGOs in India have played a vital role in raising awareness about the issues related to environment and development, and in mobilizing people to take action. They have employed a variety of techniques and media. The Kerala Sastra Sahitya Parishat, which was the catelytic agency involved in mobilizing public opinion agaisnt the Silent Valley hydroelectric project, uses traditional and folk media to communicate its messages. The Centre for Science and Environment (CSE), New Delhi, has brought out three widely circulated volumes on the state of India's environment, in addition to several other publication. CSE has also played a key role in bringing in the South perspective in International discussions of environment and development issues. Eklavya, Bhopal, develops innovative and relevant school programmes and material. The Assam Science Society which has a membership of professional and students, attempts to enhance science education.

The Narmada Bachao Andolan has brought together

scattered voices of protest against the damming of the river Narmada and has raised awarness not only in the affected area and in the rest of India, but alos among the international community. The Vivekanand Kendra, Tamil Nadu, trains hundreds of workers in the fields of health, education and development. A major focus of its activities is in Arunachal Pradesh where it runs 14 residential schools for tribal children. The People's Commission on Environment and Development, New Delhi, is a forum creatd to bring together and articulate citizen's concerns to put before the UNCED. Kalpavriksh, New Delhi, organizes awareness programmes and carries out campaigns on specific issues by lobbying, holding demonstrations and fighting legal cases.

The Ministry of Environment and Forests has instituted a number of awards to recognize outstanding contributions of individuals and organizations in various environment related endeavours.

National Awards for Prevention and Control of Pollution have been instituted to recognize the achievements of industries for their contribution in the prevention and control of pollution.

Indira Priyadarshini Vrikshmitra Awards are given to individuals and organizations for outstanding work in the field of afforestation and wastelands development.

Indira Gandhi Paryavaran Puraskar is awarded to either an individual or organization for contribution in the field of environment.

Pitamber Pant National Fellowship recognizes excellence in research in any branch of environmental science.

The Centre for Mining Environment at Dhanbad (Bihar) was establised in 1987 by the Ministry of environment and Forests to generate scientific data for sustainable mining in the country. The Centre conducts postgraduate and doctoral level courses, as well as training programmes for in service professionals. Research areas include land use management, noise and vibration problems in mining areas, air pollution in fire areas and its effects on health.

Remote sensing for survey of resources is carried out by India's earth observation satellite system, the IRS series of satellites. Projections of crop yields, land-use mapping, monitorin of forest cover and biomass, identification of agro-climatic zones are today possible, and provide a basis for micro-level planning. Drought monitoring on a real time basis is also becoming possible, as is the use of remote sensing for mitigating damage due to floods. Detailed remote sensing surveys have also helped to considerably narrow down areas for groundwater exploration. Satellite based glacier inventory of the Himalayan states has been found promising for planning and operating mini and micro hydroelectric stations.

Fishers prospect charts, derived from satellite monitoring of sea surface temperature anamolies, are in regular use. Remote sensing has also been used extensively for forest mapping, in India. It is through this that a correct picture of the extent of forest cover and the relative changes in it have been obtained.

The National Natural Resource Management System of the Ministry of Environment and Forests involves utilization of remote sensing technology for accurate inventory of resources such as land, water, forests, minerals, ocean, etc., and to utilize this information for monitoring changes in ecological systems.

The objective of all development is to add to the economic well-being of the people so that their standard of living can be improved. Development projects are, therefore, taken up to convert the natural resources into right at the inception stage to prevent the erosion of the resouces base itself. Impact assessment is a handy tool to assess the environmental compatibility of the projects in terms of their location, suitability of technology, efficiency in resource utilisation and recycling etc. Impact assessment was introduced in 1978 and now covers almost all major projects.

At present environmental impact assessment is being done for the following types of project: (a) (i) river valley; (ii) thermal power; (iii) mining; (iv) industries; (v) atomic power; (vi) rail, road, highways, bridges; (vii) ports and harbours; (viii) airport; (iv) new towns and (x) communication projects, (b) projects which require approval of the Public Investment Board/Planning Commission/Central Electricity Authority; (c) projects referred to the Ministry of Environment and Forests by other ministries; (d) projects which are sensitive and located in environmentally degraded areas; (e) public sector undertakings of the Centre where the project cost is more than Rs. 50 crore. A notification has been issued in January 1994 which makes Environmental Impact Assesement statutory for 29 categories of developmental projects under various sectors such as industrial, mining, irrigation, power, transport, tourism, communication, etc. The notification contains details aimed at rationalising and standarding the procedure for environmental clearance. Extensive delegations to the stae governments are also provided in this notification. An amendment to this notification stipulates inter alia that all applications complete in every material aspect have to be examined and decision conveyed to the applicants within 30 days in the case of site clearances and 120 days in the case of environmental clearnce of projects. Once an application has been submitted by project authority the preliminary scrutiny of the project is done by the respective technical divisions and the overall appraisal of the projects is undertaken by specially constituted environmental appraisal committees of experts. In addition, special groups/committees and task forces are constituted as and when needed for expert inputs on major projects. After a detailed scrutiny and assessment, the appraisal committee makes its recommendation for approval or rejection of the projects. Depending on the nature of the project, certain safeguards are recommended. For monitoring and timely implementation of safeguards suggested, six regional centres have been set up by the Ministry at Shillong, Bhubaneswar, Chandigarh, Bangalore, Lucknow and Bhopal.

Under the Forests (Conservation) Act, 1980 diversion of forest land for non-forest purpose requires prior approval from the Central Government. While proposals involving forest land less than 20 hectare can be decided by the state forest departments, proposals involving more than that are appriased by the Advisory Committee of the Ministry, constituted under the Forests (Conservation) Act, 1980 as amended in 1988.

When a project requires both environemental and forest clearance, the proposals are simultaneously processed under the Single Window Celearance Scheme. All cases with complete environmental data and action plans are decided within three months. In the case of diversion of forest land, the decision is taken within six months.

Major environmental impacts of river vally projects which need consideration are: (i) degradation of catchment areas; (ii) command area development; (iii) rehabilitation of those affected; (iv) incresed incidence of water-borne diseases; (v) reservoir induced seismicity; and (vi) deforestation and loss of flora and fauna including gene-pool reserves.

Major environmental impacts of mining operations are: (i) degradation of land; (ii) pollution of surface and ground water resources; (iii) pollution of air; (iv) deforestation including loss of flora and fauna; (v) rehabilitation of affected populationincluding tribals; and (vi) impact on historical monuments and religious places. A major component of the mining operations in India is the opencast mining which severely affects land use pattern. Mining operations have serious adverse impact on the growth of vegetation and general landscape. Minerals extracted interact with surface and ground water thus polluting the water resources. Loss of top-soil due to deforestation also depletes ground water resources and results in drying up of perennial sources like springs and streams especially in hill areas.

Major environmental impacts of thermal power projects include; (a) air pollution; (b) water pollution; (c) deforestation; (d) rehabilitation; and (e) land degradation. Flue gases emerging from stacks containing sulphur dioxide, oxides of nitrogen, carbon monoxide, etc., are detrimental to human beings and vegetation. Water pollution from thermal stations can due to release of slurry which is a mixture of flyash and water. Thermal pollution is due to release of cooling water which can affect acquatic life. Solution to disposal of ash problem is in its recycling by converting it into building blocks and its use in other construction works. Another step which helps in abating pollution cuased by ash is stabilisation of ash dumps through suitable vegetation.

Major environmenal impacts of industrial projects include (i) are pollution; (ii) water pollution; and (iii) disposal and utilisation of solid waste. Impacts of projects in specific areas are examined in great detail and suitable control measures suggested. Linkages of project requirements to utilisation of resources in an optimal way is an essential pre-requisite. Concept of recycling, reuse and adoption of clean technologies is increasingly becoming predominant.

Projects considered under the transport sector include laying of railway lines, roads and bridge construction, airport construction and establishing of ports and harbours. The environmental parameters affected by the transport projects have been classified into (i) natural physical resources; (ii) natural ecological resources; (iii) human/economic development resources; and (iv) quality of life values including aesthetic and cultural values. Adverse impacts on above environmental parameters are to be identified and mitigation measures provided for to offset such impacts.

Under the Environment (Protection) Act, 1986, a notification on Coastal Zone Regulation has been issued declaring coastal stretches of seas, bays, estuaries, creaks, rivers and backwater within 500 meter of High Tide line as Coastal Regulation Zones. Setting up of new industries or expansion of existing industies except those directly related to waterfront, manufacturing, handling, storage or disposal of hazardous substances and setting up and expansion of units/mechanisms for disposal of wastes and effluents etc., are prohibited in these Costal Regulation Zone. All the seven coastal states are required to prepare coastal management plans which would provide protection to ecologically fragile coastal areas rich in biological diversity and provide for land use zoning. The Coastal Regulation Zone notification, 1991, has been amended.

In nuclear power plants, safety from radiation during the operation of the plants and after, and disposal of nuclear wastes are of prime concern. Major environmental impacts of nuclear power projects which need consideration are; (i) radio-active contamination of air, water and soil; (ii) thermal pollution due to discharge of cooling water; (iii) deforestation and loss of flora and fauna; (iv) rehabilitation; and (v) radio-active waste disposal. Exposure to radio-active radiations in excess of the prescribed limits are detrimental to human beings, aquatic life, flora and fauna. The long half life periods for radio-active decay necessitate sealing of the reactor vessel and components for a dormant period of about 30 years after decommissioning of the plant.

Indira Gandhi Nahar Project in Rajasthan, though completed partially has rejuvenated the economy of the Thar desert region by improving the living conditions and brining prosperity. The completed stage I of the project provided irrigation and drinking water and raising the annual agricultural production to the level of Rs. 800 crore. Consumption of fertilizers and modern cultivation methods result in the per hectare yield of 1820 kg. of cotton and 1810 kg. of ground nut, which are the highest in the country.

The conversion of desert land into fertile land has led to phenomenal appreciation in land value and the widespread green fields is the growing indication of visible prosperity. A number of mandies have sprung up facilitating disposal of farm produce. A large number of agro based industaries have come up and allied activities like opening of banks, insurance companies, warehouses, chilling plants etc. are indications of development and growing employment opportunities.

At present the stage II of the canal is under construction. The main canal comprising 649 km was completed in 1986, including 256 km in stage II. On completion of 5780 km of distribution system and five lift canals by the year 2005, a further area of 13.16 lakh ha will be brought under irrigation.

The Indira Gandhi Nahar Project (formerly) known as Rajasthan Canal Project) was conceived by Rajasthan to utilise its share of surplus Ravi-Beas waters, with the objective of improving the living conditions in the Western Desert region of Rajasthan. After the inter-state agreement of 1955 regarding allocation of Ravi-Beas waters, the project report was first formulated and submitted in 1957 for an estimated cost of Rs.66.43 crore. The first revision of the project was done in 1963, evisaging construction of the entire project in two stages, stage I and stage II.

A sum of Rs.1425 crore has already been spent in canal construction since 1958, out of which three hundred crore area on stage I. According to official sources the total estimate expenditure of 1993 constant prices is going to be Rs. 2600 crore, whereas it will be Rs. 3522 crore incuding escalation when the project is completed in the year 2005.

Any project of such a big dimension having multipurpose objectives cannot be free from problems and Indira Gandhi Canal is not an exception.

The allotment and sale of land in the command area is being governed by Rajasthan Colonisation (allotment and sale of government land in Rajasthan canal colony area) Rules, 1975. The policy has laid down certain priorities for allotment of land. In stage, an area of 6.66 lakh has and in stage II, 2.58 lakh has been alloted so far. More than one lakh families have been benefited.

Twelve hundred cusecs of drinking water is earmarked for use in stage I (300 cusecs) and stage II (900 cusecs). The State government has so far implemented schemes to supply water to 40 villages in Jodhpur district, 30 villages in Jaisalmer district and 140 villages in Churu district. The Kanwar Sain Lift irrigation Scheme is already providing drinking water to about 180 villages. The Jodhpur water supply scheme which has been completed is to provide 10.6 cusecs of water to 158 villages and 80 cusecs to Jodhpur town.

There has been a constant demand of funds for this project. Being a project of inter state nature, this has acquired national importance. One of the reasons for delayed completion of the project is lack of funds. The Government of India has been liberally assisting the project since the Seventh Plan under various programmes. Under the Border Area Development Programme an amount of Rs. 254 crore has been provided since the beginning of Seventh Plan. The Government of India has assured continued assistance for an early completion of the project. The Rajasthan government too is making substantial plan provision so that the project does not have financial constraints. The Indira Gandhi Nahar Project all these years has not received any financial assistance from World Bank or any other international financing agency.

The project once completed in the year 2005, will improve household income and expenditure structure by bringing substantial changes in attitude and life style of people.

Afforestation, horticulture, pasture,l agro forestry are the areas which will attract huge investment. Innovative scientific and technology inputs for irrigation, production technology growing of commercial and pharmaceutical crops, coming of agro based processing units are going to be the predominant field of growth.

The State government is making sufficient provisions for Command Area Development Works in stage II, which were commenced in VII Plan.

Once stage II of the project is completed, it is going to yield immense benefits to the economy of the region. An additional irrigation in 9.64 lakh has yielding an annual agricultural production of the value of Rs. 2200 crore, making available drinking water for 14.0 million of human population and big stock of cattle besides bringing an area 3.62 lakh ha under afforestation are going to be the laudable achievements of this project. Alongwith meeting the requirements of human beings, making available fooder for 5.2 million herd of cattle and generating employment are the other benefits which will accure. It is estimated that direct employment to five lakh people will be provided. The rejuvenation resources, establishment of large number of industries, and thus being an allround socio-economic development of the region.

Though there was no uniform pattern of outlay and investment, it is evident that the performance of social forestry programme in terms of investment (as a proportion to targeted amount) was fairly high, largely due to the devaluation of the Indian rupee but, there was a sharp decline in terms of investment (both in absolute terms and as a proportion of targeted amount) between 1992-94 reflecting the resource crunch on the part of the government and a lack of interest in the scheme.

The basic feature of the scheme being to plant seldings where CPRs were available, afforestation was carried out in the State on different categories of land.

Since the commencement of the programme, the Karnataka Forest Department has brought a larger area under this scheme. Up to the end of 1993-94, 50,234 ha of land were planted under different models. A major proportion of this was achieved under the World bank sponsored programme in the first two phases. After the end of the World Bank sponsorship, the State continued the scheme. It is too early to judge whether the State government would be able to carry on the programme effectively considering the fact that there was a drastic cut in the investment during 1992-94. Whatever amount was spent during this period has mostly gone to maintenance of the existing plantation rather planting new area. Of the total plantations raised under various categories of land (for which the data is available category wise up to 1991-92), the C&D lands account for the largest area with 16,291 ha, closely followed by Gomal land (11,383 ha) and tank foreshore (7,669 ha). Though a large area was under the component of C&D lands, it still fell short of the targeted area. The same is the case with other categories of land. According to an estimate, up to 1989-90, the total area available for development of forest was 499, 498 ha (Wasteland Development in Karnataka). Out of this, only 50,234 ha wre covered by trees which account for only six per cent of the available potential.

It is also significant to note that in the first phase of the scheme (1983-84 to 1987-88) aided by World Bank and ODA, annually about 5,703.33 ha of land were brought under plantation. However, a fairly sharp decline in the area brought under plantations during the II (in spite of devaluation effect) and III phases (during which the State government took on itself the responsibility of financing the SFP) reflects on the government dependence on the agency funds (though the government claims that a huge portion of the funds has to be spent towards maintaining the existing plantations and hence the decline in the fresh area brought under plantations).

In Katnataka, 13 villages spread over a few districts were selected for the study. In each village, a structured questionnaire was employed at different levels. Information was also collected through informal discussions with village elders, village-level officers and through our own observation.

It was observed that most people in Karnataka were not aware of the SFP. All that they knew vaguely was that the Forest Department had planted some trees on the village commons and the villagers were not allowed to graze their livestock in the enclosed lands; and the efforts of the forest officials in enducating the people on the importance of social forest through displaying billboards in some strategic points have had little impact on them.

Before taking up common lands for regeneration, the government felt the need for setting up Village Social Forestry Committee (VSFC) consisting of members drawn from different sections of society. The VSFC was conceived as a link between the Forest Department and the local community. The committee was to be responsible for all decisions—from identification of plantation sites to laying down of norms for the distribution of usufructs.

It was also envisaged to make the social forestry scheme a community-based one, as the success of revival of CPRs depended to a large extent on the co-operation of the people.

But it was noticed that there were problems in the formation and composition of VSFCs. In most of the sample villages, the VSFC was not formed before undertaking the plantation work. In Karnataka, of the 13 sample villages, only a couple of them—Siddapura in Chitradurga district and Bathsandra in Tumkur district—had VSFC formed before start of the work. In Siddapura, a non-government organization—Taralabalu Rural Development Foundation (TRDF)—managed to form a VSFC thanks to the head of the community and involved the village community in the development of the plantation right from the beginning. But in Bathsandra, the VSFC existed only on paper with hardly any meeting convened during the year. In one village, Chilkur in Hassan district, Efforts made by the Deputy Conservator of Forests to form a VSFC failed due to sheer indifference on the part of the Zilla Parishad and the village leaders concerned.

We are faced with a sort of paradoxical situation in that though recent trends indevelopment administration are ine favour of strengthening democratic institutions at the grass roots level for ensuring sustainable development, it was observed that in the sample villages in Karnataka, people were against inclusion of Mandal Panchayat members or other politicians as members of the VSFC because this wuld, as they perceived, politicize the institution. Further, some of the committee members were generally not interested in implementing the programme. Inclusion of politicians in VSFCs, belated formation of VSFCs and the indifferent attitude of the members have, to some extent, affected the effective management of the SFP in the State.

It is also observed that the Forest Department has initiated efforts to hand over the forests raised under the SFP to decentralized governments for maintenance, so that they can get a substantial portion of income when the forest produce is harvested. But many Panchayats have not come forward to take up the responsibility as maintenance requires some expenditure which they claim is difficult to bear, as they always face a 'resource crunch.'

In Karnataka, in the absence of VSFCs barring a couple of villages, forest officials did not consult local people in choosing plantation sites and seedlings to be raised on the proposed plantations. The reasons advanced by the forest officials were that there was the possibility of the people objecting to such an idea on the ground that they might lose access to common lands for graxing livestock and for collecting fodder, firewood, etc. The forst officials also felt that private encroachers might go to court for redressal thereby delaying the project. Such fears on the part of the forest officials led the villagers to think that their common lands were being taken away the Forest Department. In this ironical situation, community participation in CPR development suffered a set-back.

Normally the VSFC at its meeting passes resolution requesting Social Forestry authorities to undertake plantation on common lands. But, it was observed that indoing so, the VSFCs allocated sites far away from habitation and devoid of access to water source. Since achievement of the target was the main driving force, big plots were selected rather than appropriate ones. Here again care was seldom taken to look into the soil suitable or environmental problems.

Enroachment of common lands was found to be quite high in the sample villages of the State. Of the 4.654 acres of of CPRs available across the sample villages, the poor people had encroached on about 525 acres (accounting for about 11.3 per cent of the total available CPRs), while the rich had enroached on about 1,220 acres (about 26.2 per cent). As the common lands belong to the village community, the big farmers who usually wield considerable influence over village affairs by virtue of their position in society, encroached on these lands as if it was their natural right. The small and marginal farmers also encroached on these lands as they provided foood to them. The efforts of forest officials to evacuate the encroachers met with little success. Thus privatization of CPRs reflected a total lack of societal responsibility to protect what was common property.

The massive plantation scheme has posed a big problem to the village community in general and the

IRDP beneficiaries in specific as they are not allowed to graze their large and small runinants on the plantation areas at least in the first three to four years. Faced with a scarcity of grazing lands, the villagers are forced to graze their livestock on these plantation areas (in the initial years of plantation) resulting in the destruction of saplings and frequent quarrels between the rural community and the forest authorities.

Forest officials allow people to collect loppings and dry twigs from plantations after a certain stage of growth. However, it was brought to the notice of the research team that most of the housedolds were not allowed by the forest officials to collect dried tops from the plantation areas. When the issue was discussed with the officials, they came out with the observation that the people felled trees illegally while collecting dried leves, lops and tops from the plantations. In some sample villages in Karnataka, people belonging to SCs/STs brought toour notice that just because they belonged to lower castes, they were not allowed to collect even fodder from the plantation areas. (This needs further probing).

One of the objectives of the Social Forestry Programme was to provide employment to rural people during off-season. But observations in coastal and Maland Karnataka reveal that though there was substantial labour force available in rural areas, it was not enough to meet the needs of plantation work during critical periods as most labourers would be busy in agricultural operations, demand for which being very high during rainy season. To carry out plantation work during he rainy season, therefore, it was necessary to bring in workers from neighbouring areas and this invited objection from the local community. Thus overlapping of social forestry activities and agricultural operations defeated the very purpose of providing employment to the local people. On the contrary, the farmers in southern Karnataka expressed that their agricultural operations would get affected due to SFP. They say that under the scheme, several local rural agricultural labourers were employed for the purpose of digging poits, boundary trenches, planting of seedings, weeding and maintenance of forestry. This type of work isusually carried out during the rainy season. The higher wage rate offered by the Forest Department for plantation operations attracts local labourers. This has considerably affected the agricultural operations during the sowing and weeding season. The scarcity of labour during the sowing season not only forced some of the farmers to go in for other crops which require less labour input but also force them to switch over from labour-intensive crops to labour saving crops. This may be one of the reasons for the declining trend in investment in agriculture. (See Business Standard, December 30, 1994). In this kind of controversial situation, it is difficult to say whether the villagers are benefited by the programme or not. Therefore, an in-depth study is required to explore further.

Removal of silt and sand from tank-bed plantations by villagers is causing soil erosion and withering of trees. Sand and limestone are carried away by people, mostly for house construction and pot-making. Even government agencies take sand to fill up seepages and breaches in other places. In hillock plantations, government as well as private parties remove blocks of granite.

The village social forestry workers and plantation watchers ae the bridge between officials and local people. They interact closely with village people and as such there is greater scope for spreading the message of social forestry to all the villages thrugh them. But unfortunately, the drop-outs among them are more as the nature of the job is temporary and very tiresome.

It was observed that massive planting operation was carried out wherever wasteland was available. The roadsides have been extensively used for raising various species such as eucalyptus, subabul and most of tank foreshores have been planted with Acacia Nilotica as it has the capacity to survive prolonged drought conditions and prolonged submersion. Although these species may have solved, to some extent, the problem of firewood and small timber to the local people, such amicro help is inadequate in a growing society; perhaps people could have benefited to a large extent if the Forest Department had planted fruit-bearing species such as mango and tamarind on a large scale along with other species.

7

Recent Environmental Concerns

In a wide spectrum of industry and agriculture and the entire gamut of services, there has been great progress in the country during the post-Independence era. The growth in several sectors have indeed been spectacular and in several others it has been modest while in a few others outright dismal. On Monday, 10 November 1996, the foundation stone for the automobile plant of the Hyundai Motor Company of South Korea, was laid at Irungattukottai, some 40 km from Chennai. The plant involves an outlay of $ 700 million (around Rs. 2500 crore) in the first phase; and another $ 400 million (around Rs. 1440 crore) in the second phase. A production capacity of around 100,000 passenger cars in the 1300 cc-1500 cc range is envisaged. The first car is expected to roll out of the assembly line by October 1998. Most importantly, HMC promises a 70 per cent indigenous content from the first car. Which means prospects for dozens of additonal collaboration arrangements and investments for the production of components. At full production, the turnover of HMC will be in the region of Rs. 6000 crore.

This is the third mega investment in the automobile sector involving outlays exceeding Rs. 1500 crore each. The other two relate to the Mahinndra-Ford India Ltd. project to produce passenger cars of similar capacity and in same medium segment; and by Ashok Leyland Ltd., planning to invest on facilities to expand capacity to 100,000 commercial vehicles.

In recent months total investments promised in Tamil Nadu exceed Rs. 5000 crore–an outlay that perhaps exceed all investments made on new projects in the first instance all through the past 50 years.

In all these areas, and in a wide spectrum of industry and agriculture and the entire gamut of services, there has been great progress through the years of Independent India. The growth in several sectors have indeed been spectacular and in several others, it had been modest; and in a few others outright dismal. The bench-making has been done both in regard to the potential offered by India and by developments in several other countries which started on industrialisation much later than we did. South Korea offers a ready example.

In looking at growth, over the last five decades, we can segment these into five distinct phase that roughly correspond with decennial slots.

India has made rapid strides in industrialization, and today is one of the ten most industrialized nations of the world. But industrialization, as in the rest of the world, has brought with it unwanted and unanticipated consequences. These include unplanned urbanization, pollution and risk of accidents. Industrialization moreover not only affects the immediate environment, but has consequences for a larger region whose resources get intimately tied to new industrial development.

Yet as the country continues to industrialize and new plants come up, some of the underlying issues remain. Dirty industries continue moving South. Hazardous chemicals are dumped or brought for reprocessing to developing countries. Often, in developed countries, different values are attached to human life in the North and in the South. Different standards are applied, and processes and factories being discarded in developed countries get relocated in the developing ones.

The Bhopal disaster, when methyl isocyanate crept into the houses of sleeping residents on the morning of 3 December, 1984, killing over 3,000 people and maiming countless others for life, brought many of these issues into sharp focus. It was a tragic testimony of just how much could go wrong. The hazardous side of industry became painfully apparent to countless people in India and abroad. It questioned location policies, safety requirements of industries, the responsibilities of North-based multinational corporations, the preparedness for dealing with disasters, citizens' right to know about the industrial process and the risks involved.

Near the industries, water and air pollution problems are very serious. Water pollution not only affects surface water but also groundwater. It is estimated that 70 per cent of India's surface water is seriously polluted and 80 per cent of the population does not have access to safe drinking water. For instance in Patancheru in Andhra Pradesh, over 60 factories—most of them chemical units—discharge their toxic wastes into freshwater streams. In Bichhri in Rajasthan, chemical effluents from textile and chemical industries pollute the waters of rivers and wells. The health impact of such cases is serious and the incidence of cancer, lung and skin diseases, and deformities is high in these areas. While they are restricted in extent, air pollution levels are high in industrial areas. For instance the average levels of particulate matter in the four metropolitan cities exceeds 360 mg/m while the WHO standard is 150 mg/m.

Another concern relates to occupational health incertain industries. Asbestosis, byssinosis and pneumo-noconiosis are some of the occupational diseases reported. Silicosis has been reported in mines and other industries.

Several central and state statues, such as the Industrial Development Act, the Labour Acts, the Factories Act and the Municipal Acts have environmental provisions in them. However it was the enactment of the Water (Prevention and Control of Pollution) Act, 1974, and the Air (Prevention and Control of Pollution) Act, 1981, which made these environmental factors the principal object of legislation. The Bhopal tragedy caused a surge in environmental legislation and an umbrella Environment (Protection) Act was passed in 1986. This covers hazardous activities in addition to pollution.

Under the Environment (Protection) Act, 1986, the Central Government is responsible for laying down procedures and safeguards for handling hazardous substances. Rules have been made for the manufactures, storage and import of hazardous chemicals, their management and handling, as well as for the manufacture, use, import and storage of micro-organisms and genetically engineered organisms. Radioactive waste disposal is controlled through a regulatory board managed by the Bhabha Atomic Research Centre. The Government has also established a Central Crises Group Alert System with a control room at New Delhi to deal with major chemical accidents in the country.

Many industries and large projects need environmental clearance. The State Pollution Control Boards monitor industrial areas. The Government of India has made it mandatory to assess the environmental impact of new large undertaking in the country. The impact assessment covers not only air, water and soil polluiton, but also damage to historical monuments, wildlife, forests, and to natural resources in general. Unique to India is the recently enacted Mandatory Public Liability Insurance which makes it imperative for units dealing with hazardous substances to take insurance cover against damage to health or property of the community in the vicinity of the industry.

Industrial location policy is a crucial element in determining the impact of industry on the environment. Unplanned industrial growth has in some cases led to industrail conglomerates and urban sprawl. This has often led to prime agricultural and forest land being diverted for urban and industrial use. Near forests, urban areas have led to deforestation. For certain industries, a two-stage clearance procedure has been adopted by the Ministry of Environment and Forests, considering the site specific nature.

While legislation today has enabled authorities to step in, this alone cannot lead to improved environment in and around industries. For this to happen public awareness, as well as awareness and concern among the decision-makers is required. Where people have been consicous they have protested and not let polluting industries spoil their environment. Where industries have been conscious they have got together and taken initiatives for effluent treatment. A typical example of joint efforts by industry in the safe disposal of effluents is the Baroda Effluent Channel in Gujarat, managed by the Gujarat Industrial Development Corporation.

There is urgent need to create widespread awareness. Towards this end the Ministry of Environment and Forests has made a beginning by introducing a scheme for an Ecomark to lable environm-ent-friendly products. NGOs too have several programmes to create environmental consciouness. School programmes to involve students in environmental quality monitoring have begun.

But finally environmental factors will only be taken into account where alternatives are availabel. Today with Indai opening up its economy to greater internationl participation in the industrialization of the country, it si important to ensure that the best and cleansest technologies are available for htis growth, so that industrialization occurs with the minimum of negative consequences.

In accordance with the prevailing thinking, the First Five year Plan stated that the objective of industrial planning was to make good the deficiencies in production of key industrial items and to initiated development, which would enable cumulative expansion of such basic production. There was better appreciation in the First Plan of the need for coordination of industrial planning with the formulation of other economic policies, such as customs and excise tariff structure, import and export policy, investment and technology policy and monetary and financial policy. The Second Plan and later plans have been encreasingly concerned with the allocation of public resources and much less with indications and policies to direct the whole economy indesired directions.

The Industrial Policy Statement of 1973, inter alia, identified high-priority industries where investment from large industrial houses and foreign companies would be permitted. The Industrial Policy Statement of 1980 focussed attention on the need for promoting competition in domestice market, technological upgradation and modernisation. The policy laid the foundation for an increasingly competitive export base and for encouraging foreign investment in high priority technology areas. This found expression in the Sixth Five Year Plan, which emphasised the need for productivity to be the central concern in all economic and production activities.

Nevertheless the sector continued to provide the thrust for the development of heavy industries. In critical areas such as power, railways, coal, petroleum, steel and fertilisers, the public sector has been intensely involved in setting the pace of development. Apart from public investments in basic industry and infrastructure, the expansion of the private sector in line with Plan objectives and priorities were greatly facilitated by financial institutions. An elaborate network of specialised development banking institutions with the Industrial Development Bank of India at the apex was established to help finance industrial investment in the private sector. These institutions, numbering over 50, have become the major source of long-term finance for the corporate sector.

As the statement on Industrial Policy, 1991 says, "These policies created a climate for rapid industrial growth in the country. Thus on the eve of the Seventh Five year Plan, a broad-based infractructure had been built up. Basic industries had been established. A high degree of self-reliance in a large number of items–raw materials, intermediates, finished goods—had been achieved. New growth centres of industrial activity had emerged, as had a new generation of entrepreneurs. A large number of engineers, technicians and skilled workers has been trained."

The Sixth Plan had achieved augmentation of new capacity more or less in consonance with the targets in alarge number of insdustries including, among others, aluminium, zinc, lead thermoplastics, yarn, petrochemical intermediates, electrical equipment, cement and consumer durables. However shortfall in production had taken place in some basic industries, such as steel, cement, non-ferrous metals, fertilisers and certain other industries, including textiles, jute manufactures, sugar, drugs and pharmaceuticals, commercial vehicles and railway wagons. Production targets were exceed in a few industries like machine toos, passenger cars, motor cycles and scooters, consumer electronics and communication equipment. Domestic imbalances resulting from shortfalls in production hasd to be corrected through imports of essential commodities, like steel, cement, fertilisers and sugar.

A technological thrust was given during the Plan period in certain industries in the engineering sector. The first 500 MW thermal generating unit was commissioned and the manufacture of 500 MW turbo generators and boilers had commenced. There has been a systematic upgradation of production technology for other equipment, needed by the power sector. The manufacture of equipment for 1350 tonnes per day fertiliser units and blast furnaces of 3200 cubic metres capacity for steel plants was being undertaken in the country. A strong base had been laid for the rapid development of the electronics sector.

The Seventh Plan recognised the need to consolidate on these strengths and to take initiatives to prepare Indian industry to respond effectively to the emerging challenges. A number of policy and procedural changes which were introduced in 1985-86 aimed at increasing productivity, reducing costs and improving quality. Production capacity restrictions on the industries were gradually reduced and broad banding, which enabled a manufacturer to choose and produce any product mix which suited him in the context of the prevailing market conditions was introduced. In 1986, as against a policy of re-endorsement of existing capacity, the scheme of minimum economic scale of production was introduced with Letters of Intent prescribing a minimum economic size for a single unit. The accent was on opening the domestic market to increased competition and readying the industry to stand on its own in the face of international competition. The public sector was freed from a number of constraints and given a large measure of autonomy. The technological and managerial modernisation of industry was pursued as the key instrument for increasing productivity and improving competitiveness in the world.

As a result of the policies pursued since Independence, the long term trend of industrial growth for over forty years since 1950 is a trend annual growth of just over 6 per cent. This, says rakesh MOhan in an essay in Bimal Jalan's book on Indian Economy, "is quite an achievement, given the magnitude of distortions built into the system." He divides the growth record into three distinct periods: 7.7 per cent annual growth over the first three plan periods (1950-1965), four per cent annual growth over the holiday (1966-69) and the Fourth and Fifth Plan periods (1969-79), and finally the recovery to about 7.7 per cent growth over the Sixth and Seventh periods.

The period 1966-1980, says Mohan is effectively the dark period for Indian economy. This period encompassed a number of exogenous shocks: the devastating three-year drought of 1965-68, the aftermath of increased defence espenditures resulting from 1962 was with China and two wars with Pakistan, the oil price shocks of 1973 and 1979, and the downturn in the availability of foreign resources. During this period, the Indian economy was constantly struggling to adjust.

As a result of policy changes, the composition of Indian industry had undergone great transformation. At Independence, the consumer goods industry accounted for almost half of all industrial production. In 1991 such industries accounted for only about 20 per cent. In contrast, capital goods production was less than 4 per cent of total industrial production. In 1991, it had gone up to 24 per cent. Similarly basic goods share had increased from 20 per cent to 40 per cent.

Metals and minerals

India is richly endowed with minerals. Under the Constitution, minerals rights and the administration of mining laws are vested in the state governments. The Centre, however, regulates the development of minerals under the Mines and Minerals (Regulation and Development) Act, 1957 and the rules and regulations framed under it. This Statute empowers the Centre to formulate rules for: (i) the grant of prospecting licences and mining leases for schedule minerals, (ii) the conservation and development of minerals., and (iii) the modification of old leases. The Act, came into force on 1 June 1958. Amendments to this Act were made in 1972, 1986, and 1994.

Principal mineral found in the country along with their estimated reserves are given below.

Coal is India's largest mineral resource and presently India is the fifth largest producer of coal in the world. Vast deposits of coal of Gondwana formations occur in West Bengal, Orissa, Bihar, Madhya Pradesh, Andhra Pradesh, Uttar Pradesh and Maharashtra. It also occurs in tertiary formation in Assam, Arunachal Pradesh, Meghalaya and Nagaland. Total known reserves of all types of coals in Gondwana and tertiary coalfields estimated stands at 192 billion tonnes. Out of these, reserves of prime-coking coal have been estimated at 5.3 billion tonnes. Total reserves of lignite stands at 6.5 billion tonnes, located in Tamil Nadu, Gujarat, Rajasthan, Kerala, Pondichery and Jammu and Kashmir.

The total recoverable reserves of bauxite in the country are placed at 2,525 million tonnes while the total in situ reserves are 3,037 million tonnes. The conditional resources of bauxite are about five lakh tonnes. In addition, prospective resources are placed at 90 million tonnes. Orissa, Andhra Pradesh, Madhya Pradesh,

Gujarat, Maharashtra and Bihar are the principal states where bauxite deposits are located. Major reserves are concentrated in the East Coast Bauxite deposits of Orissa and Andhra Pradesh.

Total recoverable reserves of chromite are estimated at 8.8 million tonnes. Deposits of economic significance occur in Andhra Pradesh, Bihar, Karnataka, Maharashtra, Manipur, Orissa and Tamil Nadu. However, refractory grade reserves of chromite are very meagre.

The total recoverable reserves of copper ore in the country are 415.86 million tonnes equivalent to 4.14 million tonnes of metal content. The all-India conditional resources of copper are 695.29 million tonnes (1.99 million tonnes of copper metal) and prospective resources are 769.9 million tonnes of copper ore. Major and important copper ore deposits are located in Singhbhum district (Bihar), Balaghat (Madhya Pradesh) and Jhunjhunu and Alwar (Rajasthan). In addition, small copper ore deposits are in Andhra Pradesh, Gujarat, Karnataka, Sikkim, Orissa, Uttar Pradesh and West Bengal.

There are three important gold fields in the country, namely, Kolar Gold Field, Kolar disrict, Hutti Gold Fields in Raichur district (both in Karnataka) and Ramgiri Gold field in Anantpur district (Andhra Pradesh). Total gold metal ore reserves are estimated at 176.9 lakh tonnes.

The total recoverable reserves of iron ore in the country are about 9,606 million tonnes of haematite and 3,143 million tonnes of magnetite. Haematite resources are located in Andhra Prades, Bihar, Goa, Karnataka, Madhya Pradesh, Maharashtra, Orissa and Rajasthan. Magnetite resources are located in Andhra Pradesh, Bihar, Goa, Karnataka and Kerala.

Lead-zinc resources are located in Rajasthan,

Gujarat, West Bengal, Andhra Pradesh, Meghalaya, Orissa, Sikkim, Tamil Nadu and Uttar Pradesh. Total recoverable reserves (all grades) of lead and zinc ores are 198.5 million tonnes comprising of metal content of 2,390 thousand tonnes of lead and 9,866 thousand tonnes of zinc metal. The conditonal resources of lead-zinc are 200.29 million tonnes in the country.

The total recoverable reserves of manganese ore are 233.33 million tonnes out of which 41.05 million tonnes are proved , 142.03 million tonnes probable and 50.25 million tonnes of possible category. Main reserves are in Karnataka followed by Orissa, Madhya Pradesh, Maharashtra and Goa. Minor occurences of manganese are in Andhra Pradesh, Bihar, Gujarat, Rajasthan and West Bengal.

The total estimated conditional resource of nickel ore is 294 million tonnes located in Orissa (285 million tonnes) and Bihar (9 million tonnes). Minor occurrence of nickel in Tamil Nadu, Maharashtra and Goa are indicated.

The recoverable reserves of tungsten ore have been estimated at 25.89 million tonnes or 77.32 thousand tonnes of WO_3 content. The main reserves are at Degana, Rajasthan. It also occurs in Maharashtra, Karnataka, West Bengal and Uttar Pradesh.

The recoverable reserves of barytes are 70.15 million tonnes. The Mangampet deposit occuring in Cuddapah djistrict (Andhra Pradesh) is the single largest deposit in the world containing 67 million tonnes of recoverable reserves. Minor occurences of barytes are located in Rajasthan, Madhya Pradesh, Maharashtra, Himachal Pradesh, Tamil Nadu, Uttar Pradesh and Bihar.

Diamond deposits occur in three types of geological settings such as kimberlite pipes, conglomerate beds and alluvial gravels. The main diamond bearing areas in India are Panna belt in Madhya Pradesh, Munimadugu-Banganapalle conglomerate in Kurnool district, Wajrakarur kimberlite pipe in Anantpur district and the gravels of Krishna river basin in Andhra Pradesh. Reserves of about a million carats, there are conditional submarginal of 265 thousand carats.

Dolomite occurrences are widespread in almost all part of the country. The total recoverable reserves of all grades of dolomite are 4,967 million tonnes. Of the total all India recoverable reserves, major share of about 92 per cent reserves is distributed in seven states– Madhya Pradesh, Orissa, Gujarat, Karnataka, West Bengal, Uttar Pradesh and Maharashtra.

Fireclay occurs as a bedded deposit, mostly associated with measures of Gondwana and Tertiary periods. Important deposits are associated with Jharia and Raniganj coalfields in Bihar and West Bengal, Korba coalfields in Madhya Pradesh and Neyveli Lignite field in Tamil Nadu. Notable occurrences of fireclay not associated with coal measures are known in Gujarat, Jabalpur region of Madhya Pradesh and Belpahar-Sundergarh areas of Orissa. The recoverable reserves of fireclay are about 697 million tonnes.

Total recoverable reserves of fluorspar in India are 2.15 million tonnes. Rajasthan and Gujarat are the only producing states in India. Fluorspar occurs in Gujarat, Madhya Pradesh, Maharashtra and Rajasthan.

The recoverable reserves of gypsum are estimated at 239 million tonnes. Out of the above, 70,000 tonnes surgical plaster grade, 39 million tonnes of fertilizer/ pottery grade, 38.6 million tonnes of cement/paint grade, four million tonnes of soil reclamation grade and the rest is unclassified. The production of gypsum is confined to Rajasthan, Tamil Nadu, Jammu and Kashmir, Uttar

Pradesh, Himachal Pradesh and Gujarat. Rajasthan is the main producer of gypsum followed by Tamil Nadu.

The recoverable reserves of graphite are 3.11 million tonnes. Orissa is the major producers of graphite. Almost the entire reserves under proved category are in Ramanathapuram district, Tamil Nadu. Resources of graphite are in Andhra Pradesh, Orissa, Tamil Nadu, Kerala, Bihar, Gujarat, Rajasthan, Madhya Pradesh and Maharashtra.

The recoverable reserves of ilmenite are 86.75 million tonnes. Ilmenite occurs mainly in beach sand deposits right from Ratnagiri coast in the west to Orissa coast in the east. These minerals are found in Kerala, Tamil Nadu and Orissa.

The all India recoverable reserves of kaolin, including white clay of all categories are about 986 million tonnes. Principal producing states are Bihar, Gujarat, Rajasthan and West Bengal. Kerala, Haryana, Orissa and Madhya Pradesh also produce significant quantities and ball clay is mainly produced in Rajasthan, Andhra Pradesh and Gujarat.

The total recoverable reserves of limestone of all categories and grades are placed at 76,446 million tonnes. The conditional reserves have been estimated at 360 million tonnes. Major producing states are Madhya Pradesh, tamil Nadu, Andhra Pradesh, Gujarat, Bihar, Orissa, Rajasthan and Karnataka.

India is the world's leading producer of sheet mica and accounts for about 60 per cent of global mica trade. Economic deposits of mica occur in three important belts in Bihar, Andhra Pradesh and Rajasthan.

The total recoverable reserves of magnesite are about 233 million tonnes of which 41 million tonnes are in theproved category. Magnesite is found in Uttar

Pradesh, Tamil Nadu and Rajasthan while minor occurrences are in Karnataka, Jammu and Kashmir and Himachal Pradesh.

The total recoverable reserves of kyanite and sillimanite in the country are 2.7 million tonnes respectively. Besides, conditional resources of 175.84 million tonnes of kyanite are also estimated. For sillimanite conditional resources of 5.9 million tonnes and prospective resources of 0.8 million tonnes have been estimated. Kyanite deposits are located in Andhra Pradesh, Bihar, Karnataka and Maharashtra. Sillimanite resources are in Kerala, Orissa, Madhya Pradesh, tamil Nadu and minor occurrences in Andhra Pradesh, Assam, Bihar, Karnataka, Maharashtra, Meghalaya, Rajasthan and West Bengal.

Deposits of phosphorites are located in Madhya Pradesh, Rajasthan and Uttar Pradesh. Besides, apatite deposits of commercial importance are reported from Bihar, Andhra Pradesh, Rajasthan, West Bengal and Tamil Nadu. Recoverable reserves of rock-phosphate are estimated at 146.95 million tonnes of all grades and of apatite at 13 million tonnes.

Other minerals occuring in significant quantities in India are bentonite (Gujarat, Rajasthan, Bihar, Jammu and Kashmir and Tamil Nadu), corundum (Maharashtra, Madhya Pradesh, Andhra Pradesh * and Gujarat), fullers earth (Rajasthan, Karnataka and Andhra Pradesh), garnet (Tamil Nadu, Rajasthan and Andhra Pradesh Pradesh), pyrites (Bihar and Rajasthan), steatite (Rajasthan, Uttar Pradesh, Andhra Pradesh, Tamil Nadu and Bihar), wollastonite (Rajasthan and Gujarat), zircon (beach sand of Tamil Nadu, Kerala and Orissa) and quartz and silica minerals are wide spread and occur in about all states. Besides, the country has vast resources of building dimension and ornamental stones such as granite, marble and slate. Granite is mainly mined in Tamil Nadu, Karnataka, Andhra Pradesh and Rajasthan, marble in Rajasthan, Uttar Pradesh and Gujarat and slate in Madhya Pradesh, Andhra Pradesh and Haryana.

Oil and natural gas

As India is one of the lowest cost refiners in the world, experts believe that it might become a net exporter of petroleum products in the coming century and a "swing producer" to stabilise global product markets. Though the first oil well in India was completed late in the last century—drilling for the oil well at Digboi in Assam was begun in September 1889 and completed in November 1890—the search for oil in a big way started only after the country gained Independence. The first well at Digboi was drilled by the Assam Railway and Trading Company. Later the Assam Oil Company (AOC) came into existence, which sold its rights to the Burmah Oil Company.

These were the beginnings of Oil India Limited, which became a fully-owned Government company in the early eighties. Thus at the time of Independence, indigenous production of crude oil was confined to Assam.

Since this was hardly enough to meet the country's needs for petroleum products, the Government of India took a conscious decision to develop the country's oil resources, both onshore and offshore.

Creating a Petroleum Division within the Geological Survey of India in October 1955, exclusively for country-wide oil exploration, was the first step. It did not take much time for GSI's Petroleum Division to grow into the Directorate of Oil and Natural Gas, and subsequently into an autonomous Oil & Natural Gas Commisssion through an act of Parliament in October 1959. Now, of course, the Commission is known as Oil & Natural Gas Corporation Limited.

The real fillip to the development of the indigenous petroleum industry was given by the late Keshav Deo Malaviya, who gave ONGC the necessary push and was also responsible for the creation of Indian Oil Corporation, India's first national refining and marketing corporation.

Later, of course, the refineries and marketing companies owned by Burmah-Shell, Esso and Caltex (not to talk of the small Digboirefinery owned by Burmah Oil Company) were nationalised giving birth to two more national oil companies, i.e. Bharat Petroleum and Hindustan Petroleum. Today there are 14 refineries (including the two mentioned above)—13 in the public sector and one in the joint sector. The Gas Authority of India Limited (GALL) was set up in 1984 for planned utilisation of gas reserves and was given the responsibility to set up the HBJ pipeline.

These are briefly the main operators in the oil and natural gas sector, which is basically a public sector monopoly now. While Oil India's operations, in the initial stages, were confined to the north-eastern region, ONGC's initial successes came in the western region. The first discovery of oil and gas made by ONGC was in 1958 in the Cambay onshore basin in Gujarat. Also in Gujarat, the first giant oilfield was discovered at Ankleshwar in 1960.

In what was termed as "Samudra Manthan" in the early sixties, ONGC decided to step up its offshore exploration activity in earnest. Seismic surveys helped in the discovery of the Aliabet structure at the mouth of the Narmada and later in "Bombay High". A big debate raged in the late sixties whether we should develop

"Bombay High" on our own or entrust the job to foreign compaines. The first option was chosen and ONGC acquired its first jack-up type rig "Sagar Samrat" (built for the Commission in Japan) in 1973. "Sagar Samrat" started drilling in "Bombay High" in January 1974 and about a month later oil was discovered at the very first well it drilled in this oilfield, which has met part of the country's crude needs for the past 15 years or so.

ONGC has travelled quite far in the 22 years since oil was established in "Bombay High". Crude oil production from offshore areas (which is solely from ONGC) has risen from five million tonnes in 1980-81 to a high of 21.2 million tonnes in 1990-91. It was around 20.2 million tonnes 1994-95. Total crude production both from onshore and offshore areas (i.e. the total output of OIL and ONGC) was around 35.2 million tonnes in 1995-96.

But the country's requirements of petroleum products have grown at a rapid rate, from 30 million tonnes in 1980-81 to almost 75 million tonnes in 1995-96. Current estimates indicate that it would reach a level of about 113 million tonnes by 2001-02.

Looked at from a different perspective. India's domestic oil production vis-a-vis petroleum product consumption indicate that the percentage of slef-sufficiency has declined from 55.6 per cent in 1990-91 to 43.7 per cent in 1995-96 and is estimated to decline further to 23.5 per cent by 2006-7. In other words, the percentage of self-sufficiency in another 10 years (which is not far away) will be half of what it was in 1990-91.

This emphasises the immense task ahead for all the institutions involved in meeting the country's petroleum product requirements. According to the report of the Strategic Planning Group on Restructuring of Oil Industries (referred to as the R group), mobilisation of Rs. 180,000 crore is required as venture capital for investment in the exploration and production sector alone in the next few years.

Several policy initiatives are required to tackle the gigantic task ahead. Delivering the Third Lovraj Kumar Memorial lecture on India's oil policy in the coming century, Dr. Vijay Kelkar, Secretary, Ministry of Petroleum and Natural Gas, visualises that in the coming century, India will be one of the great industrial powers and obviously oil policy will have to subserve this goal.

Talking about India's oil policy not only from a long-term perspective but also in the international context, Dr. Kelkar is of the view that if the 20th century was the century of oil, the 21 st century would be the century of natural gas.

Not only natural gas is more abundant in terms of reserves but also it is more evenly spread in terms of geographical distribution of these reserves and thus offering greater security of supplies. At the present rate of depletion, Dr. Kelkar points out, the global reserves of crude oil will last 43 years and natural gas 66 years.

Pointing out that India's current consumption of petroleum products is around 78 million tonnes and will be growing at the rate of about 10 per cent or so per annum over the next decades and exceed 270 million tonnes by 2020, Dr. Kelkar says that even by early part of the next century itself India would have already become one of the top five consumers of petroleum products, ahead of a number of major OECD countries such as France, U.K. and just behind China and Russia. In other words, India's import requirements would be growing faster with total demand exceeding total supply resulting in increased import dependence for oil and also for natural gas.

Comparing India's situation with other countries

which have very little domestic hydrocarbon resources, Dr. Kelkar has pointed out the first element of policy thrust has to be accelerated exploration programme within the country. In this India is fortunately placed because over the last several decades, the country has created a great institutional base in exploration, production and refining. But Indian institutions have to become more efficient, internationally competitive and try to maximise India's share in global equity oil (like some of the other countries have done who have very little hydrocarbon resources).

Another policy element is to review the present administered pricing mechanism (APM) under which a number of petroleum products are heavily subsidised. This aspect has been gone into at length by the R Group, which has suggested a phased withdrawal of the present administrative pricing mechanism, under which the main operators in the petroleum sector have little inducement to become more efficient as the return is based on a cost-plus formula.

Even from the point of view of generating more resources for re-investment in the industry to meet future demands of the country, a review of APM should form an integral part of future oil policy.

Addressing the economic editors conference in Delhi in November, Mr. T. Baalu, Minister of State for Petroleum and Natural Gas, highlighted that the cumulative outstanding claims of oil companies from the oil pool account are likely to touch Rs. 15,500 crore by March 31, 1997.

On of the reasons he cited for this mounting outstanding claims is the non-adjustment of selling prices of petroleum products in the context of increased imports and rise in international prices of crude oil.

Gross imports of crude oil and petroleum products at 47.68 million tonnes in 1995-96 were 15.4 per cent higher than in the previous year. If the value of these imports was Rs. 17,838 crore in 1994-95, the bill rose to Rs. 24,095 crore in 1995-96.

According to the R Group report, the contribution to the exchequer both Centre and States) from the oil and gas industry by way of royalty on crude oil and gas, oil development cess, excise and customs duties, corporate taxes and dividends worked out to Rs. 24,493 crore in 1994-95. If one excludes the share of the States out of these levies, the Centre is already spending more on imports of oil and petroleum products than the contribution being made by oil and gas industry to the exchequer.

Here, it must also be noted that the Central Government mopped up 47 per cent of oil revenue in 1993-94 by way of taxes, royalties, etc. Oil and gas industry is thus a large source of revenue for the Centre.

Organisational structure

A number of organisations are engaged in exploration and development of mineral resources in India. These include Geolgical survey of India (GSI), Indian Bureau of Mines (IBM) and a number of public sector undertakings under the administrative control of the Ministry of Mines.

Geological Survey of India functions as the premier national organisation for earth science, entrusted with the task of scientific survey and research for locating mineral resources (except oil, natural gas and atomic minerals), systematic generation and continous updating of geoscience information through ground, airborne and marine survey, the entire gamut of activities being related to multifarious developmental needs of the country. The survey operates within the ambit of its charter 1873 and priorities laid down by the Government. The other important functions of the organisation cover management of natural hazards like earthquake, floods, landslides, volcanism etc., providing geotechnical advice to all the major civil engineering, communication and urban development projects, geoenvironmental resource appraisal, upgradation of geoscientific expertise through training. The results of GSI investigations are documented in the form of scientific and technical reports, professional papers, maps, inventories and various types of publications.

The survey with its central headquarters at Calcutta, functions through six geographically based regions, three activity based Wings (Marine, Coal and Airborne Survey) and one training Institute. In each of the region/wings towards greater collaboration and setting up of consultancy and commercial endeavours in the third world countries.

The Indian Bureau of Mines (IBM) is the national organisation under Ministry of Mines and engaged in promotion, conservation and scientific development of mineral resources of the country other than coal, petroleum and natural gas, atomic minerals and minor minerals. It performs regulatory functions, namely enforcement of Mines and Minerals (Regulation & Development Rules and the provision of Environmental Protection Act. It also undertakes scientific techno-economic, research-orientid studies in various aspects such as geological, mining ore beneficiation and environment. IBM provides technical consultancy services to the mining industry for geological appraisal of mineral resources and preparation of feasibility reports of mining projects including beneficiation plants. It prepares mineral maps and countrywide inventory of minerals resources of leasehold and freehold areas. IBM also functions as data bank for mines and minerals and publishes statistical periodicals and brings out technical publications/monogrphs on individual mineral commodities and bulletins on different connected subjects. it advises the Central and state governments on all aspects of mineral industry, trade and legislation. It imparts training to technical and non-technical officials of IBM and also persons from mineral industry and other agencies in India and abroad. IBM is organised into six functional agencies in India and abroad. IBM is organised into six functional divisions. It has its headquarters at Nagpur and 11 regional offices and well equipped ore-dressing laboratories and Pilot Plant at Nagpur, besides, two regional ore-dressing laboratories at Ajmer and Bangalore. IBM also has a big Central Library with about 61,000 books.

Minral Exploration Corporation Limited (MECL) was created in 1972 with the main objective of bridging the gap between the discovery of mineral prospect and its eventual exploitation. Its identified major functions are to plan, promote, organise and implement programme for the exploration of mineral resources and to perform such functions as Central Government may from time to time, assign to the company in connection with exploration of the mineral resources in and outside the country. The Corporation has its headquarters at Nagpur. MECL has fulfilled its main objective by establishing over 55,000 million tonnes of reserves of higher confidence for veriety of minerals. The drilling capacity of 72,000 m per annum at the time of inception in 1972 has increased to 4.25 lakh metre of drilling and mining capacity has increased from 1200 mtr in 1972 to 9000 m in the last year of Seventh Five Year Plan. During 1993-94, the turnover of the company was Rs. 40.73 crore.

Bharat Aluminium Company Limited (BALCO) was incorporated on 27 November 1965 as the first primary aluminium producing undertaking in the public sector. The Company is operating Korba Aluminium Complex in Bilaspur district of Madhya Pradesh and Bidhanbag Unit in Asanosl in west Bengal. It has a capacity to produce one lakh tonnes of aluminium metal/products. During the past few years, the Company's production of saleable metal/products has been about 92,000 tonnes per annum. Its net profit has been going up steadily and during 1994-95, it earned a net profit of Rs. 90.51 crore (provisional). The new projects of the Company include installation of a new Cold Rolling Mill having an installed capacity to produce 40,000 TPA of thin quality sheets/coils. The Comapny is also in the process of modernisation of their smelter plant at Korba for increased productivity and reduction of power consumption, which is a major factor in input costs.

National Aluminium Company Limited (NALCO) was incorporated on 7 January 1981 with the objective to produce alumina and aluminium. Its registerd office is at Bhubaneswar. It operates a bauxite mine to raise 24 lakh tonnes per annum of bauxite from the Parnchpatnali (Koraput) deposits, an eight lakh tonnes per annum alumina refinery at Damanjodi (Koraput), a 2,18,000 tonnes per annum aluminium smelter at Angul (Dhenkanal) and six 120 MW captive power plants at Angul to feed the smelter. Aluminium Pechiney of France was the technical consultants for the project and had supplied the technical know-how and basic engineering package.

NALCO received ISO 9002 Certification from IROS for Alumina Refinery on 21 November 1994 and ISO 9002 Certification for quality system for Smelter Plan in March 1995 from RWTUV. Highest production of calcined alumina of 81,000 MT during January 1995 exceeding the rated capacity. NALCO produced 1,78,072 tonnes of aluminium and earned net profit of Rs. 294.62 (provisional) during the same period.

Hindustan Zinc Limited (HZL) was incorporated on 10 January 1966 to take over operations of the earstwhile Metal Corporation of India Limited and to develop mining and smelting capacities to substantially meet the domestic demand of zinc and lead metals. With headquarters at Udaipur, HZL's operations are spread over in the states of Rajasthan, Andhra Pradesh, Orissa and Bihar consisting of five mines with a total lead-zinc ore production capacity of 3.04 million tpa and four smelters with combined installed capacity of 1,49,000 tpa zinc and 65,000 tpa lead besides a rock phosphate and tungsten mine. The company offers a wide range of zinc and lead metal grades to its customers, besides a range of by-products. The production of zinc metal by the company during the last four years has ranged between 84,600 tpa and 1,19,810 tpa. The lead production during the same period has ranged between 30,300 tpa and 34,500 tpa. The sales turnover of the company during 1994-95 was Rs. 97,274 lakh and its net profit (after tax) during the same period was Rs. 7,643 lakh.

HZL signed a Memorandum of Understanding with M/s. Niugini Mining Limited.Australia, to identify gold resources in India and later on if resources are found viable, to set up a joint venture. It has also signed an MoU with M/s. BHP Minerals, Austrails, for exploration and development of base and procious metals in Rajasthan. Besides, HZL and BRGM, France, have reached an agreement with Vietnam Rare and Precious Metal Corporation (VMC) for setting up of joint venture for exploration and development of Pac Lang Gold Prospect in Vietnam.

Hindustan Copper Limited (HCL) is the sole producer of primary copper metal in the country. It was incorporated on 7 November 1967, to take over from the National Mineral Development Corporation, projects, schemes and studies pertaining to exploration, exploitation, mining and smelting of copper. In 1972, the erstwhile Indian Copper Corporation Limit, a company incorporated in England was nationalised and merged with HCl. The main projects of the company are: (i) Khetri Copper Complex (KCC) in Rajasthan comprising Khetri, Kolihan, Chandmari and Dariba mines (since closed), concentrators at Dariba (since closed) and Khetri, Metallurgical and fertilizer plants at Khetri; (ii) Indian Copper Complex (ICC) at Ghatsila in Bihar comprising Mosaboni, Fathargora, Kendadih and Rakha Mines, three concentrators at Mosaboni, Moubhandar (since closed) and Rakha and metallurgical plants for copper and by-product recovery at Moubhandari (iii) Malanjkhand Copper Project (MCP) at Malanjkhand in Madhya Pradesh comprising an open pit mine, concentrator and leach copper plant; and (iv) Taloja Copper Project (TCP) at Taloja in Maharashtra for conversion of cathodes both imported and part of our own into continuous cast copper wirerods as value added product. The company produces primary copper products in the form of cathodes, wirebars, wirerods and is also engaged in manufacturing of single super phosphate, sulphuric acid, gold, silver, selenium, tellurium, palladium, copper sulphate and nickel sulphate as by-products.

The current operation plants of the company are to produce and market about 70,000 Mt copper in different forms out of which 45,000 MT of refined copper is produced from indigenous ore resources. With the changed economic scenario in the country, HCL has initiated process of restructuring of companies to remain competitive. During 1994-95, the turnover of the company was Rs. 932.95 and its production of refined copper was 46,134 MT.

Bharat Gold Mines Limited operates the world famous century old Kolar Gold Mines in Karnataka State. The company was nationalised in 1956 and was incorporated as a public sector company under the Department of Mines, Government of India in March 1972. Though the gold mining is the principal activity of the company, as a corporate stategy, it has diversified into the field of mine construction and contract works, manufacture of mining machinery and components of equipment.

The company has three major activities namely: (i) Gold mining: Two mines in Kolar Gold Fields, Karntaka-Mysore Champion Amalgamated mine and Nundydroog mine, and three mines in Andhra Pradesh, Yeppamana mine, (Anantapur); Chigargunta mine; and Old Bisanatham mine, (Chittoor); (ii) Mine Project and Construction Division-Taking up mine construction and development works for other mining (coal and metal mines) industries all over India, and (iii) Workshop Diversification-The workshops manufacture mining machineries and components of certain equipment and undertake jobbing works, like machining and fabrication for major industries in the country.

The company's registered office is at Koar Gold Fields and its liaison office is at New Delhi. In 1994-95, the company produced 650.28 kg of gold. The continued financial losses over the decade has resulted in the company being declared as a sick industry and consequently referred to Board for Industrial and Financial Reconstruction (BIFR) who have appointed ICICI as Operating Agency to formulate a rehabilitation package envisaging increase in gold production from the existing shallow mines to ensure economic viability, exploration and exploitation of gold from the BGML lease-hold areas in collaboration with a suitable joint venture partner and to recover gold from old mill tailings accumulated over the years by constructing a suitable gold recovery plant by BGML.

Sikkim Mining Corporation was established as joint venture of Sikkim State and Government of India in 1960 by proclamation of erstwhile "Sikkim Darbar". the objective of the Corporation is to mine multimental ore for production of copper, lead and zinc concentrates. The Corporation has only one mine (Bhotang Mine) Situated at Rangpo (East Sikkim). During 1994-95, the Corporation produced 270 mt tonnes of copper concentrate, 85 mt of lead concentrate and 568 mt of zinc concentrate. Zinc concentrate is being sold to M/s. Hindustan Zinc Ltd. since April 1994. Hindustan Copper Limited has stopped taking copper concentrate, M/s. HAMCO Mining and Smelting Limited, Calcutta, has lifted 3,500 tonnes of lead, 200 tonnes of copper and 200 tonnes of zono concentrates on trial basis in the year 1994-95.